4 33

D1195583

Women, the Family and Peasant Revolution in China

Women, the Family and Peasant Revolution in China

Kay Ann Johnson

The University of Chicago Press
Chicago and London

Kay Ann Johnson is associate professor of political science and Asian studies at Hampshire College.

The University of Chicago Press, Chicago 60637
The University of Chicago Press, Ltd., London

90 89 88 87 86 85 84 83   12345

Library of Congress Cataloging in Publication Data

Johnson, Kay Ann.
   Women, the family and peasant revolution in China.

   Includes bibliographical references and index.
   1. Women—China—History. 2. Confucianism—China—
History. 3. Family—China—History. 4. Socialism—
China—History. 5. China—Rural conditions. I. Title.
HQ1767.J63 1983   305.4'0951   82-24748
ISBN 0-226-40187-1

To My Mother and Father

Contents

Acknowledgments

I would like to give special thanks to Edward Friedman who, as my teacher, colleague and friend, has unfailingly provided encouragement and feedback on numerous drafts of chapters throughout the long process of writing this book. I would also like to acknowledge the significant contribution to my intellectual growth, and to the final draft of this book, made by my feminist studies colleagues at Hampshire College, with whom I have designed and team-taught cross-cultural, interdisciplinary family studies courses: Margaret Cerullo, Nancy Fitch, Miriam Slater and Francis White. Each of them has provided me with insights into my own work and helped me place my "case study" into a broader comparative historical and theoretical context. Collectively, they provided the supportive colleagueship and intellectual inspiration that allowed me to finish this book amidst the relentless teaching demands of Hampshire College. Finally, I would like to thank Paul Pickowicz, Mark Selden and, again, Edward Friedman, who conducted fieldwork with me in and around Wukung village in Hopeh in 1978. A very small part of the information gathered during that fieldwork appears in this book and I thank them for allowing me to use it. Our entire collection of data will appear as a collectively authored book on Wukung.

Introduction

Few societies in history have prescribed for women a more lowly status or treated them in a more routinely brutal way than traditional Confucian China. Belief in the interaction of principles of *yin* (dark, earth, cold, negative, death, the north side of the mountain) and *yang* (light, heaven, warmth, positive, life, the south side of the mountain) formed the basis of an ancient Chinese cosmology which, it is said, presented an essentially androgynous vision of the universe.[1] However benign the origin of these notions, the Confucianization of ancient Chinese cosmology assigned *yin* to female, *yang* to male and froze them in a rigid hierarchy of submission and dominance, passivity and activity, weakness and strength. This hierarchy fundamentally permeated dominant Chinese culture and religion for nearly two thousand years. Few, if any, corners of Chinese life failed to reflect this gender hierarchy, rationalized through cosmological belief and regularized in practice through Confucian ritual.

The classics buried women's personalities and lives under the weight of the Three Bonds of Obedience: to obey fathers when young, husbands when married, and adult sons when widowed. For centuries, treatises, endlessly memorized and recited, exhorted females to servility, passivity and self-effacement. Elite ideals of female propriety encouraged the ultimate of self-negation—suicide—as an honorable response to violations of chastity.[2] Women's position in sex and work was reflected in a practice of female mutilation known as footbinding, a thousand year old institution which, among other things, stood as an expression of one of history's most powerful sadomasochistic male fantasies. Throughout their lives, women were supposed to be only slightly more than chattel, routinely bought and sold in marriage, concubinage or outright slavery.

1

The life and death consequences of being born female in traditional China can be gleaned from traditional literature, traveller's tales, personal recollections and scattered statistics, mostly from the nineteenth and twentieth centuries. They include a female suicide profile that exceeded men's at all ages and bulged during the painful years of betrothal and early marriage, relatively high rates of female infanticide in times of economic hardship, and significantly higher mortality rates among the numerous young girls who were "adopted" in childhood for marriage.[3] The unbalanced and sometimes seriously skewed sex ratios that have been reported among the population (as high as 156 males to 100 females in one Shensi county in 1928) reflect, in part at least, these types of horrors.[4]

In the nineteenth and twentieth centuries, Chinese began to turn a critical eye upon their own society, and a consciousness of the blatant abuses of women began to surface among a segment of the population. Because of the centrality of Confucianism and the hierarchical, male-dominated Confucian family institution to all aspects of traditional society, growing concerns for general political and social reform inevitably led to consideration of issues involving the family and women's status.

For centuries, Chinese rulers and Confucian scholars likened the state to the traditional Confucian family system. Proper order and hierarchy in the political realm of the state was said to be directly related to the proper order and hierarchy of the family and the family's proper moral training of obedient, filial subjects. Symbolically, the entire political system was based on the ideal Confucian family and its moral code.[5]

Throughout Chinese history, cycles of dynastic decline usually resulted in a new leadership that called for a restoration of the traditional virtues and order embodied in the ideal Confucian family and a return to an idealized past when such virtues supposedly reigned throughout the kingdom. But the decline of the Ch'ing dynasty under the impact of modern imperialism in the late nineteenth and early twentieth centuries brought forth a plethora of would-be rulers and defecting intellectuals who sought not to restore the old ways, but to build a new order to bring China forward into the modern world as a powerful nation-state. It was natural that family reform would be an important symbolic issue to these forward-looking elements who sought new solutions and significant political change for China. By the first decades of the twentieth century, various types of reformers came to believe that the traditional family and its Confucian values needed to be altered in the effort to revitalize China's national condition. Late Ch'ing dynasty reformers, liberal democrats, nationalist and communist revolutionaries, all, to a lesser or greater extent, wanted to reform the family institution and its norms.

For most of these reformers, concern with the reform of the traditional family was merely one part of a general iconoclastic, anti-Confucian critique of Chinese politics, society and culture.[6] But for a small, growing women's rights movement that emerged after the fall of the Ch'ing, family reform was a particularly crucial issue. Certain aspects of the Confucian family system were seen as shackles binding women to a life of dependence, servitude and suffering.

This study examines the policies and changes concerning women that have developed in the countryside under Chinese Communist Party (CCP) leadership during the revolutionary and postrevolutionary periods. The primary focus is on reform of marriage and the family because, as I argue in the following chapters, marriage, family and kinship practices have defined and shaped women's place in Chinese society more than any other single set of factors. Part 1 includes a brief descriptive background of the most relevant features of traditional Chinese family and kinship as well as an analysis of how the family has shaped women's behavior and of family and kinship as primary causal factors in women's subordination in society. This is followed by a discussion of the impact of the multiple crises of late nineteenth- and early twentieth-century China on the family institution.

Part 2 provides an interpretative political history of the development of marriage reform and women's rights policies during the revolutionary period. This development is traced from the earliest days of the CCP, when it was a small urban-based party (1921–23), through the first revolutionary alliance with the Kuomintang (KMT) (1924–27), which marked the Party's first serious ventures into the countryside, to the Kiangsi Soviet period (1929–34) when the Party fully ensconced itself in rural territory, to the Yenan period (1936–45), during which the CCP directed resistance to Japanese invasion from its wartime base areas in the remote border regions of the North and Northwest and, finally, through the last civil war with the KMT (1946–49).

Part 3 deals with the early years of the People's Republic of China, which included the "high tide" of marriage and family reform, a unique period in that it was the only time in which a politically active approach to promoting family reform and womens' rights gained some ascendency in CCP policy. The period from 1950–53 is analyzed closely, detailing the series of campaigns that surrounded the implementation of the 1950 Marriage Law, the main legal document of the PRC pertaining to womens' rights and family reform.

Part 4 looks at the major developments since the mid 1950s which are presumed to have had an impact on gender equality and change in womens' family status: the collectivization drives of the 1950s, the Cultural Revolution of the late 1960s, the Anti-Confucian campaign of the mid-1970s and finally, more briefly, current population control policies.

Throughout, I return periodically to some of the larger theoretical issues raised in Part 1 concerning the dynamics of change for women and the family.

1 The Prerevolutionary Setting

1 Women and the Traditional Chinese Family

The "traditional Chinese family" is of course an ideal type.[1] For centuries, the closest living model for the traditional family, with its Confucian norms and highly differentiated status hierarchy, was the large, extended multigenerational family of the landed gentry. Imperial scholars compiled many treatises on proper behavior based on the ideal functioning of this type of family. Its norms and structure were widely hailed as a model to be emulated. Yet, clearly, only a small minority of wealthy families could fulfill all of the features of the model. In practice, family structure, norms and customs varied geographically and with social class. For example, family size and complexity, norms governing women's economic activities, and the incidence of "minor forms" of marriage—forms which deviated from the presumed "ideal" or "major form"—varied considerably geographically and with class throughout the society.[2] In contrast to the elite ideal, the families of less prosperous peasants tended to be small and relatively simple in structure; women and young children were generally more economically important; deviations from "proper" forms of marriage were far more common and might even be the norm in some areas. As James Scott points out, the "Little Tradition" of the peasants is not simply a mirror reflection of the "Big Tradition" of the elite.[3]

Nonetheless, certain common structural and normative features of kinship and family could be found throughout Chinese society. Even where peasant tradition diverged from the elite tradition, the latter often provided ideals motivating or helping to explain behavior where attainment of the ideal was conspicuously absent. In China, the influence of certain elite norms as ideals toward which peasants aspired was perhaps intensified by the lack of a hereditary ruling class and the relative up and down mobility of the commercialized bureaucratic state. The commonly observed phenomenon of average peasants going deeply into debt, sometimes even mortgaging precious land, to try to maintain the ruinously expensive, ostentatious, proper ceremonies and rituals fostered by elite Confucian tradition indicates the legitimating power of certain aspects of the ideal in popular culture.

ɩOne of the features of the traditional Chinese family that cut across history, geography and class was the low status of women in a family and kinship system organized around men and male authority. The ideal traditional family was patriarchal, patrilineal and patrilocal, and was embedded in an extended male kinship network.ɩAlthough the significance and closeness of kinship ties between males varied geographically and with class, several degrees of kinship relations among males were supposed to be close and entailed definite mutual obligations. The term *liu ch'in*, the "six kinship relations," which designated socially significant relationships, usually included relations between father and sons, and relations among brothers, brothers' children, brothers' grandchildren and brothers' great-grandchildren.[4] The more distant of these relations were not likely to be intimate and might be significant primarily within the context of a larger lineage organization. In many parts of China, these surname organizations, based on claims to a common ancestor and reckoned exclusively through males, with memberships ranging from several hundred to over ten thousand, were extremely important and provided the foundation of community organization. Such lineage organizations, usually dominated by their richest members, were central to religious life and also often controlled the basic political, judicial and educational functions of communities as well. Patrilocal residence rules at marriage and the advantages of living among a supportive network of kin meant that male kin tended to live close together and remain rooted in the same community from generation to generation when economic conditions permitted. Entire villages, or whole neighborhoods within larger villages, were often composed of a single clan.ɩ

Kinship ties on the maternal side might have some significance, especially among the very rich (who could use marriage to extend political and financial ties) and the very poor (who needed mutual cooperative networks to survive and whose forced geographic mobility might leave them without strong male kin networks). But meaningful kinship relations on the maternal side rarely extended beyond the immediate natal family of a mother or wife, and even these relations were weakened by patrilocal residence, poor communication and a kinship ideology and religion based exclusively on patrilineal lines. Indeed, many customs were aimed at symbolically or literally severing the ties of married women to their natal kin.[5] Overall, affinal kinship and biological ties through women were unusually weak in the Chinese kinship system.

The family, as the basic and most intimate unit of kinship, gained much of its strength, stability and importance from its connections with the broader kinship networks.[6] As with the larger networks of the clan, the size and solidarity of the family household was both a cause and effect of wealth. The elite ideal was to maintain a large joint family household organized according to a strict hierarchy based on age and gender. According to this ideal, a father, all his sons, grandsons, great-grandsons and their wives remained within the same household. Having "five generations (of males) under one roof" was considered great fortune and was one of the most valued signs of status, wealth and moral worth. Of course, very few could attain this extended, multigenerational household ideal. It required prosperity, long-term economic and social stability and low mortality rates. Even among the wealthy, family discord and partible inheritance practices often led after a few generations to the division of large households and distribution of property among brothers, although close relations among the separate households were usually maintained. A relatively small joint or stem family (perhaps including surviving parents, one son, his wife and their small children) was far more common, although the very poor might fail to attain even this.[7]

Yet even among smaller, more simple families, patriarchy, patriliny and patrilocality were characteristic. Women lacked all rights of property ownership and management and carried no formal independent decision-making authority in matters affecting the family and clan. Indeed the patriarchal-patrilineal-patrilocal configuration, in China, as elsewhere, made women marginal members of the entire family system. They were temporary members or future deserters of their natal families and stranger-intruders in their new husbands' families. Structurally, women existed as outsiders within the male-defined family system, no matter how central their actual role in propagating and maintaining the male family.

This outsider status was accentuated for young Chinese women by the prevalence in most areas of surname exogamy and often village exogamy—that is, customs and taboos which prohibited same-surname and often same-village marriages (even where villages contained more than one surname).[8] These unusually restrictive customs, coupled with rooted residential patterns based on patrilineally related males, meant that women were frequently enjoined to marry outside their own native communities. Thus women not only had to leave their natal families at marriage, but were also geographically separated from their community, natal kin and all of the social relationships they had developed

during the first fifteen to twenty years of their lives. In entering her
husband's family as a stranger, a woman also entered his and his kin's
village as an outsider, without established interpersonal networks to
rely on. ।

   This handicap was particularly serious considering the importance of
firmly rooted interpersonal relationships and close kinship networks as
a resource in rural societies in general and in Chinese society in
particular. Moreover, cross-cultural studies suggest that when women
are denied access to legitimate roles of authority within family and
society, they rely heavily on developing and manipulating informal
interpersonal relationships and emotional ties to gain influence over
their lives and to partially overcome the imposed handicaps of male-
dominated authority structures.[9] But in an extensively exogamous,
patrilocal system, even the development of these informal avenues of
influence is hindered when young women had to begin married life as
outsiders, spending years establishing themselves in an unfamiliar
community, kinship network and family.

   ।The status and power of women in the Chinese family did, however,
vary with different phases of their lives. Within the male-defined
family, women gained some status and respect through bearing children, particularly male children. After the marriage of a son, a woman
gained some formal authority in the family as a mother-in-law by virtue
of generational age among women. The birth of children also allowed a
woman to overcome her emotional isolation by developing ties of
affection and loyalty with her offspring, building what Margery Wolf
calls an informal, mother-centered "uterine family."[10] Although the
uterine family was unrecognized by the dominant patriarchal-patrilin-
eal family norms and ideology, it was crucial to women's lives and, as
we shall see later, to the political dynamics of family reform. ।

   The most difficult and degrading phase of life for a woman was
immediately after marriage. Under the major form of marriage, a
teenaged woman entered a blind marriage arranged by her parents
through a matchmaker. Lacking status in her new family, lacking the
protection of any established affectionate ties with her husband,
lacking the protection and solace of kinship or interpersonal relationships in her new community, the young wife came abruptly under the
authority of husband and in-laws. In day-to-day affairs she was most
directly under the authority and supervision of her mother-in-law, who
controlled the women's work within the family.

   The nature of marriage exchanges between patrilineal families both
reflected and reinforced the bride's subordination within her husband's
family. The groom's family usually paid a "bride price" (*li-chin* or *p'in-
chin*) to the bride's family, symbolizing the transfer of rights to control
the woman's body and her labor from her natal family to her new

husband's family.[11] In some cases, the bride price amounted to an unadorned purchase of female "property." In other cases, the "purchase" was mitigated by a dowry sent by the bride's parents to the new husband's family. Among wealthier families, there was social pressure to send a large dowry at least equal to the bride price in order to display publicly the family's wealth.[12] In such cases, an "indirect dowry" system operated which might help equalize the expenses between the two families, even though the dowry usually did not, as in some societies, provide the woman with control over significant personal property in her husband's family.[13] Among the poor, evidence suggests that dowries tended to be much smaller than bride prices, or they were not involved at all.[14]

A major study of the 1930s indicates that for China as a whole the male's family's overall wedding expenses (including bride price) exceeded the bride's family's expenses by 50 percent, with regional variations.[15] In the poor, winter wheat-millet regions of the Northwest, expenses of the groom's family exceeded those of the bride's family by nearly two and one-half to one. On the other hand, in the northern winter wheat-kaoliang regions expenses were equal, and in the Szechuan rice area average female family expenses exceeded the male's, suggesting that dowries were the dominant practice.

The issue of bride price practices versus dowry practices and their differential relationship to women's rights and social status is complex and problematic. Bride price and dowry practices have been understood by most scholars as dependent variables related to women's economic roles and status.[16] Cross-culturally, bride prices tend to be dominant where women play a relatively active role in subsistence agriculture, and are thought to reflect women's economic worth. On the other hand, dowries tend to be dominant where women's economic role is more restricted.

The apparent dominance of bride prices in most parts of China does not quite fit the general patterns observed elsewhere, for, as will be discussed later, Chinese women generally had relatively low participation rates in the agricultural economy. But, with the major exception of the Northwest (where women's participation rates were the lowest but the bride price/dowry ratio was apparently the highest), variations within China did seem to follow the expected pattern; that is, dowries were inversely correlated with women's agricultural participation rates.[17] Thus bride prices in China, as elsewhere, tended to be positively correlated with a variable-economic participation—that is usually considered important in raising women's status and increasing their rights and freedoms.[18]

Yet while dowries often reflect a woman's low economic worth and low status, and bride prices a woman's valued role in agriculture, bride prices logically do more to undercut a woman's rights and status in her husband's family than do dowries, for they symbolize the sale of these rights by her parents to her husband and in-laws. In China, cultural images of women as chattel seem to have gained particular strength from bride prices. "A woman married is like a horse bought; you can ride them or flog them as you like" was a well-known adage in parts of China. When male families paid dearly for women in marriage, they could be expected to exert great pressure and control to get value from their investment.

The ceremonial and often ruinously expensive transfer or exchange of money and gifts was most characteristic of the "major form" of marriage. But deviations from the major form that occurred in response to social and economic circumstances no less reflected and reinforced the control of women by and for the male-defined family even if they did not involve such great expense. There were two significant deviations: the matrilocal marriage and the minor marriage.

The most radical deviation in form was the matrilocal marriage, although its purpose and goals were the same as the major form—to maintain the patrilineage.[19] When a family had only daughters, parents would seek a son-in-law who would be willing to move into their family to work and to provide them with male heirs and eventually support in old age. In extreme cases, the man agreed to be fully adopted as a son, changing his own surname and taking on all the rights and obligations of that role. In other cases, there simply would be some arrangement to assure that one or more of the male offspring of the couple take the descent of the mother's father.

Thus, in the absence of sons, daughters might be valued as a link in the family chain and enjoy lifelong ties to natural parents and native village. However, matrilocal marriages were generally viewed as second-class arrangements. The man who was willing to enter into such a marriage was likely to be viewed as morally flawed and socially inferior to men who remained filial sons to their own patrilineage. Sometimes a man with several older brothers might be available to enter a matrilocal marriage because of special family or economic circumstances. But more often those willing to enter a matrilocal marriage were rootless men without family, land or financial resources—that is, those who had no prospects of a proper marriage.[20] Daughters destined for a matrilocal marriage therefore were likely to feel consigned to an inferior and improper marriage, despite the fact that matrilocal marriage spared them many of the traumas and disadvantages of the proper major form of marriage.

Probably the most common deviation from the major form of marriage was the minor marriage, the practice of taking a "little foster daughter-in-law" (t'ung-yang-hsi).[21] Under a minor marriage a girl was transferred to her future husband's family at a very young age, sometimes in infancy. She was then raised by her in-laws and, after physical maturity, became the wife of her "foster brother." Although in-laws bore the expense of raising their own daughter-in-law, they gained early control over her labor and avoided the greater ceremonial and bride price expenses of a major marriage. The minor marriage also had the advantage of avoiding the potential disruption of ongoing family relationships which a new adult daughter-in-law might bring. The incidence of *t'ung-yang-hsi* seems to have varied widely throughout China, ranging from being virtually nonexistent to being the preferred form of marriage.[22] In parts of China, this practice seems to have been most often found among the very poor who could not afford the expense of a major marriage and it apparently increased during hard times. In other places, however, the minor marriage appears to have been the preferred practice, not merely one forced by difficult circumstances.[23]

For the "little foster daughter-in-law" the practice could be particularly brutal. Although she avoided the difficult period of being an outsider in a strange family and village, the ill treatment of these girls was notorious. They were sometimes viewed as little more than family slaves and frequently denied the affectionate relationships which a natural daughter could expect with her parents.[24] Indeed, the bitter conditions of these poor girls sometimes were reflected in substantially higher mortality rates than for either sons or natural daughters.[25]

Regardless of the way a woman was married, she was considered the property of the patrilineal family, to be used to perpetuate and serve its paramount ends. The "exchange of women" as practiced under the traditional Chinese kinship system made female-initiated divorce virtually impossible. Bride prices which predominated as the mode of "exchanging women" in most areas of China made divorce particularly difficult.[26] Because of the great expense of acquiring a wife for a son, the marriage of a son which was crucial for the continuation of patrilineal, patrilocal family was often dependent on obtaining a bride price for a daughter. In minor marriages, though high bride prices were not involved, a son's marriage might depend on a direct exchange of his infant sister with another family's. Daughters, directly or indirectly, were a means of acquiring wives for sons; where there were no sons, daughters were the means of bringing in a substitute son. Few families had the means or the motivation to free unhappy daughters from arrangements that were determined for them by the central needs of the male-defined family. Even less could women themselves be vested with the power to disrupt family arrangements at will.

Even if a woman's husband died when she was very young (or, sometimes, even if he died after their betrothal), the woman's in-laws retained control over her. Confucian norms proscribed the remarriage of widows: a widow was supposed to remain faithful to her dead husband, his family and ancestors for life. In practice, however, the remarriage of widows was not uncommon in parts of China, especially among the poor.[27] But whether or not a widow was remarried remained a question to be decided by her in-laws, who might keep her or sell her to another man to suit their family needs. If she was remarried she had no right to take any family property nor did she have any claims to her children, who belonged exclusively by law and custom to the patrilineal family of their father.

Elite values concerning women's work paralleled their dependent, lowly status within the kinship system and emphasized seclusion and the control of women's lives by men and family. Ideally, women's daily lives were confined to the domestic realm and their contact with nonfamily members carefully limited. Proper women's work mainly involved the service and nurturance of children and family members, the manufacture and processing of materials supplied by men for household consumption and sometimes handicraft work or various other tasks that could be done in or near the home.

In reality, the extent to which women's lives reflected these elite ideals varied a great deal. For example, in some northern areas where women did little field work except during the busy season, even the lives of many peasant women might have generally reflected these norms in times of economic stability. Where women did little work outside the home, their general freedom of movement probably was more restricted; norms of proper seclusion were stricter and penetrated further down the social ladder. A woman raised in a modest (but not impoverished) family in Shantung in the late nineteenth century recalled

> We were not allowed, my sister and I, on the street after we were thirteen. People in P'englai were that way in those days. When a family wanted to know more about a girl who had been suggested for a daughter-in-law and asked what kind of a girl she was, the neighbors would answer, "We do not know. We have never seen her." And that was praise.[28]

Thus a foreign missionary travelling in nineteenth-century China could observe that women "never go anywhere to speak of, and live . . . the existence of a frog in a well."[29]

In many parts of China, however, norms of female seclusion were far more lax, especially among poorer peasants, and women's economic roles deviated considerably from the elite ideals restricting women to purely nonremunerative, domestic work. In many areas in the South, women regularly participated in field work and frequently went "outside" to work. Among the Hakka, a culturally distinct Han group that settled mainly in the South and Southwest, women apparently predominated in agricultural work and other kinds of physical labor.[30] A local study of several Chinese villages in Yunnan Province conducted in the 1930s also reported that women did more agricultural work on family farms than men.[31] Furthermore, in a variety of places throughout the country, women made major contributions to family income through work in income-earning cottage industries; indeed, women predominated in the early development of the important traditional textile industry, just as they predominated as laborers in the early industrialization of that industry in the twentieth century.[32]

ⵏ Such variety and range of participation levels make easy generalizations about women's traditional economic roles difficult and fraught with dangers of oversimplification⌡ As we shall see later, Chinese Communists have emphasized the view, derived from Friedrich Engels, that women's oppression in traditional family and society was rooted in their exclusion from participation in productive economic activities outside the home and their resultant economic dependence on men. Yet the commonly held notion that women in traditional Chinese society were restricted to the home and were never allowed to participate in "productive" labor is an exaggeration. There is also reason to suspect that various writers and demographers may have underestimated women's economic contributions due to pervasive cultural biases which would lead informants to undervalue and understate work done by women.[33] While evidence does indicate that women generally played "secondary" economic roles and this was, no doubt, one factor in their lack of power within the family, the range of participation was considerable and the effect on women's status of higher or lower rates should not be oversimplified.[34]

As is true in most nonhorticultural, plow agricultural economies, women's participation in the main activities of agriculture—the basis of the traditional economy—was, on average, significantly lower than men's. The only comprehensive national data on women's participation in agriculture in pre-1949 China comes from the massive study done by John L. Buck in the 1930s.[35] The overall rates and the general pattern of regional variation he found roughly fit the patterns of women's participation in agriculture which economist Ester Boserup has found to prevail elsewhere in the world.[36] Buck's figures show that for all of China women averaged 13 percent of agricultural labor, and that women's role in agriculture ranged from almost total exclusion in some northern and northwestern areas (where more extensive, dry plow agriculture prevails) to being a very significant if still secondary one in some southern areas (where more intensive, wet rice cultivation prevails). Aside from some ethnic minority and Hakka areas, nowhere in China did women participate to any significant extent in the "main" tasks of farming, such as plowing.

More important than participation rates, however, was the fact that women's work generally was dependent on and controlled by men who, through the corporate patrilineal family, monopolized control over the means of production and over the fruits of women's labor. Therefore, even women with high rates of participation in agriculture or in other "productive" work were unlikely to be able to translate their labor into significantly greater independence or leverage.[37]

The brutal custom of footbinding was an obvious physical manifestation of the restrictions placed on women's lives and of women's subordination to men and family authority, underlining women's role as "goods for exchange."[38] For nearly a thousand years, footbinding painfully crippled and partially immobilized millions of Chinese women for their entire lives.[39] The custom apparently began as an elite court practice in Central China around the T'ang dynasty because of its erotic appeal to men who developed a sexual fetish for abnormally small feet.[40] It gradually spread throughout China and eventually even penetrated down to the poorer classes in many places.[41] Although we lack national statistical data, the pattern of footbinding roughly seems to have reflected the pattern of women's participation in agriculture. Footbinding obviously limited women's ability to work in the fields. Where families least needed women's labor in agricultural work, footbinding was likely to be most widespread; yet in some areas, bound-footed women could be found working in the fields as best they could during busy periods or even on a regular basis.[42] In many areas, footbinding was considered a requirement for any proper marriage; only girls destined for the life of a slave or indentured servant might escape the painful, maiming custom. Whatever its origins or erotic, even sadomasochistic, functions for men, it is clear that footbinding also served the purpose of controlling women: physically restricting their freedom of movement and further solidifying their dependent position vis-à-vis men and the family. One of the best known of the numerous manuals that expounded on the proper behavior of "virtuous women," *Nuer-Ching* states, "Feet are bound not to make them beautiful as a curved bow, but to restrain the women when they go outdoors."[43]

The need to restrain women is a concern that runs through many myths and much of traditional literature and popular culture. The corollary of such a concern is an acknowledgment of women's potential power. It can be argued that underlying the history of women's subjugation are ever-present male fears of the threat women pose to the male-dominant social order. Thus, Chinese culture traditionally reflected dichotomous and even contradictory images of women.

While women were seen as naturally weak and submissive, they were also often portrayed as dangerously powerful.

In a variety of contexts women were regarded as ritually unclean and harmful to others. Images of women's power usually involved their sexuality or their role in reproduction. Woman, as the object of man's erotic desires, had the sexual power to sap him of his strength and virility. Traditionally men were advised to regulate carefully their sexual contact with women.[44]Folklore and medical wisdom often held that frequent ejaculation could result in a dangerous loss of *yang* (male) essence and a *yin* (female) imbalance in males, leading in extreme cases to death.[45] Yi-tse Feuerwerker points out that in traditional writings the femme fatale is a common theme and popular tales of history are full of powerful female figures who have brought great ruin through their lust and the manipulation of men.[46] In the well-known novels, *Chin P'ing Mei* (*Golden Lotus*) and *Shui Hu-chuan* (*Water Margin*), the "fascination and horror" which men show towards women's sexuality make women the target of misogynous outbursts of violence and ritual exclusion through which men reassert control and dominance.

Cross-culturally, images of sexually irresponsible and dangerous women juxtaposed against cultural ideals of the nurturant, submissive mother-wife are common.[47] But this pattern is perhaps most pronounced in societies with extended patrilineal, patrilocal kinship systems.[48] Such kinship systems make women outsiders to the primary kinship groups of society, but they are outsiders who live within the group and whose reproductive powers are central to the group's continuation. As such, women, particularly new brides, may be viewed with suspicion and as a potential threat to group solidarity. When a woman becomes a mother, her emotional hold over her husband's children may continue to make her uncertain loyalty to the patrilineage seem threatening. Woman's sexuality and reproductive capacity appear to be simultaneously the source of her greatest value to the male group and the primary source of her power to disrupt it.

It can be argued that there was a reality behind fears of women's disruption of the male-defined family and male authority, despite the enormous weight of law and customs that prescribed a "frog in the well" existence for women. Studies of women's behavior in male-dominated family systems indicate that women are rarely as passive as norms dictate. Rather, women often actively attempt in patterned ways to influence their own lives and others even as they overtly accept the broad restrictions on formal rights and authority imposed on them by the system.[49] Because women are barred from overt power and their efforts to achieve power are perceived as dangerously disruptive, they must work in informal, indirect or concealed ways, often relying on the development and manipulation of interpersonal relationships to influence men. In societies where any exercise of power and influence by women is considered illegitimate, even subtle and dimly perceived patterns of female influence might well give rise to or reinforce negative images of women as dangerous and threatening to proper order.

Margery Wolf's analysis of women in traditionally structured Chinese peasant families provides important insights into women's strategies of influence as well as the ways the patrilocal, patriarchal Chinese family structure shapes these strategies.[50] Her analysis and its implications deserve some detailed discussion for they help illuminate some of the dynamics of family reform which will be discussed later, especially the phenomenon of "female conservatism."

The main vehicle for women's exercise of influence, according to Wolf, was the uterine family, which women created in order to mitigate their outsider status in Chinese kinship and their lack of legitimate family authority. A woman's uterine family existed within her husband's family but was centered around herself as mother and was based primarily on her affective relationship with her children. This informal, officially unrecognized family became woman's primary source of influence, security and personal belonging. Thus while males within the Chinese family system were simply *born* into families and social networks of kin and village, women worked much of their lives to *create* networks to overcome their loneliness and lack of influence in the formal structures.

Although the uterine family was a mother-centered group created by women to serve the needs of women, it clearly reflects the dominant patriarchal norms that value sons over daughters. Because of patrilocality and because formal authority belonged only to men, a woman's uterine family needed sons as much as man's patrilineal family did, although for somewhat different reasons. To a man, having a son fulfilled his sacred obligations as a man to ancestors and provided one further link in a patrilineal chain that existed before him and would exist after him. To a woman, a son provided a permanent mother-child relationship upon which she could center a family that would be tied to her for the rest of her life. Sons also provided a conduit through which a mother could hope to influence the world of male authority. The ideal son for a Chinese mother was one who, above all else, was personally loyal to her and who would serve as her "political front man" in domestic and even public affairs. A woman therefore invested a great deal in binding her son to her as she raised him.

In socializing her son, a mother was likely to stress the importance of one of the central patriarchal values of traditional Chinese culture—filial piety—although with a twist. While the classics and men would interpret filial piety as the obligation of a man to place the honor and interests of the patrilineal ancestors and the patriarch above all else, a mother was likely to emphasize to her young son that filial piety involved a man's life-long personal loyalty to the self-sacrificing mother who gave him life and nurtured him.

There were numerous other patriarchal norms useful for women's strategies of survival and influence as well. Arranged, blind marriages and the suppression of romantic love served to keep the conjugal bond secondary and helped a mother protect her relationship with her son from what might otherwise be its most serious threat—a daughter-in-law, especially one who was a strong-willed, seductive, adored young wife.[51] The ideal bride for a son was a submissive, healthy, and hard-working girl unlikely to challenge the mother's wishes and relationship with her son. Because of a mother's overriding interest in protecting her bond with her son, Wolf argues that minor marriages were extremely popular among mothers and were perhaps a "woman's creation." Adopting and raising an infant daughter-in-law allowed the mother to bind her son's future wife to her and further lessened the possibility that the daughter-in-law as an adult would threaten the mother-son relationship.[52] Evidence also suggests that the minor marriage suppressed the potential for romantic or intimate sexual bonding between husband and wife even more thoroughly than the major form of arranged marriage[53]—a consequence perhaps known and appreciated by mothers who depended so much on the filial devotion of their sons. While the final, formal authority to arrange a marriage rested with the patriarchal male, arranging a marriage was also by all accounts women's business in peasant communities. It seems likely that women used this influence not with an eye toward furthering the interests of the patrilineal family, but to protect their own uterine families.

While women primarily relied on building influence through the uterine family and sons, they might also gain informal influence through social networks established outside their husbands' families among women in the village. In many male-dominated peasant socie-ties, informal nonfamilial women's communities formed around the sex-segregated work patterns in villages provide an important means for women to affect family and village affairs indirectly through gossip and the mobilization of social pressure.[54] Chinese men fear "losing face" by having their behavior discussed in public and in their neighbors' households, and women's networks often had the power to make embarrassing public issues of other's behavior, even if men disparaged the opinion of individual women.[55]

Although most of the informal, interpersonal means of influence used by women favor older women who are established in the village women's community and who have grown sons, younger wives might also find some relief from severely abusive family behavior by mobilizing the sympathy of women's networks. In large families, wives might also manipulate domestic squabbles and act through their husbands to influence affairs. The division of large joint households in patrilineal patriarchal societies is often blamed on the inability of brothers' wives to live in harmony due to women's "quarrelsome nature." But such behavior probably reflects more clearly the fact that women act primarily to enhance the consolidation of their own uterine families at the expense of, or in disregard of, the larger patrilineal group cherished by dominant male family ideals and religious beliefs. While men gain economic and political power by binding their kinsmen together, women, young women especially, can gain greater influence and freedom by undermining the larger kin unit in favor of the one in which they are emotionally and personally central. As one scholar has put it, women may indeed be the worm in the apple of patrilocal domestic groups.[56]

Thus, in a variety of ways, it is important to avoid seeing women as passive and as devoid of influence as formal patriarchal family structures, laws and ideology would lead us to believe. Rather, one might assume that in fairly regularized ways the influence of women often went beyond their legitimate limits in informal and sometimes surreptitious ways.

This perspective allows us to avoid an oversimplified view of women as purely passive victims of Chinese history. This latter view has characterized many of the contemporary portrayals of women in traditional Chinese society, including those of Chinese revolutionaries and many Western feminists. The view of woman as victim obviously has merit, but alone it is too superficial and static to illuminate the complexities involved in reform and the behavior of the oppressed, which has often disappointed reformers. The question of what the oppressed themselves have invested in and wrested from the system is rarely asked, leaving obscure the larger issues of what needs to be changed to fundamentally alter their situation.

The work of Wolf, Collier, Lamphere and others invites us to consider the extent to which women who lived within a particularly virulent patriarchal system were nonetheless able to carve out some space in which their behavior and own sense of identity would not be totally dictated by dominant ideals of passive submission to male authority.[57] Through the subtle manipulation of interpersonal relationships and the successful creation of uterine families and informal social networks among women in the community, women avoided, and sometimes actively subverted, totalitarian male control. Women not only actively used accepted patriarchal norms and culture for their own nonpatriarchal purposes, but also subtly shaped their meaning in the process.

One should not, of course, overstate the case. Without legitimate authority and independent economic means, women could not escape the reality of male dominance. While women's strategies manipulated patriarchal norms for female purposes and sometimes subverted male goals, they clearly did not fundamentally threaten male hegemony. The concept of "hegemony," to borrow a term from Marxist Antonio Gramsci, implies inherent conflict between dominant and subordinate groups, but conflict which is safely contained within the bounds of structures and ideologies that represent the interests of the dominant group, in this case males. In the very process of using available mechanisms for greater influence and protection, women's strategies directly and indirectly reinforced the traditional Confucian family system. Ironically, women, through their actions to resist passivity and total male control, became participants with vested interests in the system that oppressed them.[58]

Women could not adopt and manipulate patriarchal norms for their own purposes without simultaneously supporting the broader patriarchal system those norms upheld. In order to ward off threats to the solidarity of their uterine families, older women usually had to become the most stalwart defenders of the patrilineal family structures within which their own uterine families necessarily resided. In the process, women not only supported the patriarchal system, but older women also found themselves pitted against the interests of younger women, including their own daughters. To protect her crucial bond with a son, a woman could be driven to give away her own nursing infant daughter and then force an adopted daughter to marry a "brother." The extremely narrow, highly personalized ties that women had to rely on for influence and survival—primarily ties with sons who were at the same time younger women's husbands—necessarily created conflict among women and divided oppressed against oppressed. While mothers dreamed of docile, hard-working daughters-in-law, young women dreamed of being married to a man who had no mother.[59] Traditional Chinese culture is full of tales of the notoriously cruel mother-in-law as well as the sexually powerful and irresponsible younger woman. Both cultural images find a real basis in women's desperate need to create uterine families and manipulate men. And both images perhaps express the fears of women as much as the fears of men.

The behavior of Chinese women and their response to change in the twentieth century must be understood, then, not only in terms of the massive oppression they suffered over the centuries, but also in terms of the ways they created a stake for themselves within a family system that denied them full human status. Female conservatism, along with a greater proclivity toward personalism and particularism, is understood to be a near-universal phenomenon by many anthropologists.[60] These characteristics have often been attributed to Chinese women in the traditional family, and, as we shall see, have vexed feminists and family reformers periodically throughout the twentieth century.[61] This conservatism is often explained by Marxists and many others in terms of "false consciousness" or some variant of the "psychology of the oppressed"; after years of socialization and confinement to the narrow, domestic sphere, women were left full of negative self-images, ignorant of the outside world, fearful of changes they could not comprehend.[62] From the perspective of our analysis, however, female conservatism and particularistic and personalistic approaches to the world are characteristics which develop logically out of women's strategies of influence and survival within patrilocal, patriarchal structures. They are perhaps less the product of ignorance and distorted, underdeveloped psyches than they are of resourceful behavior under extremely disadvantageous circumstances. Our perspectives also would lead us to expect that "conservatism" is not a general static female orientation, but is directly related to woman's life cycle and the development of her interests through her uterine family. It has already been argued that younger women and women in extended households often act, to the extent they are able, to undermine important traditional male goals. Even the conservatism of older women may be less than it appears, for as argued earlier, women's use of patriarchal norms and structures are likely to be for their own nonpatriarchal purposes—the enhancement of a mother-centered uterine family.

None of this is to deny the importance of the deeper psychological impact of subordination and the internalization of denigrating self-images. Nonetheless, my analysis argues that the specific structural features of the traditional Chinese family and kinship system are crucial starting points for understanding Chinese women's behavior, their means of survival and the perpetuation of some of the most basic aspects of their subordination.

This emphasis on kinship and family structures, rather than economic structures, as the primary locus for understanding Chinese women and their subordination in society receives theoretical support from a number of sociological perspectives on the family, most notably the conceptual framework of Claude Lévi-Strauss and Gayle Rubin's feminist interpretation of his work.[63] Beginning with the basic principle that all societies impose cultural organization on sexuality and biological procreation, Rubin puts forth the concept of a "sex-gender system," a realm outside of (but usually interacting with) the economic system, which transforms biological sex into gender and produces and reproduces gender organization. Drawing on Lévi-Strauss's argument that the creation of kinship marks the origin of culture and society, that marriage based on some degree of exogamy (i.e., incest taboos) is a first principle of kinship structure, and that the "exchange of women" between biologically related groups of men is the basis of marriage, Rubin argues that kinship systems are, among many other things, primary empirical expressions of sex-gender systems. Furthermore, while Rubin maintains the theoretical possibility that sex-gender systems could be sexually egalitarian, empirical investigations indicate that most known kinship systems in some way involve exchanging women (rather than men or men and women), although it seems the "completeness" of this exchange varies (e.g., when matrilocal residence or matrilateral inheritance is practiced or where children may take the mother's family's name). Hence, known kinship systems are typically stratified, male-dominant sex-gender systems. Men, those who exchange, are the primary subjects of social organization; women, those who are exchanged, are human objects of social organization who move between and link male groups. According to Lévi-Strauss,

> the total relationship of exchange which constitutes marriage is not established between a man and a woman, but between two groups of men, and the woman figures only as one of the objects in the exchange, not as one of the partners. . . . This remains true even when the girl's feelings are taken into consideration, as moreover, is usually the case. . . . She cannot alter its nature. . . .[64]

In order to apply the suggestive ideas of Lévi-Strauss and Rubin to advanced industrial societies, where kinship has been stripped of many of its functions, we would need to carefully investigate how sex-gender systems have been maintained and transformed through this process.[65] Furthermore, there are some kinship arrangements in preindustrial settings which seem considerably looser than the ideal type suggested by Lévi-Strauss's analysis. However, nowhere can one find a more "ideal" example of kinship a la Lévi-Strauss and Rubin than in traditional China. In China, the exchange of women between groups of men who composed the basic units of local social organization was clear and complete. The overwhelming dominance of patrilineal kinship ties and the weakness of affinal relations and women's ties to biological kin accentuated the extent to which women were not a recognized part of social organization, culture or society. In this sense, society was composed of male groups, and women existed in the interstices between these groups, not fully belonging to either the group in which they originated nor the one into which they moved at marriage. There have been, perhaps, very few family systems in history where exclusively male principles of kinship organization—patrilocality, patrilineality and patriarchy—have been more pure and unmitigated in jural and customary practices.[66] At the level of ideology,

Confucian doctrine and its spiritual dimension—ancestor worship—
was at its core an ideology of patrilineal, patriarchal kinship.

Not only was the traditional Chinese family and kinship heritage
more unmitigated in its exclusively male principles than many other
known systems, its continuous existence as a dominant ideal form was
historically longer. Recent scholarship on ancient and early traditional
China has argued that kinship rules and customs were not uniform in
either law or practice throughout all periods.[67] This is undoubtedly the
case. Yet few would dispute the relative longevity and continuity of
general Confucian family principles. These principles already were
being asserted as ideals in elite circles by the end of the Han dynasty
(206 B.C.–220 A.D.), a period which saw the rise of Confucian family
moralists whose writings became the basis of ritualized moral treatises
for centuries.[68] They were followed by the gradual elaboration and
codification of the Confucian family ideal from the end of the Han to
the T'ang dynasty (618–907). The continuous existence of a strong,
central state system (the longest in history) officially wedded to
Confucianism provided these Confucian family ideals with a fairly
consistent body of jural and doctrinal support, backed by state
sanction, for over one thousand years. This long period of state power
and support no doubt helped to standardize actual kinship practices
and to further their penetration throughout society. While many have
speculated that during the prestate and "feudal" periods of ancient
China, family and kinship were far less male-dominated (and certainly
less rigid), few if any vestiges of this distant historical period survived a
millenium of imperial state rule.[69] By the middle of the Ch'ing dynasty
when the first rumblings of modern reform for women faintly began to
be heard, Chinese women were embedded in perhaps the oldest, most
highly developed, male-dominated kinship system in history.

This introductory description and analysis of the traditional Chinese
family has stressed the importance of family and kinship in defining
women and shaping their lives and behavior. Within this context we have
analyzed women in the Chinese family and kinship system as both subject
and object, participant and victim. Women were subjects in their social
world because, like other subordinate groups, they struggled to make
themselves subjects through informal and indirect ways, even though the
world they could successfully act upon was extremely narrow. By making
themselves subjects, women also inadvertently were complicit in a small
part of a larger social system that subordinated them. Within the larger
system of patrilineal family, kinship and state, women were more nearly
objects and victims, unable to act on or alter the fundamental normative
contours and structures of basic social organization within which they
were mere vehicles rather than members.

Edward Friedman has argued that among the rural poor, the way in which economic, social and political forces disrupted the rural family was central to creating a significantly large, potentially revolutionary force in the countryside.[9] There is debate as to whether or not average per capita rural income was falling in the first decades of the twentieth century.[10] Yet, it seems likely that peasant conditions were gradually worsening from the eighteenth century onward owing to a combination of increasing population pressures on the land and the nature of the elite structure that had developed by the late imperial period.[11] By the early twentieth century, these factors—coupled with natural disasters, political instability and civil strife, foreign encroachment, increasing commercialization and the impact on rural China of the worldwide depression of the 1930s—created conditions of starvation, pushed people off the land, forced massive migrations and otherwise disrupted the normal functioning of village, clan and family in large parts of China.[12] Under such conditions, countless families were weakened, separated and failed to reproduce themselves, thus destroying the patrilineages of the poor. To be the generation that presided over the breaking of an ancestral line was traditionally the most unfilial and unforgivable of all acts; and to live among strangers—that is, with no kin—made a difficult life all the more precarious and left one with the prospects of a death with neither dignity nor hope of salvation in the afterworld. Socioeconomic disruptions that broke the family were profound personal and spiritual tragedies.

Nearly every village study and personal account from the period tells the tale of such people—daughters and wives sold to pay off debts, children lost to starvation and hungry wolves, sons pushed into a warlord army, husbands forced to distant places to find work, rootless young men without families and without hopes for posterity.[13] In some areas a high percentage of poor males found themselves unable to afford marriage and increasing numbers of people were forced to accept marriage and family forms that deviated from the preferred traditional norms.[14] Extreme hardship and famine caused massive migrations to the Northeast and to the less populated poor mountainous areas of various provinces in the early twentieth century, inevitably breaking up millions of families.[15] Even in more stable and relatively prosperous areas, less dire signs of traditional family and lineage decay were evident in the weakening and corruption of lineage functions in village life.[16]

Thus the prism of experience through which millions of peasants perceived the twentieth-century family crisis was fundamentally different from that of May Fourth youth. The relatively privileged youth who had early access to modern education fought to free themselves from the decaying bonds of the past and to destroy the corrupted presents a scathing critique of the "ideal" Confucian family system, showing how its norms and authority structures crush the spirit of its youth and, both literally and figuratively, destroy the lives of its women. The central theme of the novel is the struggle of the youngest family members to save themselves from the human destruction wrought by the traditional family. The youngest son, who is the novel's hero and represents Pa Chin, finally takes the necessary, yet difficult, final step: he leaves the household forever to "go out into society" and join like-minded youth with dreams of a new world.

Within the context of the anti-Confucian struggles of the May Fourth era, many young intellectuals became increasingly aware of the disproportionate toll that the traditional society and family system took on women. One of Mao Tse-tung's earliest articles, typical of May Fourth critiques of the family, concerned the suicide of Miss Chao, a young bride in his home town.[5] In desperation, Miss Chao had committed suicide rather than submit to a dreaded arranged marriage. Mao asserted that her death and the deaths of many others like her resulted from the "iron net" cast around them by the old family system and the society that supported it. The famous May Fourth writer Lu Hsun described this system as a "flesh-devouring" monster because of the physical and mental destruction it wreaked, especially on women. One of Lu Hsun's most powerful short stories, "New Year's Sacrifice" (Chu-fu), tells the tale of a pathetic woman who was driven mad by the inhuman practices and superstitions fostered by the traditional Confucian family system.[6] May Fourth writers also reflected the way poverty imposed especially dehumanizing forms of suffering upon women because of their lowly status in family and society. Jou Shih's short story "Slave's Mother" portrays how the dire economic conditions that prevailed in parts of rural China led to female infanticide and men's use of women as a final piece of property to barter against debts and starvation.[7] What the May Fourth writers sought for their own lives and for the nation was a family more in line with the reform ideals of the West: a conjugal family based on gender equality, mutual love and free choice. This type of family was believed to be better for the individual and society. It would allow women and youth to fulfill their personal potential and it would free energies previously spent in narrow family obligations and rituals to serve the larger society.[8]

But, of course, intellectuals alone do not make revolutions. The successful Chinese revolution that gained power in 1949 was built on a coalition of many of these radical intellectuals of May Fourth with an impoverished stratum of peasants, marginal peasants and former peasants. This mass base of the coalition was also experiencing a "family crisis," even though it was of a very different sort. Indeed, self-conscious critique of the Confucian family system, and with it came the emergence of modern feminism in China among urban intellectuals.

This critique of the family system and women's position in traditional society was an integral part of the anti-Confucian, iconoclastic intellectual ferment of the May Fourth movement, an urban-based movement of the late teens and early twenties calling for national rejuvenation through cultural revolution.[2] The May Fourth movement, named after a student demonstration on May 4, 1919, protesting the bartering of Chinese territory by imperialist powers at the Paris Peace Conference, marked the turning of a generation of young, disaffected intellectuals toward radical mass political activism. The defection from the old order by intellectuals—primarily sons and daughters of the old gentry and rising commercial classes—began in the late nineteenth century and added to the forces unleashed by dynastic decline, escalating population pressures, forcible imperialist encroachment, and the rise of new, often disruptive, modes of production to weaken the moral, political and economic foundations of Confucianism. These multiple crises demonstrated to the urban intellectuals who spearheaded the rise of social radicalism in the first two decades of the twentieth century the inability of Confucian values and social structures to meet the challenges of technological progress, foreign incursion and ruthless international competition. Their questioning inevitably encompassed the Confucian family, which was long held to be a miniature reflection of the traditional order. The active search for alternative values and ideals to revitalize China and create a more just society was fueled by new Western ideas and modern education that introduced notions of equality, democracy and individual freedom. In the hands of educated youth, these notions became intellectual battering rams with which to storm the Confucian citadel.

Many of the educated May Fourth era youth were also engaged in a personal struggle to free themselves from the fetters of the patriarchal authority and values of their own families.[3] Believing that the hold of old family values and normative ties stifled the potential of youth and women and prevented them from making the necessary commitment to build a new world, many came to believe it was necessary to break completely with the past, including their own families.

The popular autobiographical novel *Family*, by Pa Chin, is a classic statement of the social concerns and personal struggles of May Fourth youth, among whom Pa Chin himself figured prominently.[4] The novel, set around the period of the May Fourth incident (although Pa Chin did not finish and publish it until a decade later), portrays the life of an old, wealthy, but declining, gentry-cum-mercantile capitalist family. It

2 The Twentieth-Century Family Crisis

When revolutionary forces turned to issues of family reform in the 1920s and 1930s, they confronted a traditional family system which was already under considerable pressure and, among some segments of the population, showing signs of disintegration. A variety of economic, social, political and intellectual forces were creating strain for the family. Some of these pressures were old ones, symptoms of economic and social disruption that always accompanied the cyclical decline of dynasties. Others were new and unique to the twentieth century, deriving directly and indirectly from the onslaught of imperialism and the rise of a radical, iconoclastic intelligentsia seeking to destroy the old Confucian order and create a new world. The family crisis that resulted from these interacting forces provided the context in which CCP attitudes and policies toward family reform first emerged, and it has had important, and contradictory, implications for the way those policies have evolved.

Although there was very little criticism of the traditional Confucian family system prior to the late nineteenth and early twentieth centuries, criticism was not totally absent. Several of the popular epic novels of the Ming dynasty (1368–1644), such as *Dream of the Red Chamber* (*Hung-lou meng*), *Journey to the West* (*Hsi yi ji*) and, to some extent, *Golden Lotus* (*Chin p'ing mei*), present implicit or explicit critiques of certain aspects of the family system, particularly the suppression of romantic love and the distortion of human relationships. By the 1830s, several scholars had explicitly criticized aspects of the traditional treatment of women, including footbinding, harsh and unequal standards of female chastity, concubinage and restrictions on the development of women's abilities.[1]

But the last years of the Ch'ing dynasty (1644–1911) and the early years of the republic (founded in 1911) saw the first blossoming of a

27

There are several general points which flow from this analysis that are particularly relevant to understanding changes and evaluating policies that have developed with the Chinese revolution. One of the major theoretical and practical issues raised by Chinese Communist policy (and by recent scholarship on this subject) concerns the extent to which one can explain, and alleviate, women's subordination to men by dealing mainly with their traditional exclusion from, or subordination within, the system of economic production. My analytic perspective suggests that women's secondary roles and relatively low participation rates in major areas of the economy deprived them of important means of influence and narrowed the sphere in which they could act. But it did not in itself cause the basic subordination of women, which derived from fundamental principles of kinship organization and family formation, both of which in turn organized society.

To say that women's subordination in the basic social networks formed by family and kinship is not a derivative of their role in the economy is not to assert the opposite, nor is it to assert a lack of interaction between the two realms. Rather, it is to stress that those who would seek to fundamentally alter women's traditional subordination to men would have to make reform of the ideology, norms and structures of family and kinship central to their efforts. These efforts would have to involve altering unquestioned cultural assumptions of men and women, especially older women whose own subordination had led them to both internalize and use patriarchal norms in order to survive. At the same time, efforts to alter the structures of family and kinship would be a necessary counterpart to gradually changing consciousness, to opening people up to new assumptions and values concerning women and gender equality. Women were subordinate and held to be inferior to men not only because of misogynous cultural values and attitudes of disdain, but also by structural patterns inherent in marriage and kinship, patterns that made men the rooted basis of community networks and made each new generation of women "outsiders" to social organization. As long as these patterns remained undisturbed, parents, kin and village would look differently upon the value of males and females and their social position even if major economic changes made males and females equal in their income-earning activities.

Finally, the nature of the traditional family and kinship system—its longevity, its unchallenged agnatic principles, its place at the core of an all-encompassing social, political and religious ideology, and the dynamics of female behavior produced by its structures—ensured that effective reform would be difficult and would require an enormous, long-term investment of energies in a variety of direct and indirect ways. Reformers would, of course, find it difficult to win over men and women to fend for themselves and hence to find greater independence. Rural families sent increasing numbers of young peasant girls to urban areas to work in new textile industries in order to obtain additional sources of income, necessitated in some areas by the deterioration of traditional rural cottage industries.[28] Although these girls were often tied to contracts negotiated between their families and labor contractors, many derived a new degree of independence from their wages and from their distance from direct family control. They also gained some exposure to the modern influences of the treaty ports, which were centers of May Fourth activity and, later, labor movement agitation.[29] A tiny minority of small towns and rural areas also saw the introduction of girls' education, primarily through Western missionaries, who sometimes induced the poor to send their daughters in return for food.[30]

But the fresh cultural currents of the May Fourth movement generally failed to reach rural areas beyond the immediate vicinity of urban centers. And for most poor rural women, their "liberation" from traditional family controls under the conditions of early twentieth-century China must have been experienced as brutal, degrading, and life-threatening. Women forced to rely on themselves or to support a destitute husband could expect to find little other than demeaning work offering the barest subsistence. The more fortunate might find work in domestic service, most others as the lowest paid laborers, beggars or prostitutes. The suffering of women under conditions of poverty and family disintegration took especially cruel forms; if not drowned in infancy, they often found themselves bartered and sold, deserted and starved.[31] As the lowest, most dependent members of traditional society, they were the most vulnerable and suffered the most from its disruptions.

Numerous first-hand accounts reveal the vulnerability of women who could not rely on stable family relationships. Underlying such accounts is the added pain that comes from a sense of living a life that violates what is understood to be proper and moral. Not uncommon is the following account of a peasant woman born in Shensi Province in the early twentieth century who recalled the tragically familiar encounter with the slave dealer and the scourge of opium, which foreign traders had imposed on China by the mid-nineteenth century.

> Ours was a poor family, and when I was sixteen I was married off to a peddler and tinker, who took me with him to Hopeh. He began smoking opium and stopped working his land so he lost it. He began going round the villages mending cooking vessels. He was often away for long times at a stretch.
> I looked after our house in Wuan hsien. I don't know what he paid for his opium, but I got less and less from him and in the end

I was getting nothing at all. As I did not want myself and our daughter to starve to death, I took a place with a farmer. . . . with his own land. I worked there for four months. I had no pay, but food for myself and my daughter.

When I was twenty-two I was sold. [Weeps.] My husband came one day and fetched me and my daughter and took us to a slave dealer called Yang. [Weeps.] My husband sold us so as to get money for opium. I never saw him after that. So years ago I was told that he was dead. When I had been two days with Yang, the slave dealer, he sold me. He sold me and my daughter for 220 silver dollars to a farmer called He Nung-Kung.

I was very unhappy. Mr. He was an old man. He was twenty-three years older than I was. We did not love each other.[32]

Under normal, stable circumstances, the quality of peasant women's lives depended heavily on the threads of the interpersonal ties they wove within the family and village. When, in the face of severe poverty and its dislocations, these frail threads snapped, women had pathetically little to fall back on other than their own personal strengths. Therefore, many women must have longed for a stable traditional family life, to be properly married wives and mothers, living within a familiar framework which provided an opportunity to build those traditional ties that gave hope of some dignity and security in old age. For too many rural women, the weakening and disintegration of the traditional family and the loss of the ability to live properly by its norms did not have liberating consequences, but led to greater humiliation, poverty and insecurity.

The fundamentally different ways in which intellectuals and poor peasants experienced family crises and change in the decades just prior to the creation of their revolutionary coalition led to a conflict of aspirations and values that would have an important impact on the pursuit of family reform and women's rights during and after the revolution. Yet the situation was not as simple as a dichotomous split between two forces, one seeking restoration and the other reform. On the one hand, despite defensive and restorationist impulses among the disrupted peasantry, there were forces in the countryside that were predisposed to certain reform appeals, predictably among those most oppressed by the traditional family system—young women. On the other hand, the intellectuals who emerged from the May Fourth movement were neither fully united nor single-mindedly committed to the pursuit of women's rights and family reform as political priorities within the revolutionary movement. The move from intellectual agitation to organized political activism marked by the founding of the CCP highlighted tensions between the feminism of the urban women's movement and the Marxist categories and political priorities of the predominantly male CCP leadership, even though they basically agreed on the goals of gender equality and family reform. These tensions in many ways paralleled the classic conflict between so-called bourgeois feminist concerns and orthodox Marxism that emerged among Bolsheviks in Russia by the early 1920s, a conflict over the proper relationship between gender and class oppressions in theory and practice.[33] Indeed, these tensions have continued to characterize theoretical and political debates about feminism, Marxism and the "women's question" ever since.[34]

Thus, the political predisposition toward family issues among revolutionary urban and rural political forces in early twentieth-century China was neither simple nor completely dichotomous. Tactically speaking, cross-cutting alliances to further or hinder the promotion of women's rights and family reform policies were possible from the outset. But there is no doubt that the political and cultural obstacles confronting women's rights and family reform advocates within the revolutionary movement increased when the CCP's revolutionary strategy shifted in the late 1920s from the more socially and culturally hospitable urban areas, where it was based primarily on workers, students and intellectuals, to rural areas where the primary constituency was poor male peasants caught in the throes of social disruption. The resolution of the dual family crises was bound to be controversial within the revolutionary movement.

2 Women and the Family in the Chinese Revolution, 1921–49

3 Women and the Party: The Early Years, 1921–27

While the most important forces shaping Communist Party policy and practice toward women and the family during both the revolutionary and postrevolutionary periods lie primarily in the Party's rural experiences, the Party's ideological origins, as well as its early top leadership, developed out of the radical intellectual ferment that was centered mainly in Chinese cities in the early twentieth century. The CCP was founded in Shanghai in 1921 and first developed in China's growing urban areas. It was initially the creation of those urban students and professors whose earliest dissident intellectual and political activity was as participants in the iconoclastic New Culture and May Fourth movements of the late nineteen-teens. It is clear that the urban forces shaped by the May Fourth era have had a stronger influence on articulated Party values and long-range goals than on Party practice concerning women's rights and family reform. The contradictions and tensions which arose from the successful revolutionary coalition of radical intellectuals and peasants that came together in the 1930s and 1940s is reflected, in part, by an enduring tension between ideological goals and practice on women's issues.

The early history of the CCP shows there were also tensions among progressive urban forces concerning women's rights and family reform, primarily between the independent women's rights movement and the Marxist CCP. While the conflicts that emerged later in the rural areas were more fundamental and important in shaping CCP policy and practice, the early urban experience of the Party (1921–23) and the first revolutionary alliance with the Kuomintang (KMT) (1924–27), during which both parties made their first tentative moves into the countryside, remain relevant to understanding Party attitudes, debates and policy approach. Some of its later attitudes can be traced to the Party's initial reactions to the early urban-based women's movement and to the way its Marxist ideology influenced these attitudes. Moreover, during this period, compelling pressures pushed activist women away from the reformist women's rights movement toward revolutionary struggles based on a class analysis which demanded a radical restructuring of ruling groups and society. It appears that in making the transition from reformist feminism to broader revolutionary activities there were pressures on activist women to shift their concerns away from combating gender oppressions to concentrating on other types of class oppression. In this sense, rather than becoming more inclusive, women who began to join in the revolutionary activities of the two left-wing parties, the KMT and the CCP, were urged to concentrate more exclusively on economic class oppressions. The class analysis of the two political parties, especially the CCP, asserted not only that abolishing the oppression of women had to be predicated on the success of the class struggle, but also, implicitly, that the oppressions of women as women were somehow less severe and intrinsically less important as targets of change than the oppressions of workers as workers and peasants as peasants, with these generic categories being largely defined in terms of the males who filled them. The fairly rigid Marxist orthodoxy of the early CCP failed to address the fact that for most class categories Chinese women were anomalies, if class is defined in terms of property ownership and one's relationship to the means of production. As we have seen, women as a group had no real property rights and, with few exceptions, exercised no control of the means of production and very little control over the fruits of their own labor. One could argue that, in this sense, nearly all women, as women, were a propertyless class, or *wu-ch'an chieh-chi*, the Chinese translation for the term proletariat.[1]

The earliest contacts between the Communist Party and women's rights groups and issues reveal the initial ambivalence in their relationship, as well as their compatability on basic long-term goals concerning issues of gender equality. On the one hand, as Marxist revolutionaries and inheritors of the May Fourth movement, the Party leaders sought the support of progressive women and officially recognized the universal validity of their demands for equal rights as just, ultimate goals. Yet at the outset, the Party distrusted the feminist groups themselves as "elitist," "bourgeois" reformers and distrusted their emphasis on "sexual politics."[2] Whether or not the CCP was influenced by the antifeminist thrust of Russian Communist Party resolutions that emerged in 1923, the CCP's ambivalence reflected a more general tension that has existed between orthodox Marxists and feminists. In the minds of many Party members, feminism has never lived down its early historial association with liberal, middle-class reform movements. And the term "feminism" rarely occurs in Chinese Communist writings without a qualifying term such as "narrow" or "one-sided" (*p'ien-mien te*).

The first time the Chinese Communist Party officially turned its attention to women as a group was a year after its founding at the Second National Congress held in the summer of 1922. The congress decided to establish a special Women's Department to help organize and lead women in revolutionary political activity. Hsiang Ching-yu, one of Mao's fellow student activists from Hunan and the only woman on the Central Committee, was placed in charge of this new department. In addition to establishing the Women's Department, the Manifesto of the Second Congress included among its objectives "the unlimited right to vote for all workers and peasants, regardless of sex," protection for female and child labor, and the abolition of all legislation restricting women.[3]

According to one of the congress's participants, some of the impetus for establishing this new department came from a decision taken by the Third International.[4] But this decision also certainly reflected the influence of politically active urban forces in China at the time. Many of the first Communist Party members had already indicated a concern for raising women's status and reforming traditional norms which restricted women during the May Fourth movement. The manifesto also showed the influence of women's rights groups that were active in the early twenties although significantly, it did not specifically mention the marriage and family rights raised by these groups. These groups, such as the Woman Suffrage Alliance, the Alliance for the Women's Rights movement, and various provincial alliances, argued for such things as the right to self-determination in marriage, equal husband-wife relations, equal property rights for women, the right to vote and hold office, and the right to work and to obtain an education. Similar small groups had been agitating for reform through petitioning and public demonstrations during the preceding decade.[5]

But while the Party generally espoused the democratic demands of these groups, it did not seek to establish organizational ties with them, and many Party members negatively evaluated the groups themselves. Hsiang Ching-yu, the Party's top woman leader, criticized the various women's rights groups for being Westernized, bourgeois, reforming elitists who lacked strong organization, failed to relate to women workers and the poor masses, and ignored the need for revolution.[6] These "bourgeois feminists" were also criticized for concentrating on sexual politics, incorrectly identifying men as the oppressor, rather than concentrating on the ruling class and the entire social system as the root cause of both male and female oppression.[7]

Most of these groups did seem composed mainly of women from the educated, urban minority, although some groups tried to enlist a broader constituency.[8] A larger number of active women in these groups were the Christian-educated daughters of landlords, business-men and educators.[9] This is not surprising since foreign mission schools and the YWCA were pioneers in offering girls educational opportunities. These schools provided many middle- and upper-class girls with a rare opportunity to escape the immediate authority of family and in-laws and often exposed them to liberal views on gender equality and politics.

Some of these women's rights groups did, however, try to relate their work to women workers. In the early twenties, increasing numbers of women workers were becoming politically active in unions and strike activity, calling attention to their wretched living and working conditions. Some women's rights groups aided women work-ers through educational work and provided support work for their unions, for example, by writing leaflets or petitions. Christian women's groups were apparently the most active in developing these kinds of links and in carrying out welfare and educational work among women workers. Indeed, a number of important women leaders after 1949 (such as Li Teh-ch'uan, Soong Ching-ling and even Chiang Ch'ing) were associated in some way with these Christian women's groups and their welfare work among workers.[10]

Nonetheless, these women's groups appeared to many of their Communist Party critics to be irrelevant to the revolutionary politics which the Party believed had to be rooted in the economic struggles of the working class. Thus at this early stage feminism became identified as irrelevant bourgeois politics by many leftists and Communists. Feminism, it was thought, overlooked the larger social and economic issues and the reforms it sought were futile without revolution, being predicated on a nonexistent democratic process.

Some prominent women activists, however, did emerge from this women's rights background, becoming more committed to the need for revolution in their general politics and also less singularly concerned with feminist issues. They came to view the oppression of women as but one evil of an economic and social system which needed to be totally revolutionized through mass action. Teng Ying-ch'ao, who married Party leader Chou En-lai in Canton in 1925, came from this background. One of the handful of top CCP women in the early years, Teng had been active as a student in the May Fourth movement organizing female students and was involved in the women's rights movement as a teacher in Tientsin in the early twenties.[11]

In the early years of its existence, the CCP's Women's Department under Hsiang Ching-yu concentrated on organizing women laborers. The Party was then emphasizing an "urban strategy" and women made up a sizable proportion of the proletariat. Indeed, in many cities, the majority of industrial workers were women, owing to the predominance of light industry, especially textile industry where work was closely related to traditional women's work and a traditional women's handicraft industry—spinning and weaving.[12] Furthermore, in 1922 labor activity was growing and women workers already were becoming active.[13] The first notable women's strike occurred in twenty-four Shanghai silk factories in 1922. An estimated 20,000 women participated, demanding a ten-hour work day (instead of fourteen) and a five cents per day wage increase.[14] The strike lasted three days and was apparently a failure, but it drew attention to the potential for labor organization among women. Given this worker activity, given the Party's overall emphasis on workers, and given Hsiang's negative views of the other existing women's groups and her distrust of women intellectuals, it was natural that she would turn most of her department's attention to working with women workers. It was claimed by Hsiang's sister-in-law, Ts'ai Ch'ang (sister of Mao Tse-tung's close friend, Ts'ai Ho-sen, and later married to Li Fu-ch'un), that the Party organized 100,000 women, mostly in Shanghai, Canton and Hong Kong, under the Women's Department between 1922 and 1925.[15] Ts'ai, who took over the leadership of the CCP's Women's Department around 1925, characterized Hsiang's early activity as giving a new direction to the women's movement:

> Before Hsiang Ching-yu founded the real woman's movement in China, there had been only a scattered Feminist tendency deriving from the May Fourth Movement. This had been conceived in terms of the bourgeois fight of women against men, the emancipation of women as a sex from the oppression of men. Hsiang Ching-yu changed the leadership of the whole movement into a Socialist channel in a new direction. Her idea was that the low social position of Chinese women was due to a backward social system, and that the emancipation of women can only come with a change in the social structure, which freed men and women alike.[16]

While the women's rights movement of the teens and twenties was perhaps too small, too isolated, and too naively reformist to be a real women's movement, Hsiang and Ts'ai seemed to be working more for a "worker's movement of women" as their notion of what a real women's movement should be. While one could not dispute Ts'ai's assertion that a change in the entire social structure was necessary, Ts'ai and Hsiang's ideas about the women's movement seem to have lacked any tactical concern for specific women's issues. Indeed, from 1925 until her execution in 1928 at the hands of the Kuomintang in Hankow, Hsiang, known posthumously as the "Grandmother of the

Revolution,'' was no longer directly connected with the Women's Department at all, but with general labor activity.

During 1925–27 when the CCP and KMT joined in alliance, an alliance which the CCP considered part of the "bourgeois democratic phase" of the revolution, the organization of women within the revolutionary movement grew in numbers and seemed to broaden from the narrow, orthodox approach first adopted by the CCP. At the first congress of the reorganized KMT in 1924 a Central Women's Department was formed, headed by Ho Hsiang-ning, married to an important left-wing KMT leader, Liao Chung-k'ai. Ho was the first women to join Sun Yat-sen's Revolutionary Alliance in 1905. Like Hsiang and Ts'ai, she had not directly participated in the independent women's rights groups. But her work with the Central Women's Department showed a greater concern for women's rights issues and Ho herself seems to have been strongly influenced by her close associations with women's rights leaders, which included those involved with active Christian-sponsored reform groups. Ho readily invited Communist women to work through her KMT department and in 1925, Teng Ying-ch'ao, with an established background in the women's rights movement, joined Ho in Canton as a secretary of the Central Women's Department.

The Central Women's Department operated as an active united front organization only until 1927 when Chiang K'ai-shek brutally turned on its mostly left-wing and Communist membership. During its existence, the organization of women not only expanded but also more actively incorporated feminist issues than Hsiang's and Ts'ai's CCP Women's Department had. In this brief period, it appeared that feminist issues might become more firmly established as active issues within the revolutionary movement.

According to Ho, the purpose of her department was twofold—bringing women into the revolutionary movement and obtaining women's rights from the Nationalist government.[17] Unlike Hsiang's department, Ho's was especially concerned with marriage reform. Perhaps partly as a result of the influence from Ho and her department (Ho and Teng were both members of the KMT Central Committee), in 1924 and 1926 the KMT passed resolutions declaring equal rights for women and freedom in marriage and divorce, abolishing the legal slavery of women and girls through the purchase-marriage system. Footbinding, which had been officially discouraged since 1911 but was still practiced in many areas, was also prohibited. The task of the Central Women's Department, as Ho saw it, was to give some substance to these resolutions. As Ho told Anna Louise Strong, "The women do not even know that the new laws exist; we must have propaganda to tell them. . . . The question of divorce is the most difficult and complicated question in China."[18]

Under the KMT-CCP department, various women's groups were organized among workers and students in the Canton and Hankow area. But, for the first time, efforts also simultaneously moved into rural areas behind the successful march of the Northern Expedition, a joint KMT-CCP military effort to destroy warlord power and unify China under a single national republic. By 1927, Ho claimed that a million and a half women were organized in ten provinces under various "women's unions" and mass organizations.[19] She claimed that not only women in the cities but also women in the countryside were beginning to be awakened by revolutionary activity.

As part of this effort, Soong Ching-ling, the widow of Sun Yat-sen, set up a Women's Training Center in Hankow for the purpose of training young women propagandists who then became cadres for educating and organizing women in KMT-CCP-held territory. These propagandists, and the district women's unions they helped establish, were active enough to establish a reputation as defenders of new rights among local women. Although short of funds and political influence, various unions were frequently sought out by run-away slave girls and child "foster daughters-in-law" who had heard that they might find refuge with the unions.[20]

As Ho had indicated, the most serious problems faced by the women's unions concerned marriage reform. As propagandists went out to organize and educate women about the revolution and their new rights as advocated by the KMT and CCP, many women sought escape from family oppression by coming to the women's unions for a divorce or other help. But succor for abused women often caused conflict with the traditionally dominating men and male peasant leaders whose control over women was thereby threatened. To such men and those who sought to organize them, feminist issues seemed a divisive matter for the revolutionary movement, especially in the countryside.

This problem emerged in what is claimed to be the first peasant women's union. This union was established around 1924 in the Hailufeng area located in coastal Kwangtung. The area was initially organized by the famous landlord-Communist P'eng P'ai, independently of either the central CCP or KMT. There were two women's unions established, the Women's Peasant Union and the General Women's Union for teachers, students and workers, as well as peasants. Together, the unions grew to two or three thousand members. Most of the members were young, as was typical later of many other women's unions. The women in this area were said to be unusually aided by local tradition, due perhaps to the local influence of Hakkas, a cultural minority group whose women worked in the fields with men, did not bind their feet and were known for their strength and independence.

But even though the men of Hailufeng were accustomed to more independent women than elsewhere in China, many of them hated the women's unions because, as one participant stated, they "defended the rights of women and took care of the divorce problem."[21] The union investigated women's complaints about family maltreatment, trying to make sure the women received either better treatment or a divorce. The union thus became known to its detractors as the "Bureau of Divorce and Remarriage."

In Hailufeng at this time, as in many other areas, large numbers of male peasants were experiencing a downward mobility and economic squeeze which made their ability to hold their families together increasingly precarious.[22] While these conditions must have contributed to the appeal of P'eng P'ai's peasant movement, these same conditions also probably made it all the more difficult for insecure male peasants to accept a new kind of threat to their ability to maintain control over their families in the traditional manner.

This type of problem, often in much more acute form, emerged in one union after another. As the head of the Hankow Women's Training Center, Soong Ching-ling, explained:

> If we do not grant the appeals of the women, they lose faith in the union and in the women's freedom we are teaching. But if we grant the divorces, then we have trouble with the peasant's union, since it is very hard for a peasant to get a wife, and he has often paid much for his present unwilling one.[23]

This conflict was a continuing problem in organizing peasant women within the revolutionary movement. The CCP, though committed to the ideology of gender equality, nonetheless had difficulty reconciling even the minimal needs of women's emancipation with organizing a unified peasant base for the revolution.

This conflict also was reflected in debates over organizational tactics and forms. Working with women through wholly separate and independent organizations accentuated the conflict by giving women more autonomy which they used to press their own needs. Several young women organizers who had been working with women in Hunan while attached to the Political Department of the Northern Expedition Army, discussed with Anna Louise Strong the current debate about the best way to organize women in order to further the revolution.

> "We ourselves work in the peasants' union, because we think women must be closely related to the peasants. For if the peasant cannot find peace and welfare, the women by no means can find it." They explained that there was much difference of opinion regarding the organization of women in the country districts, whether there should be separate women's unions or only separate sec--

tions of peasants' unions. They believed in the second method in rural districts, saying that the first problem was the economic welfare of the entire peasant family.[24]

The view of these young women organizers was apparently the one encouraged by the male Communists they worked with and was hinted at, though somewhat tentatively, in the 1926 Resolutions on the Women's Movement.[25] The unspoken consequence of this greater integration was to give male peasant leaders greater control over the direction of women's activities and thereby make men less threatened by attempts to organize women. The result of this effort to appease male fears was to place women's organizations more closely under the control of those most likely to oppose women's efforts to free themselves from traditional family restrictions.

Within the less autonomous organizational framework created under the Army Political Department, the young women organizers still tried to deal with women's special problems during the Northern Expedition. One of their tasks, after gaining the confidence of local peasant women (which was sometimes quite difficult), was to explain to them about women's new rights under the KMT-CCP and about the evils of footbinding and arranged marriages.[26] They then attempted to set up local organizations which would try to implement some of these changes after they left.

It is hard to tell how successful the three or four hundred young army propagandists were in their work. The Party itself commented that, during this period, peasant women had "displayed a high degree of spontaneity in joining the peasant movement."[27] In some cases, women's unions seemed to have attracted substantial membership, even in the face of public disparagement of such activities.[28] There are numerous reports of women who, after hearing of women's new rights under the Nationalists and Communists, sought out women's unions to help them enforce their new freedoms. Yet the propagandists also encountered stiff resistance, not only from men, but also from older, more conservative women. The strange young uniformed women who followed soldiers, walking freely about the village, talking to strangers and preaching traditionally "immoral" doctrines of "free love" (which was one interpretation of free-choice marriage), scandalized many villagers. In Honan, the women propagandists were withdrawn because of conservative local reaction to such "shocking" behavior.[29] Elsewhere, there were reports of young women leaders being beaten and murdered by angry family members or neighbors. Some organizers had to flee for their lives for fear of being turned over to local soldiers who moved in after the Northern Expeditionary forces left.[30]

Apparently the efforts of propagandists and their enthusiastic supporters often gave the revolutionary movement a bad name, associating the revolutionary cause with immoral behavior in the eyes of many local people. Mao Tse-tung addressed this problem in a report on his investigation of the peasant movement in Hunan in 1927, claiming that this problem gave counterrevolutionaries an opportunity to turn people against the movement.[31] He implied that such problems arose because of premature and precipitous actions by organizers and the failure to establish the proper sequence of revolutionary tasks.

According to Mao, peasants were oppressed by four systems of authority which comprised the feudal-patriarchal system. Both men and women were subjected to the state system (political authority), the clan system (clan authority), and the supernatural system (religious authority). In addition, women were dominated by men, the authority of the husband. Mao praised the fact that with the rise of the peasant movement, "the women in many places have now begun to organize rural women's associations . . . and the authority of the husband is getting shakier every day." But he added,

> At the present time, however, the peasants are concentrating on destroying the landlord's political authority. . . . Therefore our present task is to lead the peasants to put their greatest efforts into the political struggle, so that the landlords' authority is entirely overthrown. The economic struggle should follow immediately, so that the land problem and the other economic problems of the poor peasants may be fundamentally solved. As for the clan system, superstition, and inequality between men and women, *their abolition will follow as a natural consequence of victory in the political and economic struggles.* If too much of an effort is made, arbitrarily and prematurely, to abolish these things, the local tyrants and evil gentry will seize the pretext to put about such counter-revolutionary propaganda as . . . "the peasant association stands for the communization of wives," all for the purpose of undermining the peasant movement.[32] [Emphasis added.]

This formulation is important because its basic theme of finding the proper relationship between women's emancipation and various other revolutionary goals is raised again and again. Mao's uncharacteristically deterministic statement that equality will be attained as a "natural consequence" of establishing political power and proper economic conditions clearly implies an expectation that women will in due time attain equality without great conflict. Thus, conflict brought on by premature action is not only counterproductive but unnecessary.

Given that the political power of the Hunan peasant associations was so tenuous, it is not surprising that Mao argued that all other issues should be subordinated to the central issue of consolidating political power. But his optimism that patriarchal ideology would be easily and naturally abandoned in time seems drastically to underrate the tenacity of traditional beliefs and of the basic family structures that supported these beliefs among both men and women. Even more so, he overlooked the added strength such beliefs may gain in a situation where a successful peasant movement gives insecure peasants the means to realize their traditional family ideals.

Of course action taken by organizers before any of the women understood or supported such action was likely to cause adverse reaction and was likely to be unsuccessful, as Mao predicted. Conservative reluctance among peasant women was a serious problem for organizers.[33] Few peasant women had been exposed to ideas of equality and freedom which challenged centuries-old morality and customs. Women who had had little choice but to accept their own formally lesser place in an ordered hierarchy and who had spent most of their lives working to adapt that place to their needs and make it secure, must have found the new ideas perplexing, even dangerous. But issues of gender equality were divisive even when, probably especially when, propaganda for greater women's freedom found a base of support among the women themselves. Younger women who showed concern over the problems of marriage, divorce, and traditional family restrictions inevitably caused conflict within families and with the male-dominated peasant unions. Younger women also threatened the security of older women who feared losing control over their daughters-in-law and sons.

Although Mao recognized the immediate problems posed by disunity, he overlooked the long-term implications and dilemmas in creating gender equality which would continue long after the seizure of power. The strong conservative resistance so evident in the early experiences of the women's unions ironically signalled the great need for these unions to act as pressure groups for women's rights at the same time that this resistance indicated to Party men the danger of unions causing disunity and dissipating support for the movement. The dangers of disunity seemed more immediate and crucial to leaders than the long-term cause of developing women's political power or enforcing women's rights. Their solution was to subordinate the women's unions to the peasant associations and depoliticize women's rights issues whenever conflict arose, emphasizing instead common interests of men and women in establishing a new political and economic order.

In 1928, after the destruction of the KMT-CCP alliance and the Central Women's Department in 1927, the CCP moved firmly in the direction of calling for the subordination of women's organizations to the peasant associations, a position which the Party would maintain thereafter. A resolution passed at the CCP's Sixth Congress, held in

Moscow, stated explicitly that "conditions in China [were] not suitable for the organization of independent women's associations." Therefore, according to the resolution, the Party should not undertake this work and where independent women's organizations still existed, they were supposed to be incorporated into the peasant association.[34]

It is unlikely in any event that many of the women's unions set up during the 1925–27 period survived the KMT-CCP split and the right wing militarist reaction that followed. The right-wing KMT turned on the CCP and moved to suppress both urban and rural revolutionary mass organizations. KMT and warlord armies entered villages to destroy the peasant associations, labor union activity was suppressed or taken over, Communist organizers were killed or forced underground. Regardless of party affiliation, "liberated" women and girls were sought out for bloody revenge, sometimes being identified merely by their bobbed hair and, in some places, their unbound, large feet. The KMT Central Women's Department which had been controlled by left KMT and Communist women in Canton and Hankow was officially dismantled.

Whether or not the Party could adequately handle the tensions and conflicts around issues of women's basic rights without abandoning its ideological commitment to reform when it re-established itself with a firmer base in rural areas was a severe test yet to come. The Kiangsi Soviet period (1929–34), which we will examine next, provided the first real test of CCP commitment and ability to implement more rights for women, since it was the first time the Party exercised political control over a sizeable rural area.

4 The Kiangsi Soviet Period, 1929–34

After the serious setbacks of 1927–28, Communist guerillas of Mao, Chu Teh and P'eng Teh-huai gathered in the mountainous Hunan-Kiangsi border area. From this stronghold Mao and Chu moved into Kiangsi and western Fukien in Central-Southeastern China, establishing a government calling itself the Soviet Republic of China, or the Kiangsi Soviet, centered on the town of Juichin and comprising parts of Kiangsi, Fukien and Hunan. There were a few other scattered base areas set up elsewhere at this time, but the Kiangsi Soviet area was the largest and most successful. Here, despite enormous difficulties in defending against continual KMT attack, the Communists gained their first extended experience in governing and reorganizing rural society. Communist armies held the area for about five years, during which time peasants were politically organized and various social policies such as land reform were instituted. These also included policies aimed at changing the legal status of women and enlarging the scope of women's activities to help support the government's war effort and the economy.

The main emphasis in the Party's work among women throughout the Kiangsi Soviet period was on rear-area support for the war effort as necessitated by the continuous need to fight against the KMT "encirclement and annihilation" campaigns.[1] This was emphasized in a March 1931 "Plan for Work among Women" drawn up by the Special Committee for Northern Kiangsi of the CCP Central Committee:

> The most important task of the Women's Movement is to mobilize the broad masses of toiling women to join the revolution in order to keep abreast with the main task [which is to resist the attack of the imperialists and the Kuomintang against the Red Army, and to struggle for the consolidation and expansion of the power of the

51

Soviets]. We must make the women understand that only the extension and consolidation of the Soviet area and the intensification of the attacks on the enemy, can protect the interests gained and still to be gained by the women within the Soviet area.[2]

It was important to win over women to the revolutionary cause because they could in various ways influence men's decisions about joining the army. Several Kiangsi documents mention that where women had not been mobilized to support the war effort, they often tried to hold back their sons and husbands from the army.[3] Some women reportedly threatened to leave their husbands if they joined the army. Yet, where the Party's women's work was done well, women were credited with playing a major role in encouraging men to join.[4] Organizing women to learn farming skills and take over agricultural work and mobilizing women's groups to aid the dependents of Red Army soldiers also greatly helped the Party enlist men into the army.[5] A successful recruitment policy required that the Party be able to tap the resources of the entire family unit. This made women a key link in war mobilization and support. When the Party recognized this and invested its organizational energies in mobilizing women, women proved to be an invaluable resource for the revolutionary effort.

In these efforts the Party was aided somewhat by local traditions. Traditionally, women in parts of this southeastern area of China had higher rates of participation in agricultural labor than in any other part of China.[6] Also, in some parts of the Soviet area, such as Hsing-kuo County, a model area, footbinding was no longer practiced and perhaps had never been very prevalent.[7] These factors no doubt facilitated women's ability to take over for absent men. In this respect, parts of Kiangsi and Fukien provided a relatively hospitable environment for enlisting women to replace men in the economy. Even so, special organized efforts had to be made. "Plowing classes" were sometimes set up to help teach women how to perform traditionally male tasks. As a result of the war mobilization and efforts to enhance women's farming skills, some areas apparently became quite dependent on women's labor.[8]

Women contributed to the war effort more directly as well. Through the trade unions, about 10,000 women workers were organized to spend their spare time sewing for the army. Women were also organized into defense corps. Many women workers and peasant women were trained by the Trade Unions for Women Red Guard units or joined parallel Youth Volunteer units.[9] Though these women received some military training, they mostly engaged in rear-area services such as carrying supplies, nursing soldiers and occasionally carrying out intelligence work. A few women actually belonged to the Red Army, such as K'ang K'e-ch'ing, known as "the girl commander,'' who joined the Red Army in western Kiangsi in 1928 and later married Chu Teh. There were about 100 other young women who came to Kiangsi with the Red Army.[10] There were also instances of women joining partisans outside the Soviet area. In Szechuan a regular fighting regiment of women was active and there was later one unit attached to Chang Kuo-t'ao's armies on the Long March.[11] These women were symbolically important to many women in the revolutionary movement and established something of a reputation for southern women as spirited revolutionary fighters.[12] But they were very unusual cases, and in Kiangsi women were not allowed to do any front line fighting, although according to K'ang K'e-ch'ing some of them wanted to. The rear service activities of the Red Guard and the sewing groups were far more typical of the roles women were encouraged to take up to support the war effort.

As more men were drawn away into the army, war mobilization also indirectly provided women with an opportunity to increase their political participation in local Soviet bodies. In the model township of Ts'ai-hsi in western Fukien, an area with particularly heavy army recruitment, an investigation by Mao found that the representation of women in the local congresses reached 64 percent in 1933 as most of the young men were drawn away.[13] In another general report, Mao claimed that ''in many towns and villages women formed above 25 percent'' of the representatives elected to government councils.[14]

Although the new pattern of women's activities resulted more from the needs of the war situation than from the leadership's commitment to emancipate women from restrictive traditional roles and dependencies, it was nonetheless maintained that these new activities had implications for changing the public image and self-image of women. One woman leader spoke with great pride about how women had shown themselves capable of performing every kind of economic work, including traditionally male work, in the rear areas.[15] Mao typically proclaimed that the women's economic, political and war mobilization activities had clearly shown that women were a great and significant revolutionary force in the Soviets, contrasting sharply with the traditional image of women as useless in formal community affairs.[16]

While it seems that most practical work in organizing women emphasized the war effort and the need to maintain the economy, official policy and legislation did not ignore the range of women's rights issues which had concerned the young women propagandists before the 1927 suppression. These issues appealed to many young women and young men in the Soviet and helped the Party gain their allegiance. In the area of legislation, the Party leadership, less timid and much more in control than during the Northern Expedition, used its power to establish a fairly radical legal framework for women's rights in the Kiangsi Soviet. The provisional constitution adopted at the First Congress of the Chinese Soviet Republic in November 1931 guaranteed woman suffrage and stated:

> It is the purpose of the Soviet government of China to guarantee the thorough emancipation of women; it recognizes freedom of marriage and will put into operation various measures for the protection of women, to enable women gradually to attain the material basis required for their emancipation from the bondage of domestic work, and to give them the possibility of participating in the social, economic, political and cultural life of the entire society.[17]

Several other pieces of legislation affected the legal status of women. The Land Law provided that women had equal rights to land allotments, thus giving legal property rights to women as part of the "material basis required for their emancipation."[18] The Labor Code adopted by the Soviet Congress included the demands previously advocated by women delegates to the National Labor Conference in Hankow in 1927.[19] It contained an "equal pay for equal work" clause and a series of special regulations providing for paid maternity leave, nursing facilities for mothers plus a guarantee that women could not be dismissed during or immediately after pregnancy.[20]

The most important and revolutionary legislation affecting women was the Marriage Regulations passed by the Central Bureau of the Soviet Areas at the First Congress, and its passage was probably controversial among congress participants.[21] Evidence suggests that the passage of these regulations may have been owed in part to the recent arrival of the underground Shanghai wing of the Party which was forced to flee to Kiangsi by the early 1930s. According to a later account by a woman Party cadre, many of the new arrivals from Shanghai objected strongly to the views and practices of some other Party groups in Kiangsi who favored the restriction of marriage and divorce rights.[22] The more liberal, progressive outlook of these urban-oriented leaders no doubt helped tip the balance within the leadership in favor of strong marriage legislation containing no restrictions, mediation clauses or ambiguous qualifications.

The Marriage Regulations codified the principle of freedom of marriage and divorce, prohibiting coercion or the interference of third parties. Polygamy, the sale of women as wives, the practice of taking a "foster daughter-in-law," and all forms of child marriage were prohibited. The provision for divorce was terse and unqualified: "When one party is determined to claim a divorce, it shall have immediate effect."

This very liberal divorce clause was the single most radical clause in the regulations, going as far as any formal law could go in providing women with the legal basis to nullify the patriarchal power of exchanging women and to establish their own "rights in themselves" with regard to marriage. Upon divorce, the woman retained her full property rights; she kept her land allotment and an equal share of any property gained during marriage. Totally contrary to the customs of patriliny, the woman was favored in the custody of young children, which would be crucial to any Chinese woman with a vested interest in her uterine family. In recognition of women's economic disadvantages, the man, if necessary, had to help support her and her children by tilling her land. Without this provision, divorce would have been economically impossible for many women. The law thus recognized that most women had not attained the "material basis required for their emancipation." The law also involved the state in marriage affairs for the first time in China by requiring registration of marriage and divorce with the government. In part, the registration was supposed to serve as a minimal check that the law was complied with.

Although official documents established strong principles of reform and thus created potentially powerful legal weapons for reform activists, when actual implementation and actions were involved, clear signs of political conflict and ambivalence arose. Party documents, concerned that efforts on behalf of women's rights, especially those involving family relations, were potentially divisive among the ranks of the peasantry, issued warnings that it was necessary to maintain "a unified working class" in the struggle for women's rights and marriage reform.[23] Hidden in such demands for "unity" was, it seems, the desire for delay. Women who emphasized the need to deal with women's family oppression and marriage problems were criticized for leading the women's movement "away from the general movement" and "becoming isolated" from the class struggle; it was claimed that such women "concentrated on marriage problems, thus facilitating the emergence of a contradiction between the sexes which could obstruct the land reform."

The issues which were of concern to young women activists threatened the poor male peasants who were the favored constituents of the land revolution and the Red Army. Poor men, if they were able, bought their wives in the traditional manner. Now, as they were struggling to break the chains of their own oppression, gaining the means to improve their livelihood and hold their families together, their traditionally defined control over their "female property" was being threatened by the propaganda of women organizers. If the marriage law was actually enforced, in some cases poor peasant men might not only lose their wives, but also their wives' land. In order to avoid having to deal with such potential and complicating conflicts, many party leaders might well prefer suppressing the efforts of women leaders to help women solve their marriage problems and gain greater freedom.

The issue of men "losing their wives" was not taken lightly by Party leaders. Mao, in a 1931 investigative report, expressed the view that one of the cruelest aspects of the old society was that many of the male poor were unable to "get wives."[24] These men were thereby unable to meet the basic, minimal criteria of manhood in traditional society. Mao, understanding the central importance of such deprivation, hoped to present the Red Army's revolution as a force capable of redeeming the manhood of this prospective revolutionary constituency. Initially at least, Mao also hoped to dovetail this appeal to poor men with the leadership's commitment to marriage reform. He therefore argued that marriage reform would help improve the situation for poor men because it undermined the "purchase marriage system" that allowed the rich to monopolize more than their share of women while making marriage a ruinous financial burden even for middle peasants. Mao and the Soviet government therefore invited poor unmarried men to use the new marriage freedom to find women and marry despite their inability to meet traditional requirements.[25]

The terms in which Mao expressed the appeal, however—for poor men to "get wives"—underscored the problem for marriage reformers who were under political strictures to maintain a unified base of support. For marriage reform in essence was not a means of "redistributing females to the poor," like land reform or rent reduction, but an attempt to redefine qualitatively the nature of marriage by allowing women to "get themselves" through self-determination in both entering and leaving a marriage. While the most wretched poor males who were unmarried, and hence had no stake in the old marriage system, might have accepted these new terms, the more "respectable" poor peasant and middle peasant men who had managed at great cost to buy wives in the proper way were bound to see it differently. Such men were probably a majority of males in most of the Soviet areas and to them the Marriage Regulations, contrary to Mao's argument, might seem to pose a new threat to their struggle to hold their families together.

Too much concentration on freeing women from traditional family restrictions when carrying out women's work was also attacked because it was said to "give rise to decadent ideas concerning marriage."[26] References to "anarchistic immoral behavior" among cadres and young people indicated that people within the Party were concerned that new ideas about relations between the sexes were leading to moral degeneracy. One document, written in March 1931, from a Conference of the Secretaries of Women Committees of the Communist Youth, Northern Branch, revealed similar concerns and criticisms.[27] The document asserts that Communist Youth women leaders, many of whom were probably students, had difficulty relating to peasant women as well as to men, presumably because poor peasant women were not interested in women's rights. They were accused of "separating the women's movement from class consciousness" by stressing women's rights in order to win over "petit bourgeois" women, a charge that recalled the criticism of the women's rights movement in the early 1920s, discrediting "feminism" and women's rights by linking them to "petit bourgeois" politics. Some young women leaders were said to have succumbed to "romanticism," thus engendering the "disgust of the masses." It seems that even within the Party, young women were expected to shun public and personal contact with young men, in accordance with repressive traditional double standards of female "chastity." Ironically echoing, in the guise of "socialist morality," traditional patriarchal norms which held it both immoral and a threat to authority for young people to pursue romantic love or choose their own mates, some Party organizations criticized young people for being decadent and corrupt if they showed any personal interest in the new issues of marriage and freedom in love.[28]

It is difficult to tell the extent to which complaints about anarchistic and sexually immoral behavior actually reflected significant changes in behavior following the initial efforts to loosen the chains of traditional mores and norms. We know from reports from other places that even minimal movement towards greater freedom by women and young people often brought shrill accusations of moral degeneracy and sometimes resulted in brutal suppression.[29] In Kiangsi there is evidence which suggest that, in some places, women were in fact able to use the liberal marriage regulations to obtain divorces and, seemingly, to marry of their free choice. A report on two counties in the Soviet areas of northeastern Kiangsi indicated that the divorce rate was extremely high there during the spring of 1931, perhaps equivalent to a per annum calculated rate of 30 per 1,000 population or higher.[30] Reports by Mao on investigations of Ch'ang-kang Township also mentioned that free marriage and divorce for women were being put into practice.[31]

Yet one must be cautious in assuming that a significant change or a significant improvement in women's situation had occurred in many of these areas. It seems that private sexual behavior among peasants in parts of the Kiangsi Soviet area had deviated sharply from public traditional norms even before the arrival of the Communists. The woman cadre mentioned earlier reported that prior to the arrival of revolutionary forces, sexual and family relationships in some areas were "chaotic."[32] Similarly, Mao's Ch'ang-kang investigations indicate that in some areas "secret love affairs" had long been common among the peasants. In 1927 in the neighboring areas of eastern Hunan Province, Mao also found that "trilateral and multilateral" sexual relationships were common among poor peasants.[33] It seems likely that this situation was a symptom of the developing family crisis among the rural poor discussed earlier—reflecting the large numbers of the poor who were unable to afford proper marriages and the increasing inability of poor married men to control their family women. It is possible that some of the unstable nonmarital liaisons which were already common among some strata of peasants were now simply being reflected in the family registrars as marriages and divorces.[34] If this was the case, the widespread accusations that marriage reform and women's rights activists were creating conditions of "moral degeneracy" were not only unjust, but obscured the real dynamics of the situation.

There was another kind of "excess" which was also associated with reform efforts and which also seems to have served to discredit such efforts. Some male cadres and other men construed efforts to criticize traditional restrictions on women as a new means to further exploit and sexually abuse women. For example, some members of the Communist Youth in the Soviet districts of western Fukien were accused of forcing women to "sleep pell-mell with men" under the pretext of "combating feudalism."[35] Elsewhere it was reported that the local Soviets in some districts in Juichin forced widows to remarry within five days of a husband's death.[36] This latter offense was likely encouraged by the concern that poor men had been "deprived of wives," in the same sense that they had been deprived of property, so that cadres perceived "family reform" as a means of restoring "rights in women" to poor males. In the absence of concerted educational efforts and attention to reform work, it is not surprising that such "deviations" occurred. Indeed, they were predictable. But, it is ironic, to say the least, that such actions, which totally misconstrued the spirit of reform, would be used to argue for the need to downplay efforts to promote the reform regulations. Yet some of the documents which refer to "anarchistic immoral behavior" were making precisely this argument.

It seems likely that the greatest problem with the Marriage Regulations was not that they were "abused," as their detractors claimed, but that many women and young people had difficulty using them at all. In addition to the conflicts and problems already discussed, there was a general shortage of trained cadres to carry out central policies.[37] Among women, this shortage must have been even greater. War mobilization, land reform and economic construction were all considered more urgent priorities demanding cadres' attention. Women who were concerned with marriage reform and women's rights were asked to walk an impossibly fine line: to promote freedom of marriage and divorce, but oppose "absolute freedom"; to promote greater equality and protect women's rights, but avoid conflict with men; to set examples as politically active, emancipated women devoted to the revolution, but avoid offending those moral sensibilities inside and outside the Party which were conditioned to the view (however hypocritical) that proper women's activities should be largely confined to domestic family concerns, without public contact with strangers and men. Since women were warned by various Party groups against concentrating too much on women's rights and marriage reform, in addition to all of their other obstacles, it seems unlikely that much attention was paid to enforcing the Marriage Regulations.

Not surprisingly, a central government resolution in May 1932, indicated that among government organs there was a "tendency to suppress the interests of women" and to reject their appeals concerning the Marriage Regulations.[38] The provisional government was directed to investigate these tendencies and a provincial Soviet government report which appeared later in 1932 illustrated some of the problems.[39] For example, it said that in some of the counties of Kungplueh and Yungfeng, women were not allowed to ask for a divorce. In parts of Kanhsien, cadres not only refused to grant divorces, but put those requesting divorce in prison. Even in Hsing-kuo, the model county in Ch'ang-kang Township where Mao had earlier reported that marriage and divorce were free, some cadres still would not carry out the government's regulations on divorce. Another report resulting from an investigation of work in Ningtu County claimed that women who requested divorces were sent back home by local cadres tied up like criminals.[40]

Unfortunately, it is unlikely that the Soviet government had much opportunity to deal adequately with these problems after officially uncovering them. From 1932 on, the Soviet faced increasing military pressure, compounded by serious economic problems resulting from a successful KMT blockade.

Even so, in the midst of the fifth and final encirclement campaign, the central government promulgated a new and revised marriage law in April 1934.[41] The rationale for the revised law seems to have been to reconcile the government's official marriage policy with its urgent need to recruit more men into the Red Army. Most of the 1934 revisions were minor ones, making explicit what must have been implicitly understood anyway: for example, that a destitute man cannot be required to help support his divorced wife and children; that if a divorced woman has a "definite occupation" and can support herself, the man's burden of support is correspondingly lessened. The only major change involved a new clause which stipulated that if a soldier's wife wanted a divorce she must first obtain her husband's consent. Only if her husband fails to communicate with her by letter over a long period (two or four years, depending on how difficult communications were) may she request the government to register a divorce, the government having the authority to reject or accept it at its discretion.

The woman's legal right to free herself from a marriage into which she probably was sold interfered with army morale and the ability of the Red Army to enlist male peasants. Some men no doubt feared that their wives might take the opportunity afforded by their absence in the army to seek a divorce. Thus the government sharply curtailed the legal rights of soldier's wives, a group that by 1934 probably constituted the majority of young married women in the Soviet areas. For most of the army and Party leaders, the needs of women and the commitment to abolish the enforced traditional restrictions placed on them seemed neither as urgent nor as central to revolutionary success as assuaging the sensibilities of their men. It was probably argued that the soldiers, who were risking their lives for the revolution, should not at the same time have to worry about losing their wives with the aid of the government they were serving. On the contrary, it was the duty of that government to protect the property, including wives, of its revolutionary fighters and to help maintain their families in their absence.

On these issues Mao himself was caught in the contradictions which arose between his multiple revolutionary goals. While Mao was an early supporter of women's struggle to free themselves from the bondage of traditional morality and to assert new rights, he also understood the central importance of the poor male peasant's aspirations to attain his dignity and manhood through building a stable ongoing family. Mao had already argued that marriage reform, which promoted women's rights, would simultaneously benefit these poor men because it would abolish the economically ruinous bride price system. But when faced with a serious conflict between his goals, Mao, like most other leaders, usually sought to resolve the conflict by downplaying, compromising or moderating efforts to promote women's struggle against traditional male and family authority. Thus, in an effort to protect the morale of his fighting men, Mao personally supported the clause abrogating the divorce rights of army wives.[42]

This pattern of compromising efforts to promote women's rights in the face of conflict which seemed to threaten other revolutionary objectives is only partly a problem of dealing with temporary, compelling wartime conditions. And it is only partly a matter of dealing with problems developmentally in "stages." The pattern of compromise is an enduring feature of women's rights and family reform policy in China. The conflict has its roots in the contradictory aspirations of the different constituents of the revolution and in the dual nature of the experienced family crisis which helped to create revolutionary conditions. In the initial years in Kiangsi, Mao and other leaders hoped to be able to straddle the two sides of this experience—the intellectual's iconoclastic struggle against a decadent tradition and the poor peasant's struggle to hold on to some semblance of the old norms of decency and legitimacy. Yet when there were sharp conflicts between advocates of women's rights and the poor male peasants, Mao, like most of the Party-Army leadership, empathized with the latter, who constituted their most crucial constituency. This pattern which tenuously and somewhat ambiguously emerged in Kiangsi, later became fully articulated, entrenched and dominant when the Party center moved to the more conservative environment of the Northwest.

Even though the record of the Kiangsi Soviet period is mixed, when viewed in historical perspective, it seems that, compared to the later revolutionary period, women's rights advocates in Kiangsi were relatively more successful in influencing policy and, to a lesser degree, in actually implementing policy. Although the evidence is far from conclusive, it seems that upper-level policymakers persisted in officially supporting a fairly radical policy toward women's rights and family reform until the last months of the Soviet despite pressures from conservative elements. Efforts by middle- and lower-level officials to place restrictions on the new practices were rebuffed by the leadership when they passed the radical 1931 Marriage Regulations and the worst abuses at the lower levels were thereafter occasionally criticized.

The relative strength of women's rights advocates during the Kiangsi period relates in part to the relative strength of urban-oriented political forces, the freshness of the rural revolutionary experiment and the fact that culturally conservative and backward-looking rural elements had not yet fully entrenched themselves as the major constituency within the revolutionary movement.

In some ways the local social environment in the Kiangsi area also may have been more conducive to family reform efforts and women's rights than in many other parts of China. At the time of the arrival of the Red Army, there seems to have been a degree of sexual freedom for women in some of the Soviet areas which did not exist in many parts of rural China. Also in parts of the Soviet, women not only had among the highest agricultural participation rates in China, but they seemed able to take up unusually active political and community roles compared to women in villages elsewhere. The apparently advanced degree of disintegration of family ties and the relative looseness of marital relationships for a portion of the population, coupled with these particular cultural, social and economic factors, perhaps created conditions more favorable to women's rights and family reform activists than they would find anywhere else. The distinctiveness of the Kiangsi area in this respect is indicated by statistics from the early 1950s which suggest that Kiangsi had probably the highest divorce rate in China at that time, four to five times the national average.[43]

Of course the strength of family reform advocates in Kiangsi should not be overstated. The headiness and radical nature of official family reform policy in the first major area where the Party held power is striking mainly when contrasted to the later Yenan period and even the post-1949 period.

Finally, it should be noted that the abridgment of rights for soldier's wives in the 1934 Marriage Law turned out to be more than a temporary transitional adjustment to suit difficult war conditions. The clause appears in all subsequent versions of the law including the 1950 law and its peacetime application up to the present—long after joining the army was considered a hardship and a sacrifice. The cruel reality for the Red Army in Kiangsi was that few of the soldiers ever saw their families after October 1934 anyway. Of the 100,000 soldiers who left on the Long March, over 90 percent died during the ordeal. It has been claimed that none of the survivors were ever able to find the families they left behind in Kiangsi, many of whom were murdered by the KMT troops who occupied Kiangsi after the Red Army left.[44]

5   The Yenan Experience and the Final Civil War, 1936-49

In the fall of 1935, the Communist armies began to arrive in the small isolated guerilla base in northern Shensi, called the North Shensi Soviet. This area was later known as the Shensi-Kansu-Ninghsia Border Region (Shen-Kan-Ning) and its capital town, Yenan, became Communist headquarters during the Anti-Japanese War (1936-45). The local situation for organizing women in this poor, remote and mountainous area of the Northwest was in many ways less favorable than it had been in Kiangsi. This area was widely considered more conservative and restrictive in the prevailing norms governing women's behavior. Moreover, the Buck study done in the 1930s showed that women in the northern winter wheat-millet growing regions had the lowest rates of participation in the agricultural economy, only 5 percent compared to nearly 30 percent for women in parts of Kiangsi Soviet area.[1] Footbinding was still practiced on many girls at this time and nearly all older local women had bound feet, except the minority groups who lived near the Mongol border.[2] According to Helen Snow, who was in Yenan in 1937, the bound-footed northern peasant women looked askance at the strange "big coolie feet" of the urban and southern women who came to Shensi.[3] In the more conservative atmosphere of the mountainous Northwest, women's rights issues were considered by many Party leaders to be even more sensitive and potentially divisive than they had been in Kiangsi. Official policy toward family reform became more conservative. The low-priority support given to implementing women's rights and marriage reforms in Kiangsi narrowed further in the wartime base areas and eventually turned to active suppression of those who attempted to raise such issues within the Party.

Prior to the arrival of the Red Army, no substantial reform efforts had been undertaken in the North Shensi Soviet.[4] A Long March participant who had been a high-level Communist cadre in Kiangsi (and who later betrayed the Communist Party) observed that the top-level North Shensi leadership did not entirely share the Kiangsi leadership's views on these issues.[5] He noted that Liu Chih-tan, Kao Kang and other leaders in the North Shensi Soviet continued to be "influenced by old Chinese ethics" on issues related to family reform. Therefore there had been no attempts to change marriage and family relationships in the area. After the arrival of the Red Army, Shensi leaders apparently expressed concern about the radical reform ideas of the Kiangsi Soviet. At a government meeting in the spring of 1936 a section chief of the Central Internal Affairs Department openly complained that everything the Red Army stood for was good except for the marriage law it had brought from Kiangsi, which was very bad and would result in a "high tide of divorce."[6]

In September 1936, the Central Organization Department issued resolutions aimed at developing mass organizations in the border region, including women's associations. But the report indicated that little had yet been accomplished in building a women's movement and it urged further caution in developing a movement for women's rights because of its potential divisiveness.[7] Greatest efforts were to be devoted to building a broad peasant association, including middle peasants, and creating an Anti-Japanese Salvation Association to mobilize a mass base for a second united front.

In the next few years, large numbers of women were organized into women's associations, study groups, and production units within the villages. In 1937 and 1938, when other base areas were created in the North and Northwest, similar activity was carried out among women. In 1937, the current director of the Women's Department, Li Chien-chen (a Long March veteran, originally from the Tung-kiang area of Kwangtung), claimed that 130,000 women in Shen-Kan-Ning had been loosely organized into women's associations. This was about 15 percent of the women. But apparently many of these memberships were nominal. Li found that about 80,000 were active enough to "attend meetings regularly."[8] In early 1938 the women's associations of Shen-Kan-Ning claimed a membership of 173,800.[9] Again, a large percentage were probably members in name only. It is hard to judge how politically active or meaningful these organizations were. In 1938, various mass organizations, including women's associations, were consolidated into the Rear Area Enemy Resistance Association, and it appears that activities of individual organizations lapsed. It has been suggested that while such mass organizations as village peasant associations were important and vigorous during the major mass campaigns for land reform and rent reduction, between these periods their membership became more formal than real.[10] Since the women's associations received less encouragement than peasant associations, one suspects that many existed largely on paper.

In some areas, initial organizational efforts were accompanied by some propaganda for women's rights, such as for better treatment in their families and against wife beating.[11] But the main organizational efforts were aimed at increasing women's role in production to help support the economy and the anti-Japanese effort. Some training centers were set up to train local women leaders and familiarize them with Party policy. These local women then helped organize small village cooperatives and encouraged women to take up work in their spare time in their homes, most commonly, spinning, weaving and sewing. These were traditionally women's tasks and in the past they had formed the basis of a textile handicraft industry performed by women in their homes. But in many areas in the North and Northwest, such handicrafts work had dwindled in the last few generations because of the loss of markets to more efficient modern and foreign industry.[12] The few women who had retained these handicraft skills were therefore encouraged to train others in small groups. As a result of such efforts the number of women engaged in household production of cloth in Shen-Kan-Ning increased from 5,000 in the late 1930s to 13,500 at the beginning of 1943.[13] Mobilizing women to make shoes, blankets, socks and uniforms for the Red Army was even more important. These were the skills most women utilized in their own domestic work and this made it easier to enlist their efforts. Li Chien-chen also reported that some women were learning to do agricultural work and that thousands of women were involved in cultivating the land for the first time.[14] As in Kiangsi, this was particularly stressed in areas where the male population had been drawn away by army recruitment, although it is unlikely that more than a small percentage of women fully took up field work, especially in the Shen-Kan-Ning area where footbinding seems to have persisted longer than in other northern base areas.[15] It seems that, for the most part, efforts to increase women's production minimized the degree of change from traditional patterns necessary to mobilize women's labor and harness it to the war effort.

Obviously, the main motivation behind the policy to increase women's production was to mobilize "underutilized" or "nonproductive" forces to improve the economy, making the base areas more self-sufficient in the war effort and helping to compensate for the loss of male labor power. But women leaders also pointed out that this remunerative work improved women's social position. By contributing directly to the family income, rather than indirectly, as with traditional domestic work, women were expected to increase their status and respect within the family and gain some economic independence.

There were also periodic efforts to encourage women's political participation. Political enfranchisement was a new development for many poor men as well as for women, but the step was of course a much larger one for women. Women in the Northwest and North were perhaps particularly handicapped by the strength of conservative norms which excluded them from involvement in important public affairs. In Shen-Kan-Ning, the 1941 election campaign was accompanied by much propaganda extolling models of politically active women and urging local women to vote and become candidates.[16] Afterwards, 8 percent of the township council seats in that area were held by women, compared to many parts of the Kiangsi Soviet where 25 percent or more of the elected representatives were reported to have been women.[17] Li Chien-chen states that there were also 7,000 women Party members active in all of the Soviet districts in the summer of 1937.[18] This figure probably represented about 15 percent of the total Party membership at that time.[19] Li implied that, for the most part, these women had "no family connections," suggesting that the normal family responsibilities of peasant women precluded active Party membership. One can therefore surmise that a very large number of the Party women in these districts were not local women but students and Party members who had come from other areas to join the base areas. Although the Party did encourage local women to vote, it seems to have implicitly accepted that traditional roles and responsibilities of family women generally excluded them from recruitment into the Party. This effectively limited the female population considered available for training Party activists and reinforced traditional obstacles to women's equal political participation.

Efforts to promote marriage reform, while not totally absent at first, were accorded a very low priority among the various tasks to be carried out among women. Although the 1934 Kiangsi Marriage Law formally remained in force for a while and was occasionally used, mostly by women, there was no effort mounted to popularize and implement the law.[20] By the early 1940s, various local versions replaced the relatively strong Kiangsi version of the law in each of the different areas.[21] Although all these laws reaffirmed free-choice marriage and women's property rights, they were in many ways much weaker and more conservative than the Kiangsi law. They all qualified divorce by specifying grounds for divorce and giving the local government or courts discretion in granting them. Since old judicial personnel were probably retained and relevant government positions manned by untrained local cadres, this discretion was likely to result in the greater use of traditional standards in deciding divorce cases—standards, in other words, that strongly discriminated against women. Several of the laws treated betrothal in the same manner as marriage, so that betrothals were considered legally binding and breaking a betrothal had to be requested as if it were a divorce. Regulations for the Shansi-Hopeh-Shantung-Honan Border Region prohibited young women from breaking a betrothal with army personnel. Women were no longer favored in child custody except with nursing infants, and a Shen-Kan-Ning provision favored the father in the traditional manner. The man's obligation to support a divorced wife was also more qualified in these laws, and, in some cases, if the wife was considered at fault in certain ways (one law includes impotence) the man has no obligation. The early 1944 Shen-Kan-Ning law makes the most obvious concessions to traditional practices. It makes no specific reference against "purchase marriage," against taking foster daughters-in-law, against child betrothal, or against third party interference. It simply states that marriage must be based on "free will."

Since there is little evidence that any of the laws, including the 1934 Kiangsi one, were widely enforced, these local changes perhaps had little practical effect for most women. They did, however, indicate that leaders in the base areas were dissatisfied with the stronger Kiangsi law and believed that the formal legal framework for reform (whether implemented or not) should be more moderate in its potential impact on traditional family relations.

In late 1942, P'eng Teh-huai, deputy commander of the Eighth Route Army and secretary of the CCP North China Bureau, delivered an important report on work in the North China Base Areas in which he expressed the need for great caution in promoting women's rights and gender equality.[22] At a meeting of middle- and upper-level cadres of the T'ai-hang districts, the liberated areas along the mountain range that straddles the Shansi, Hopeh and Honan border regions, P'eng stated that the slogans and the implementation of policies of the women's movement must be determined by the development and success of various other phases of the peasant movement. He distinguished between raising policies as slogans and actually implementing those policies, saying that at times slogans could and should be raised but implementation efforts should not be undertaken. He warned that "freedom of marriage" should not even be put forward as a slogan until the peasants had been fully mobilized, the economic position of the poor improved through the rent and interest reduction movement, and women's "political consciousness" raised. Prior to these developments, P'eng said, the main slogan of the women's movement should be family harmony. The general slogan of "equality between men and women" could be raised in the abstract, but efforts to actualize the slogan should not be undertaken. P'eng added, somewhat defensively, that the importance of the family harmony slogan for women should not be denigrated, because it included opposing the traditionally

widespread mistreatment of women within the family. The postpone-
ment of other women's rights issues was necessary because until the
bitter economic situation of poor males had been ameliorated and
women's "political consciousness" raised, many of the wives of the
poor would try to leave their husbands and find better-off families. The
likelihood of this happening was increased by the fact that poor males,
due to their harsh lives, were more likely to beat and mistreat their
wives. Such men would naturally fear and mistrust marriage reform
and would act to prevent their wives from participating in revolutionary activities if they felt their wives could leave them.

This statement, later issued as an internal Party directive, candidly
posed the cruel dilemma faced by the Party. It was precisely the fact
that poor women would welcome and use their new rights that made
these rights dangerous to the Party's cultivation of its primary constitu-
ent—the poor male peasant. The Party's policy choice was clear: it
would temporarily withhold the right of divorce and free marriage from
poor women, whose miserable lives were admittedly often made worse
by family mistreatment. In the meantime, the Party hoped that
women's treatment within their families would gradually improve with
the improvement of poor families' economic situation and with propaganda to promote "family harmony." In this context, raising the
"political consciousness" of women meant persuading dissatisfied
poor women to remain in their husbands' families and try to make the
best of the situation.

The report said that once the masses were gradually brought to a
point where they were ready for marriage reform—that is, after some
economic improvement had been attained following rent and interest
reduction and after the "political consciousness," especially of poor
women, had been raised—"free marriage" slogans could be raised and
marriage reform implemented. Providing local cadres with the leeway
to decide when these conditions were met was more likely than not to
result in nonimplementation of marriage reform. Local powerholders
were almost entirely males whose own traditional views and position in
villages composed of male-centered family networks made it unlikely
that they would carry out family reform without clear upper-level
prodding. Those who would benefit most directly from reform were
precisely those most likely to lack access to local power. Women
therefore needed strong, unambiguous upper-level support if they were
to be able to initiate local reform efforts.

The highly cautionary tone of P'eng's report was instructive. Cadres
trained to read directives carefully, to distinguish between slogans and
action, to note different levels of urgency and upper-level pressure to
act, would read this document as providing a wide margin for inaction.

P'eng's report also advised caution on other women's issues, reiterating the distinction between raising a slogan and carrying out action to realize the slogan. For the current period, he said, and for a period well after rent and interest reduction had been carried out, women's participation in politics was to be considered a propaganda slogan only. Not until (male) peasant democratic power and political organizations had been thoroughly consolidated, should the slogan take the form of real action. Similarly, women's property and inheritance rights were to be understood only as propaganda slogans until the "sympathy of the masses," especially men, was gradually developed. In the current period the slogan, and the law giving women these rights, was to have practical meaning only for widows and for daughters who had no brothers.

In the early 1940s, the Party's policy toward women increasingly stressed production to the total exclusion of all other concerns, eventually going much further than P'eng's report in pushing women's issues into the background. While P'eng's report spoke of the need to be cautious and postpone reform, documents which appear a few months later failed to even mention the issues or were openly critical of cadres who did raise them.

The trend toward exclusive emphasis on production, and total abandonment of the other "secondary" issues, coincided with the onslaught of multiple military, political and economic crises in the border regions. By 1941 the Japanese had turned the brunt of their attacks against the Communists, shrinking the size of the base areas' population and armies. In addition to the devastation of Japanese attacks, the United Front with the KMT had for all practical purposes dissolved, resulting in the cut off of all subsidies to the Communist armies resisting the Japanese and a KMT economic blockade against Communist-dominated territories. As a consequence of these problems, the already poverty-stricken border regions faced increasing economic stagnation and inflation as the CCP government desperately tried to squeeze out sharply higher taxes and new army conscripts. Various new political and economic policies had to be devised to reorganize and rejuvenate the economy, lessen the burden of administrative cost, and enlist greater mass participation in new cooperative and productive efforts.[23] In the drive for self-sufficiency and for the alleviation of poverty, the army, in addition to its soldiering, began to engage extensively in production to help support itself and the local economy. All government and Party cadres were organized to spend some of their time performing productive tasks in agriculture or factories.

As a central part of this "production war," renewed and more widespread efforts were made to utilize family women's labor. Though there had been some previous activity in organizing village spinning groups, most of the textile production had been concentrated in state-run factories. In 1942–43, industrial expansion was coupled with decentralization and greater emphasis on village and home industry in order to stimulate and take advantage of local initiative, native skills and underutilized labor potential. Village women became the mainstay of textile production in the drive to become self-sufficient in cloth.[24]

The dire need to mobilize all human resources compelled the Party to place much greater emphasis on the crucial role which women could play. But it also provided the political context for totally dropping issues of family reform and women's rights. All issues which did not directly relate to production were to be dropped, for it was argued that they diverted energy into "secondary matters." In February 1943, the Central Committee (with Ts'ai Ch'ang the only woman member) issued an important and extremely conservative directive on women's work in the Anti-Japanese Base Areas which clearly enunciated this policy.[25] According to the directive, women were not to be called to mass political meetings. The village women's associations were to be de-emphasized and supplanted by small production groups as the basic unit for women's organization. Political, cultural and educational work was to be carried out among women only to the extent that it directly contributed to improving their production skills. There was no mention of the 1934 Marriage Law, no work to educate against child betrothal, no mention of oppressive traditional practices except those practices, such as footbinding, which it said directly hindered production. Instead, women leaders were instructed to "lessen the unnecessary mobilization of rural women" so they could devote more energy to production.

To justify this policy and defend its narrow focus against its feminist critics, the directive fully developed the notion that this singular emphasis on production was not only necessary to the war and the peasant's livelihood, but was the best, indeed the only, way to further women's own liberation. The directive criticized women leaders who questioned this rationale and who failed to act on this premise.

> To raise the political standing of women, raise their cultural level, change their lives for the better, and advance them down the road to liberation, it is necessary to begin with economic abundance and economic independence [for women]. This will be a great con-tribution to the economic construction of the base areas and [the women] can also, in accordance with material conditions, gradual-ly overthrow feudal oppression. . . . This is the new tendency in women's work in all the Anti-Japanese Base Areas.

Prior to the consolidation of power, the liberation of women had been predicated on class struggle and the revolutionary seizure of power. Now, in a governing situation under wartime conditions, women's emancipation was to be based solely on achieving "economic abundance" and on expanding their role in production. Thus narrowly conceived, the burden of change fell entirely on the shoulders of women. It was argued that women had first to begin to contribute equally to social (i.e., nondomestic) production in order to achieve gender equality and change attitudes toward women. Presumably they had to do this while still fulfilling traditional obligations and still subjected to discriminatory practices. This premise, originally developed full-blown out of the wartime economic exigencies of the Anti-Japanese Base Areas and in the particularly conservative atmosphere of the Shen-Kan-Ning Base Area, became a central theme in nearly all subsequent policy toward women, with a few exceptional periods. The particularly narrow focus on economic work at this time had to be justified on the supposed basis that it attacked the primary (and seemingly the only) cause of women's inequality in all other spheres of life. But the political context makes clear that policy was shaped far less by a narrow theoretical understanding of the roots of female oppression than by the political dynamics and leadership priorities of the period.

Even the efforts to increase women's production, however, met with some resistance from men and family members who reacted to their loss of control over women's labor. Possessive husbands complained that it was improper, even immoral, for their women to spend time working and "gossiping" together outside their own family courtyards. They objected that this interfered with women's cooking and domestic chores.[26] Since the Party paid little attention to relieving women of traditional burdens by setting up crèches or housework cooperatives, in order to take up part-time weaving or sewing, the women had to compensate by extending their working day so they could try to perform both jobs. Essential household chores, such as grinding grain, making clothes, caring for the old and young, also had to be partially compensated for by additional efforts of other family members. Predictably this burden would fall particularly on older women who were not engaged in spinning and weaving. Thus, mothers-in-law also resisted the loss of young women's labor in the house.[27]

Significantly, in contrast to other aspects of women's liberation, the Party in promoting woman's production did not pull back in the face of resistance and conflict. Apparently, after a while, and with persistent Party prodding, the added income their work brought into the family, income which was generally paid directly to the family head rather than the individual woman, overcame some of the resistance to women's new economic activities.[28]

Economically, the production movement was quite successful. In

Shen-Kan-Ning the number of women involved in home cloth production rapidly increased from 13,000 to 41,500, and production more than
doubled during the year of 1943.[29] Throughout the other base areas, the
increases were even greater. For example, in one county in Shansi, it
was reported that 8,000 of the 11,000 women did part-time spinning.[30]
Between 1942 and 1944 the production of cloth throughout the base
areas increased eight-fold and many areas approached self-sufficiency
in cloth production.[31] Aside from cloth production, thousands of
women were organized into sewing workshops to meet the army's
continuous need for uniforms, shoes and blankets. These women were
paid per piece in grain.

In addition to the success in increasing production and supplying the
army, the intensified policy to organize women for production also had
the consequence of providing a substantial minority of women with
new income-earning economic opportunities. Their material contribution to the family, although in some villages representing a revival and
expansion of traditional cottage industry and handicraft roles for
women, perhaps raised the respect they commanded in their families.[32]
The work also brought women together in groups, providing them with
an opportunity to consolidate and extend their peer group contacts.
These were the benefits which the Central Committee pointed to as
evidence of its commitment to raise women's status.

Understandably, some women leaders complained that this was not
enough, that the Party's policy was too narrow and ignored some of the
basic causes of women's oppression. Women were encouraged to take
up new work, but little was done to free women from the burdens of all
their traditional obligations. Husbands still beat their wives with
impunity, parents still sold and coerced young daughters into marriage,
in some areas the feet of girls were still being painfully broken and
bound.[33] Having passed laws which declared women's legal equality,
the Party's practical policy only indirectly affected, or even acknowledged, continuing practices of inequality. When a few women leaders
raised these sorts of criticisms in the early forties, the Party leadership
not only resisted them, but moved decisively to suppress debate. The
issues were feared as too divisive, and faced with serious military and
economic crises, the male leadership was unwilling to consider issues
which many deemed of minor significance.

The leadership's suppression of feminist criticism and agitation for
change is clearly illustrated in the Party's treatment of the well-known
radical woman writer, Ting Ling. Rebelling against a traditional Hunan
landlord family, Ting Ling had been a student in Shanghai in the early
twenties. One of the very few prominent revolutionary women who
sought to find and express her liberation in both sexual and political
terms, she became an anarchist for a time and adopted a sexually

radical lifestyle. She later married a Communist writer (who was executed by the KMT in 1931) and joined the Party herself. After being held captive by the KMT for several years, she escaped and joined the Communist forces in Yenan in 1937.[34] Helen Snow claims that when Ting Ling first arrived in Yenan, many of the wives, and probably many men as well, looked askance at her past "free love" reputation.[35] But in Yenan, Ting Ling lived a sexually conventional life. She did cultural propaganda work within the army and taught journalism. She also helped organize the Women's National Salvation Association and gained acceptance as a leading political figure.

While in Yenan, Ting Ling was sensitive to the discriminatory traditional norms and practices under which women continued to labor. She was distressed by the lack of Party effort to understand and overcome these problems in practice despite its theoretical espousal of gender equality. While leaders in Yenan tended to claim that women had achieved equality under the new laws and political system, Ting Ling's short stories portrayed women in the villages whose suffering was unmitigated. In "When I Was in Hsia Village," Ting Ling described the fate of an eighteen-year-old woman who heroically served the army as a spy.[36] She had originally been raped and abducted by the Japanese and managed to escape, but was convinced by Party cadres to return so she could gather information for the Eighth Route Army. She lived with Japanese officers for over a year, being used and humiliated by them and periodically risking her life to sneak messages out of occupied territory. When she became very ill from venereal disease, she was relieved of her secret mission and given medical treatment. Upon returning to her village, rather than receiving sympathy or praise for her sacrifices, she faced the derision and hatred of the villagers for failing the traditional norms of chastity: "Some say she has slept with at least a hundred men. . . . This disgraceful woman really should not be allowed to come back . . . ," "Now she is more useless than a worn-out shoe . . . ," "How can she have the face to meet people. . . . It is a punishment to her father. . . ." Her family, desperate to regain some face in the village, tried to arrange a marriage for her with the only man left in the village who would still have her. Significantly, the "comrade" in the village who had been involved in her spy work did nothing to defend her although he was sympathetic to her plight. The young woman, feeling humiliated and "unclean," determined that she could never expect happiness there. The only way out was to run away and "live among strangers." Even though this woman had bravely shunned old values and risked her life to fight the Japanese, the sexist attitudes of the old society chained her and deprived her of dignity. The Party had exploited her body for the war cause, but then failed to support her when she was ostracized for her selfless service.

Ting Ling's portrayal of women trapped by a society that despised, belittled and ignored them, even while using their services for the revolutionary cause, was not only a criticism of the "old society" which still existed in the base areas.[37] It was also, more subtly, a criticism of the Party leadership. On International Women's Day, March 8, 1942, Ting Ling published an article in Yenan's *Liberation Daily* which directly attacked the Party's attitude toward women.[38] According to Ting Ling, women were now encouraged to take on new roles as activists, but if they did so they were still expected to maintain traditional family obligations and roles as well. The result was that women were faced with insoluble contradictions and viewed with contempt however they acted. If women did not marry, they were ridiculed; if they did marry and had children, they were criticized for spending time with political activities instead of tending to their men and children; if they stayed at home, they were despised as "backward." The problem was not, as some leaders claimed, simply the shortcomings and weaknesses of the women themselves, but the male-dominated society they lived in. The Party had proclaimed lofty theories of gender equality, but failed to deal with the actual conditions and attitudes which held women in an inferior position. Ting Ling claimed that male leaders "should talk less of meaningless theories and talk more of actual problems. Theory and practice should not be separated." Ting Ling ended her article with a sad and bitter postscript. She said she believed that if the opinions she expressed in the article were spoken by a male leader, people would receive them well. But because these opinions came from the pen of a woman, they would probably be dismissed.

After her article was published, top ranking Party members, including Ts'ai Ch'ang, the only woman on the Central Committee and the director of the Women's Department since 1938, severely criticized Ting Ling for her feminist perspective.[39] Ting Ling, and those who agreed with her, were told that their views had been formed in the man-centered society of old China. These views were now "outdated," "harmful to unity" and unnecessary in Yenan since "full sex-equality had already been established."[40] Ting Ling was relieved of her political responsibilities for two years.

As Party leaders decided to shy away from issues of family reform and women's social and political inequality, the dissent from more ardent women's rights advocates was considered threatening enough to require a firm Party response. A year later, the 1943 Central Committee directive on women's work further reflected this policy. In a March 1943 speech welcoming this directive, Ts'ai Ch'ang followed up the attack against women cadres who held views similar to Ting Ling's.[41] She called them intellectuals who were isolated from the masses, who "express the point of view of one-sided 'feminism' " and who "pursue a system of women's work which tends toward independence from the Party." These leading cadres "arrogantly complain that the Party and the government are not helping women's work." According to Ts'ai, the cadres in the leading organs who worked in this "depraved and misleading" way, set a bad example for women cadres of worker and peasant origin, some of whom "suddenly followed this example . . . and became separated from the female masses."

Although Ting Ling was the only woman leader who was personally singled out for public criticism because of feminist dissent from Party policy, apparently many other cadres shared her views. Earlier, Li Chien-chen, who lost her position as director of the Women's Department to Ts'ai Ch'ang in mid 1937, a time when women's policy became noticeably narrower, was probably demoted in part for advocating such views. Li, the daughter of poor "coolie" parents who was sold as a "little wife" at the age of one, told Helen Snow in 1937 that the main reason she joined the Communist Party in 1927 was because of its advocacy of equality between men and women and free marriage. In her opinion, the "marriage problem" constituted one of the main problems to be solved in the emancipation of women, and, as head of the Women's Department, she advocated spending a great deal of time educating people against such practices.[42]

Ts'ai Ch'ang's own opinions, which can be traced back to her attitudes toward women's rights advocates in the 1920s, seemed to reflect the dominant Party view much more closely than Li's. In the early 1940s, she is quoted as telling women that

> our current slogans for work in the women's movement are no longer "freedom of marriage" and "equality between men and women"; but rather "save the children" and establish an "abundant and flourishing family" so as to cause each household to become a prosperous one.[43]

Clearly the narrow Party policy during the Anti-Japanese War showed little concern to directly tackle women's rights issues. Indeed, its policies by the early 1940s were aimed at hindering the development of a women's movement which might have provided some impetus for these issues in the base areas.

Policies during the Final Civil War, 1946–49

With the end of the Anti-Japanese War and the renewed outbreak of civil war, Communist social policy again became more radical, and policy toward women also broadened somewhat. In liberated areas, the class struggles which eventually culminated in land reform began and the Party became committed to the broadest possible mass participation in land reform struggles. Furthermore, the land reform policy required that land be distributed on a per capita basis, including women and children. It was therefore considered necessary for women to take part in land reform meetings to help protect their land rights as well as to add support to the class struggle.

One of the issues raised concerning women's participation in land reform was whether or not women should be mobilized through separate (but subordinate) organizations to participate in land reform. It was apparently argued by many local cadres that all would be well with women as long as the general revolutionary goals of land reform were fulfilled and that, therefore, there was no need to pay special, separate attention to women's problems.[44] Again, the fear of alienating male peasants and complicating the land reform struggles by involving women seems to have raised its head. In a report about a presumably typical village land reform movement in the Shansi-Hopeh-Chahar Border Region, the local peasant association cadres expressed the fear that if the women were brought into the meetings they would "learn bad ways." The men said, "My women cannot do it, they dare not speak. Let some one else's women do it." They felt there was no need in any case to bring the women into the matter, since the men could handle it themselves and the women could add nothing of importance.[45]

The Party leadership finally decided to undertake efforts to overcome such resistance and several reports were published in the liberated areas in 1947 and 1948 explaining the usefulness and necessity of separate but subordinate organizations to mobilize women for land reform during the initial period.[46] Land reform teams which were sent into the villages by higher levels of the Party to help oversee and guide local work were instructed to call special women's meetings and to revitalize or set up local women's associations to guide this work. Although the women's associations of the liberated areas had claimed a membership of over seven million in 1945, these organizations had not been active politically during the war years and were defunct in many areas.[47] Land reform thus provided a new impetus and importance to the women's associations. It was pointed out in the various reports that without these separate organizations and meetings, it was difficult to get women involved. Women were afraid to speak up or attend the regular peasant association meetings where often disapproving men controlled the proceedings. The all-women's meetings would provide women with a supportive forum to discuss land reform and aid women in gaining confidence and in expressing themselves publicly. The

women's organizations, however, were clearly subordinate to the loc‹
peasant associations which were the actual decision-making forum fᴏ₁
land reform and other village matters. The women's groups were
simply vehicles for arousing the women and bringing representatives
into the regular peasant association.

In some of the old base areas, the mobilization of the women's
associations for land reform and class struggle apparently posed new
leadership problems. During land reform the poor peasant women were
supposed to form the core of women's organizations. Yet often the
women's association was dominated by middle or rich peasant women.
A study of a village in northern Honan showed that since the late
1930s, in contrast to village male leadership, it was primarily the
middle peasant women who had taken the lead in women's organizations.[48] This trend had been accentuated by the production drive, for it
was mainly the middle peasant women who had been able to retain
important handicraft skills. During land reform, many of these women
were discredited because of the class status of their husbands' families,
traced back for several generations. Although this "ultra-left" attack
on middle peasants was later corrected, the women never regained
their positions.

Furthermore, the poor peasant women activists who came to the
fore to replace them presented a new problem. They were considered
disreputable women largely because their poverty had forced them into
irregular sexual relationships and made it impossible for them to
maintain the decorum of "proper women." Some had been rented out
to landlords and other men to pay off a husband's or father's debts.
Others had lost their husbands and lived unmarried with other men.
Some, without family ties, eked out an existence as prostitutes or
scavengers, one of the few ways a familyless woman could survive. As
a result of the type of traditional moral judgments which these sorts of
women were subjected to, the women's association was greatly
weakened. Even local party cadres refused to allow their wives to
attend women's meetings, threating them with beatings and getting
"kicked out of the house." As one cadre apologetically explained,
"The virtuous women weren't militant, and the militant women
weren't virtuous!"[49] It was apparently very difficult to find women
leaders who met both the class standards and the moral standards set
down by male cadres. One strongly suspects that the language was
circular—if the women were militant (i.e., outspoken, assertive, daring
to break away from traditional restrictions which kept them in their
place) they were not considered virtuous women by the men any
longer. In some places, mere participation in a literacy class could raise
suspicions that a woman was "loose."[50]

That similar leadership problems, unique to women in a sexist environment, existed elsewhere is confirmed by a report on women's associations in another liberated area in the Northeast. The report complains that at the beginning of land reform the "women's movement [had been] slack, and in a good many districts the women's leadership positions were snatched away by either landlord women or vagrant women."[51] "Vagrant" women most likely referred to those at the bottom of the economic ladder, probably similar to the poorest women in the previously mentioned Honan village. These "vagrants" were politically suspect not because of their class interests but presumably for their poor moral reputations, which probably resulted directly from their poverty and exploitation as women. Women leaders, unlike men, were highly vulnerable to this kind of double standard.[52] Such judgments could be used to cripple women's political organizations and make it impossible for poor, "lumpen proletariat" women to play a revolutionary role. Edward Friedman argues that marginal, lumpen male rural dwellers, lacking strong family ties, held the greatest revolutionary potential. The Party was successful because it drew on this potential while bringing such socially outcast elements together with more rooted villagers in one revolutionary movement.[53] But the female counterparts of these lumpen elements were more likely to be prevented from playing such a role by the Party's as well as the villagers' unenlightened attitudes.

In the liberated areas of Shantung, documents indicate that "loose women" and "broken shoes" (a colloquial term for prostitutes) even became struggle targets at peasant association meetings during the early phases of land reform.[54] The Party leaders warned against this tendency when it was taken to an extreme. But they did so not because they sought to enlighten people's attitudes toward these women nor because they felt it was wrong to condemn them, but because such targets diverted the movement away from the main enemies. According to a Party document, thieves and "loose women" were relatively insignificant targets and the movement should not get bogged down with such struggles. But if the masses demanded it, it was permissible to attack such targets, as an initial tactic, to begin to mobilize the peasants for more serious political action. Significantly, the Party, which moved firmly against women who strayed from the "main target" to attack the poor males who oppressed them, was more lenient when the peasant association strayed to attack poor women who broke traditional proper sexual norms, believing that this might be useful in some circumstances.

While generalizations are impossible, these instances appearing in some of the earlier liberated areas in the North illustrate the discriminatory and complicated social obstacles which faced women trying to enter the political life of the villages. In some respects, Party policy was cognizant of the problems and moved to correct them. In other respects, Party policy ignored the problems or even reinforced unenlightened attitudes that hampered women's political participation.

In general, the mass mobilization efforts accompanying land reform did succeed in involving women in village political life to a previously unknown extent. In some model areas it was claimed that up to 90 percent of the women actively participated in land reform.[55] In this more revolutionary atmosphere a number of women's associations began, as some men had feared, to propagandize for women's rights and reform of attitudes toward women. Women's associations sometimes became vehicles through which women were encouraged to express openly grievances against their treatment by husbands and in-laws. The public expression of individual women's pent-up bitterness could be explosive and violent. The worst husbands and fathers-in-law were sometimes dragged before meetings of women to be criticized, "reformed," and even beaten in revenge. Such men were supposed to serve as public examples to other men that women could no longer be mistreated with impunity. Collectively the women could, for the first time, find direct recourse and some external support for asserting their rights.

In Long Bow Village in southeastern Shansi, for instance, many of the young women who dared to attend the early meetings of the women's association were beaten and mistreated by husbands, fathers-in-law and mothers-in-law for going out to these meetings. To put an end to this stiff resistance, the women's association executive committee decided to make an example of one of the husbands at the behest of his bruised wife. They called a mass women's meeting, attracting over half the village women, and demanded the husband explain his actions. He inopportunely explained that he beat his wife because the "only reason women go to meetings is to gain a free hand for flirtation and seduction." Angered, the women beat him until he promised he would never again beat his wife. Several similar incidents occurred, including a two-day jail sentence for another abusive husband.[56] The Long Bow Women's Association also facilitated the first divorce ever granted a woman in that village.[57] Reports of similar spontaneous women's activities in other liberated areas indicate that this was not an isolated case.[58] Although Party documents indicate that such militant actions by seemingly powerful women's organizations were exceptional, these cases illustrate that there existed a base of suppressed discontent which could, if provided with sufficient organizational support, mobilize women into collective action on behalf of their own interests as *they* perceived them.

While central Party policy toward women did noticeably broaden during this period and did cautiously begin again to direct attention to the "feudal shackles" which bound women,[59] leaders definitely did not at this time condone the type of militant action taken by women in Long Bow and elsewhere. In 1948 the Central Committee issued a new directive on women's work which revealed the leadership's concern to broaden and intensify local efforts to deal with women's special problems but at the same time channel these efforts so as to avoid "internal antagonisms."[60] In reviewing women's activities since the 1943 directive, the 1948 directive identified two mistaken tendencies which had to be corrected. One was the tendency to ignore women's special problems, taking a "laissez-faire" attitude toward the "heritage of feudal thinking and customs" which oppressed women. The second mistaken trend was "the old mistaken tendencies with regard to advancing women's liberation which give rise to internal antagonisms between men and women and between young and old women, thus causing division among the masses." This second criticism clearly referred back to the earlier debate with the "Yenan feminists." It seems to have been aimed at the "excessive" and "hasty" tactics employed by those women's associations (such as in Long Bow) which spontaneously focused on attacking men and in-laws instead of on class struggle. The Party was then in the process of correcting such "errors" through instructions to land reform work teams and women's leaders to discourage women from engaging in feminist struggles.

An example of these efforts to check the autonomy of women's groups during land reform is provided by the actions of work teams in northern Honan. In one village, the women were encouraged, as part of the land reform process to hold "speak bitterness" meetings to publicly reveal their past suffering at the hands of local landlords. Many of the women, however, aimed their attacks at husbands and in-laws, whom they felt to be their most immediate oppressors. In response to this development, a work team was sent in to "convince" the women to forgive their "erring comrade" husbands and to focus their attacks instead on their joint oppressors, the landlords.[61] By this time it was evident that had the Party wanted to build on women's consciousness of and resistance to oppression, there were many opportunities to build upon, even in conservative, mountainous rural areas. Nonetheless, "for the sake of class struggle," the Party felt women's spontaneous efforts to express their grievances against men and family members had to be repressed and the autonomy of women's groups checked.

The 1948 directive said this "divisive" tendency was evident in only a minority of areas. The tendency to ignore women's interests was, however "relatively universal." The directive pointed out that in many areas "distinctively women's organizations had been completely done away with or existed in name only" and it was now imperative that separate women's organizations exist in all areas. The 1948 directive, like the 1943 directive, emphasized that women's production work was the core of all other work; "the 1943 Central Committee directive is entirely applicable on this point." But the narrow and exclusive focus of the earlier directive was implicitly criticized:

> We should not presume that just because we want women to participate in production, that the feudal remnants which restrict women will just naturally be done away with, that it is unnecessary to continuously do [propaganda] work. This kind of laissez-faire-ism takes the point of view of not paying attention to the special interests of women. In the process of production all kinds of mass organizations and associations should constantly promote education among the entire peasantry so as to advance the thinking and ideas of equality between men and women, criticize feudal thought and traditional customs and do away with all feudal customs which restrict women.

The directive stated that it was even appropriate to "struggle against the backward elements which constantly oppress women." But it was pointed out that these elements were only a "small minority" and that this struggle concerned ideology among the ranks of the peasantry, hence calling for methods of education and persuasion very different from the struggle methods used to discredit the landlords. By stipulating that only a minority held views which warranted an "ideological struggle," the Central Committee clearly attempted to narrow the focus to only the worst abuses against women, exempting the average male peasant who held traditional views about male prerogatives over women. Even for this most abusive minority, the directive cautions against the "illness of haste."

The main task of women's organizations was, as before, not direct mobilization and agitation against oppressive customs and routine mistreatment, but mobilizing women for greater production. While this required breaking traditional barriers and lessening some restrictions on women, it was considered by the leadership to be far less controversial than dealing directly with sexist attitudes, family reform, and enforcing women's rights. The cause of increasing production was one that the leadership could easily identify as a common interest of both poor men and poor women. And, most importantly, it dovetailed with the leadership's major concern to improve the war-torn economy at a time when new capital inputs were not available. Efforts to emancipate women were still sharply circumscribed because they were viewed, by largely male leadership, as legitimate only to the extent that they could be harmonized with the class struggle being waged by poor exploited men.

Thus, during the final revolutionary civil war and the accompanying land reform movements, Party policy toward women broadened and issues of gender inequality, such as restrictions on women's political participation, mistreatment of women by family members, purchasing wives and child brides, were again raised. But this change was tempered with caution and moderation. Marriage reform issues still seemed, as a matter of policy, to be mainly in the stage of raising slogans. Women were encouraged to organize politically, but their political activities were to be focused primarily on land reform and class struggle issues, not issues of gender equality and female oppression. When necessary, work teams were used to maintain this focus. The subordination of women's issues was further ensured by the subordination of women's organizations to the male-dominated peasant associations whose traditional views concerning women were likely to discourage any distinctly feminist activity. While the central leadership advocated reformist measures to gradually abolish the "feudal shackles" which bound women, it was opposed to mobilizing women for direct struggle against these shackles. Women who did so were discredited as "splittists" and as bad Marxists, for abandoning their class viewpoint for a "narrow" feminist one.

For poor peasant men, the personal act of struggle was considered central to breaking the authority of those who had dominated them politically, socially and economically. Only in this way could peasants break their own psychological chains of submissiveness, awe and fear. As one scholar of the Chinese revolution pointed out,

> In the very act of lashing out at local landlords, men cut the ties binding them to the traditional power structure and its values of subservience to entrenched landlord power, and committed themselves to the new order. Here was the key to the communist insistence, sometimes honored in the breach, that the people seize power with their own hands, that the unleashed fury of oppressed peasants rather than the organized might of the Red Army provide the impetus for land revolution.[62]

It is also for this reason that Mao, in Hunan in 1927, defended the often unruly poor peasants' associations from critics who charged that, while their goals were just, the peasants' struggle needed to be controlled and held back by the Party to prevent them from committing "excesses" and "going too far." Mao countered that,

> There is revolutionary significance in all the actions which were labelled as "going too far" in this period. . . . Proper limits have to be exceeded in order to right a wrong, or else the wrong cannot be righted.[63]

From this perspective, it must be concluded that the Party leadership deprived women of an important, perhaps essential, means of freeing themselves from their centuries-old subservience to entrenched male power. The Party leaders, including Mao himself, voiced support for the just cause of liberating women from their special forms of traditional oppression, but, like the detractors of the Hunan peasant associations, they constantly feared women's "excesses," their "going too far." Mao's harsh criticism in Hunan could be turned against himself and the leadership on the issue of women. In Hunan, Mao had asserted,

> Those who talk about the peasants "going too far" seem at first sight to be different from those who say "It's terrible!" . . . but in essence they proceed from the same standpoint . . . that upholds the interests of the privileged . . .[64]

The actions of many local women's groups were no doubt retarded by the Party's insistence on tightly controlling women's groups so as to subordinate them to a revolutionary strategy that accorded women's interests a low priority. Organizationally, the Party deprived women's groups of needed autonomy from conservative local interests rather than helping them attain the local independence necessary to act on behalf of women's special interests. Always preferring caution and delay to the risk of conflict, the Party missed many opportunities during the revolutionary period to promote family reform and women's rights, opportunities which might not easily come again.

6   Legacies of the Revolutionary Era

From its very beginning the Party, looking through orthodox Marxist ideological lenses, tended to see women's rights and family reform as secondary issues in the revolutionary struggle. But the Party's disposition to see the vigorous pursuit of family reform and women's rights as an obstacle to its revolutionary strategies developed as its social base shifted from urban areas to the countryside and as the Party center moved from major coastal cities to rural Central-South China and then to the remote, culturally conservative Northwest and North. Each of these shifts seems to have brought a narrowing of the social base for family reform, although it is probably more accurate to say that these shifts led to the incorporation and increasing importance of a large rural male constituency whose aspirations strongly contradicted the progressive family reform ideals of women's rights advocates. It could be argued that not only was the real need for marriage reform greatest in the countryside, but the spontaneous desire for marriage rights— particularly divorce rights—was most urgently felt among young rural women, some of whom reacted swiftly to the promise of reform even without guarantees for their future protection and security. In Kiangsi, it is also clear that some social base among women for family rights existed. But whether or not a significant social base for aspects of reform existed, whether or not the need was more urgent, the resistance and potential resistance forces grew larger and included the most strategically important revolutionary constituency. Party policy responded more readily to this resistance and by the time of the Anti-Japanese War the Party was too cautious to explore the potential social base for its espoused reform goals, fearing in fact that at least some poor women might respond all too readily if organized and encouraged.

The urban areas, where the Party began, certainly provided a more hospitable social environment for family reform ideas, at least before

84

the brutal KMT suppression in 1927. The major urban areas gave birth to the independent women's rights groups in the first decades of the century and also produced a proletariat with a large proportion of women. The culturally iconoclastic New Culture and May Fourth movements, which developed a critique of the traditional family system among intellectuals, were also largely urban phenomena. The notion that cultural revolution had to be a propelling force, as well as an outcome, of China's rejuvenation was central to their thinking.[1] When, after 1919, radical intellectuals increasingly turned toward political activism and Marxism, they brought with them the heritage of the New Culture and May Fourth movements. Marxism also reaffirmed the goals of family reform and equal rights for women which the New Culture and May Fourth movements already had raised in the context of cultural revolution.

Thus the cities provided both a contemporary iconoclastic intellectual heritage and emerging social groups which were potentially conducive to agitation on family reform and women's rights issues. Yet even in this favorable situation, as we have seen, the Party did not initially do much to agitate about or organize around these issues. Although many of the first Communist Party members had been early champions of the need to oppose the evils of the traditional family system, family reform and women's rights seemed less important to them when they moved from the realm of intellectual questioning to political action. When it came to a matter of setting priorities and investing in action, many male Communist revolutionaries, armed with a new materialist orthodoxy, would not choose to put their actions where their words had been. In order to appeal to women's rights advocates, the Party advocated full equal rights for women as ultimate goals to be realized in the socialist society. But the Party also made it clear that actions had to be aimed at other targets considered more central to promoting the revolutionary struggle.

One wonders what might have developed had the Party's urban experience been longer or had the Party been able to maintain its urban base while moving into the countryside. Under such circumstances, women's rights advocates might have been able to maintain a stronger social base of power both inside and outside the Party, while trying to link up with the most desperate elements among rural women. Some women's rights groups were beginning to try to reach out to the budding women's workers movement. In time such links might have become more firmly established. In some of the cities of major revolutionary activity, women were a majority of the proletariat. Had the urban proletariat remained an important revolutionary constituency for the Party, the leadership might have eventually developed a different approach to issues involving women's rights. While family rights and general rights vis-à-vis men were not the most immediate issues impelling working class women to revolutionary activity, they were by no means irrelevant to them. Studies in the early 1930s showed that young women workers were beginning to develop progressive attitudes on such issues even in the politically repressive urban atmosphere of those years, and women's demands in the work place often focused on their specific needs as women, such as maternity benefits.[2]

In fact the most promising pre-1949 period from the point of view of politically integrating women's rights activities with other revolutionary activities was the 1925–27 period of KMT-CCP alliance. The united front context helped broaden the Party's narrow orthodoxy and it gave greater strength to the pursuit of "bourgeois" democratic women's rights. At the same time mass movements in both urban and rural areas were on the rise. Young female worker and student activities began to venture into the rural areas to promote marriage reform and women's rights and found there elements among rural women who readily responded to the promise of change. The Central Women's Department, staffed by left-wing KMT and CCP women who had a strong background in the urban women's rights movement, considered the promotion of women's rights and marriage reform both inside the government and among the masses to be one of its primary functions. While the Central Women's Department did not always enjoy the central Party support it needed for its programs, it had the advantage of acting as a semiindependent women's interest group within the revolutionary movement. It was not a mere appendage of the male-dominated Party apparatus. It drew both strength and inspiration from urban-based women's rights groups and from activist women workers and students and it seems to have briefly found a desperate, if small, spontaneous rural constituency.

But when cut off from the urban women's movement and women's workers movement, the only mass social base available to women's rights advocates was a rural constituency that was too politically weak and socially isolated in a hostile environment to be able to act without strong central support. Under such circumstances, women's rights advocates would have to rely almost entirely upon the male leadership's ideological commitment to the long range goals of reform. This situation left the leadership relatively free to promote, postpone or ignore such goals to suit its other goals and to respond to pressures of its more powerful and favored constituencies in rural areas.

As we have seen, as the revolutionary center moved north, the Party increasingly chose to postpone and avoid sensitive family reform and women's rights issues. At the same time the Party acted to check any incipient tendency toward political autonomy by women's groups whenever it seemed to be emerging. Women cadres were repeatedly criticized for the tendency to "separate the women's movement from the general revolutionary movement." In this way the Party leadership sought to maintain its freedom to define "women's issues" and to downplay sensitive aspects of reform. The relative success of the Party leadership in depriving women's groups and women's rights advocates of any effective political autonomy aided the Party in pursuing conservative family reform and women's rights policies during the decade of the Anti-Japanese War.

That decade has been noted as a formative period particularly important for later Maoist approaches to social change and economic development.[3] The "Yenan Way," which Maoists would repeatedly recall, contributed a populist mass-line style to Leninist leadership organization, modes of cooperative, labor-intensive mobilization for economic development and the cultivation of a spirit of local self-reliance and sacrifice for the common good. Above all, the successful political and economic experiments of Yenan led to a reaffirmation of the idealized virtues of the rooted, cooperative village community as the basis of rural survival and rejuvenation. As the modal experiences of this period popularized and ruralized the ethos of the revolution, they also helped shape later national policy which would go far towards stabilizing and restoring the peasant family while doing much less in the direction of reforming it. The Yenan environment provided especially conservative constraints on policy toward women and family reform. The wartime setting and the particularly restrictive cultural traditions of the remote, mountainous areas of the North and the Northwest strengthened the most conservative and cautious tendencies in the Party on family reform issues. This environment helped firmly establish as dominant an approach to social change for rural women that emphasized almost exclusively women's relationship to labor outside the home, linking this to the economic well-being of the family and community. The promotion of legal reform, women's participation in organs of political power and noneconomic kinds of structural changes that could affect women's relationship to family and village were pushed into the background in both theory and practice. After 1949, the labor-intensive production war of the early 1940s, relying as it did on the use of underutilized female labor, was a modal experience not only for the Maoists approach to rural development, but for their approach to liberating rural women as well.

While this approach had a positive effect in involving women in the economy outside the home and in reviving and expanding women's remunerative work in traditional cottage industries, it was decidedly narrow as an overall approach to social change for women. If the Yenan period provided the most important formative experiences of the Party's rise to power, it also provided the most conservative lessons on issues of family reform and women's rights. The most important Maoist model villages in postliberation China have tended to fit the Yenan syndrome: very poor, remote, rugged mountain villages, usually with heroic histories in the resistance struggle against Japan.[4] It is in precisely these types of areas that women were likely to have the lowest rates of participation in agricultural production, that footbinding persisted the longest and that traditional cultural restrictions on women seem to have been the greatest. Over the years, women leaders in China have tended to consider such poor, remote areas to have the most culturally backward environment for issues concerning women's position.[5] The villages of the South, or even of the northern plain, would have provided more promising models from the point of view of women's rights advocates.[6] But, historically and politically, the "Yen-an Way" eclipsed the "Spirit of Kiangsi." Kiangsi's broader, more radical political impulses toward family reform and women's rights were overwhelmed as women's rights advocates lost political ground to a poor male peasant constituency whose backward-looking family aspirations were more easily harmonized with the narrow women's work approach of Yenan.

On issues of family reform and women's rights the leadership could appeal to a Marxist framework to justify this very narrow, politically inactive approach. Theoretically the Yenan approach found its clearest support in the materialist Marxist view of the origins of female subordination as elaborated by Friedrich Engels.[7] Especially since the early 1940s, the Engelsian view that women's inferior status is directly and primarily related to their traditional exclusion from "productive" economic roles, an exclusion which began with the development of private property, has provided the main theoretical basis for the dominant Chinese Marxist operational theory concerning women's status and how to change it, as indeed it has formed the basis for most socialist thinking about women.[8] Basing itself on this view, the 1943 directive, like many post-1949 policy statements, argued that general social emancipation for women, including family reform, was primarily, perhaps wholly, dependent on enlarging women's economic role outside the family and changing their relationship to production. In other words, oppressive family relationships, and the culturally defined patriarchal attitudes and family structures which support and justify these relationships, should be treated as dependent variables in the process of social change, while women's economic roles should be treated as the primary independent variables. When reduced to its simplest form this view becomes a unidirectional, unicausal economic theory of gender inequality where change arising in the economic realm will automatically induce interrelated changes throughout the "super structure" of society. In this way, Engels, like many non-Marxist modernization theorists, predicts that culturally defined ascriptive norms progressively and inexorably give way to universal achievement-oriented norms thereby democratizing, secularizing or rationalizing major aspects of traditional culture.[9]

Similarly, the dominant Chinese view of the status of women has asserted that after the political victory of the revolutionary movement, once women are brought into remunerative social (i.e., nondomestic) production, interrelated and liberating changes in all other areas of society, including family life and culture, will naturally occur. Women's traditional dependence on men will be broken, they will become both more socially valuable and valued for their economic contribution to family and society, they will wield more authority in their communities and families, and eventually the entire cultural superstructure of male superiority and female subordination will give way to new norms of equality and female worth which reflect women's new relationship to production.

Politically, then, the Engelsian approach to the problem of gender inequality could be used to advocate a very conservative and politically inactive approach toward women's other political, social and family roles. It provided theoretical justification for the tactical political resolution of tensions which existed within the revolutionary coalition between the family reform ideals of a generation of radical, educated youth and the backward-looking traditional family aspirations of a less articulate, but on these issues ultimately more decisive, poor male peasant base. During most of the post-1949 period as well, the official view of women has continued to stress heavily, and often exclusively, the economic determinants of women's status, with the major concern being to mobilize women into social production.

3 Family Reform in the People's Republic, 1950–53

7   The Politics of Family Reform

Although since the 1940s the dominant position of the Chinese Communist Party on women has been that changing women's relationship to production will, in a natural, evolutionary fashion, change their familial, societal, and political status, this has not been the only perspective advanced. The early 1950s in particular was a period in which much greater political attention was given to efforts to actively reform patriarchal family structures, attitudes and customs, even at the risk of creating conflict with male supporters. Indeed the period from 1950–53 is unique in this respect, constituting the "high tide of marriage reform." The proponents of reform efforts, who included the likes of veteran women's rights activists Teng Ying-ch'ao and Ho Hsiang-ning, criticized the overly sanguine views that dominated policy in the 1940s. They argued more forcefully than before that patriarchal structures, customs and ideology were deeply rooted in popular attitudes and had a tenacity independent of the "feudal" economic and political system which presumably gave rise to and supported them in the past. Such patriarchal structures, beliefs and customs were not, as Mao had once sanguinely predicted, likely to collapse quickly or naturally in response to the new political and economic relations being established in the villages. In terms of a theory of social change, the implicit argument of family reform advocates in the early 1950s posited that patriarchal ideology and family practices, which for centuries defined women's lowly family and social status, must themselves be treated as at least partially independent variables crucially and negatively affecting the process of change.

Family sociologist William Goode, among others, has made a similar argument about the independent role ideology can play in the process of change in shaping and furthering egalitarian changes in relations between the sexes and in creating pressures to move away from the traditional toward a more "modern" family system. In his massive comparative family study, *World Revolution and Family Patterns*, he argues that what he calls the democratic and egalitarian "ideology of the conjugal family" should be treated as both an independent and dependent variable in the process of modernization and family change. He finds that the introduction of such ideas, partially independent of economic forces and changes, can help create the conditions and direction of family change by weakening the "self-evident rightness" of the old system.[1] Conversely, in the absence of such ideological development and debate, traditional family norms and ideology may more vigorously persist and resist sets of economic forces, forces which are often posited as the "determinants" of family structure and ideology. In the West, Goode argues, ideological factors, resulting in part from the philosophic extension of Protestant notions concerning the rights and duties of the individual to women, played a crucial and independent (though very incomplete) role in the development of greater freedom and status for women.

Joan Scott and Louise Tilly have challenged the historical accuracy of Goode's view of the positive, leading role of ideology in promoting change in Europe, arguing that this process was at best characteristic only of elite and middle-class experience.[2] They nonetheless maintain Goode's critique of materialist notions of change that see values as merely dependent variables. Looking at nineteenth-century European peasant families, Scott and Tilly posit a continuity of traditional values in the process of adapting to extensive structural change. They argue that among the poor, women's increasing economic participation outside the home did not in any immediate or direct way disrupt traditional family value orientations toward women.

In some ways, both the Goode and the Scott and Tilly perspectives may be useful in understanding the dynamics of the Chinese situation and the dual nature of the Chinese family crises which shaped the context within which Chinese marriage reformers sought to promote change.

In early twentieth-century China the democratic "ideology of the conjugal family" was indeed an important aspect of urban intellectuals' questioning of the traditional family and its treatment of women. Among this group, it played a leading role in promoting and suggesting directions of change and it provided youth and women with new intellectual weapons to legitimize their own personal struggles against traditional authority.[3] Such elite debate, however, had barely entered the rural areas, and where it had, it had been suppressed or prevented from developing by the unfavorable balance of political and social forces. Marriage reformers felt that in the absence of such ideological forces in rural areas, traditional family values would more easily persist, despite structural changes. Rural women and youth would be deprived of an important source of inspiration and legitimation in their struggles for change in the face of traditional authority.

Whether or not traditional male supremacist ideology and patriarchal family and marriage practices should be treated primarily as dependent or independent variables in the processes of social and economic change was not simply a theoretical debate for Chinese leaders, if, indeed, it was self-consciously theoretical at all. The real importance of such implicit theoretical issues was that they reflected different policy choices as well as different levels of concern over "women's issues." In order to argue for a more politically activist approach to women's rights and marriage reform—an approach which had definite costs in terms of organizational time, political energy, social conflict, etc.— advocates not only had to call attention to the serious nature of women's traditional oppression, but also had to argue for a different view of the dynamics of change and of causal relationships. It was still generally accepted that increasing women's role in the economy was essential to realizing greater gender equality and self-determination for women. But, in the spring of 1950 when the National Marriage Law was promulgated, it was increasingly argued in editorials and speeches by various leaders that progress in reforming sexist "feudal" attitudes and oppressive family practices was first necessary to alleviate suffering and to help enable women to make the new social and economic contributions which the Party called on them to make for China and themselves. Such problems could not be ignored nor could it be conveniently assumed, as it was in the 1940s, that patriarchal ideology and practices would take care of themselves in the course of fulfilling other general revolutionary goals.

In a historical sense, this position might be seen as a reassertion of the more radical antipatriarchal, anti-Confucian impulses of the May Fourth tradition. Significantly, this re-emergence coincided with the reincorporation of urban areas into the revolutionary fold, including those areas that had once been the major centers of radical May Fourth activity and the site of early women's rights activities among intellectuals. Family reform advocates of the early 1950s, some of whom had themselves been youthful May Fourth movement participants, not only shared the rebellious May Fourth anti-Confucian spirit that sought a joining of interests of radical youth and young women against patriarchal authority. They also shared the May Fourth era's voluntarist intellectual orientation toward *cultural revolution* as a primary means to change and rejuvenate Chinese society.[4] Implicit in their approach to reforming the family and furthering women's rights was an enormous faith in the importance and power of ideas in shaping society.

This position toward family reform emerging in the early 1950s also appears to be similar to the position taken by Ting Ling and other so-called narrow feminists who were criticized and censored in Yenan. Indeed, Ting Ling's criticism that the Party neglected problems of traditional sexism and failed to understand the special difficulties and oppression of contemporary women was repeatedly voiced openly by others in the early 1950s. For example, in April 1950, a *People's Daily* editorial supported the view that in the old liberated areas little if any attention had been given to implementing the marriage laws and that therefore serious acts of oppression against women had been allowed to continue.[5] According to the editorial, lower level Party cadres frequently ignored, approved of or even participated directly in the perpetuation of old practices, particularly with regard to women's divorce rights. Moreover, such flagrantly illegal behavior on the part of lower-level cadres had not been seriously criticized or subject to discipline by those higher up. An Tzu-wen, head of the CCP Organization Department, later claimed that this unsatisfactory state of affairs had resulted from the Party leadership's lack of understanding, concern and attention to problems concerning women.[6]

The emphasis on the independent and dynamic role of ideology and consciousness as a casual factor in promoting change not only recalls characteristic May Fourth intellectual orientations but also has been identified by China scholars as a distinctively Maoist approach to social change.[7] Although Mao himself devoted surprisingly little attention in his writing and speeches to the problems of gender inequality (and when he did he was uncharacteristically mechanical), his emphasis on ideology, on transforming consciousness through education, political debate, mobilization and confrontation with previously accepted value systems, lent itself to a more activist approach than did the more orthodox Engelsian approach.

The marriage reform campaigns of the early 1950s—a time when women's rights were dealt with more actively than at any other time before or since—were characterized by this sort of politically directed mobilization approach. Politically, the Engelsian policy position suited a compromise between the radical, iconoclastic orientations of May Fourth generation revolutionary intellectuals and male peasant aspirations; it provided a theoretical means to maintain distant goals while avoiding direct and immediate political confrontation arising from disparate aspirations and orientations toward traditional culture. In contrast, the voluntarist, activist policy position advocated by marriage reformers sought, in the spirit of May Fourth, to do battle with the forces of resistance and to carry reform ideas to rural areas, rallying support from a constituency of youth and women. It was a time when family reform advocates sought to drive an ideological wedge into the "self-evident rightness of the old family system" in the countryside as had been done in urban intellectual circles during the teens and twenties.

To be sure, the old family system in the countryside already showed signs of disintegration. But, no doubt, many peoples' hopes for the future rested on a return to the old moral order and security envisioned in the ideal traditional family. Thus the task of marriage reformers was to try to introduce a new vision of a reformed egalitarian family system at a time when millions who had effectively lost all meaningful family relationships, and millions more who had desperately managed to maintain some semblance of the traditional normative relationships, were in the process of reknitting their families.

Western social scientists have often argued that a modern nuclear or conjugal family system is better suited to the needs of economic development than traditional, extended, patriarchal systems. In this latter system, elders organize and control the labor of younger members to suit family needs in the old ways, they demand their loyalty and transmit nonrational ascriptive norms to determine the individual's role, status and economic function. Such a system, it is argued, hinders the development of a more productive, "free" and disciplined labor force, one which can respond to the demands of the modern market place where "rational" achievement criteria must take precedence over old ascriptive criteria. Traditional particularistic family loyalties may also conflict with the broader social responsibilities and identities which the modern nation-state demands of its citizens.[8] We shall see later that state-directed development strategies may in fact benefit from maintaining the strength of the traditional family structures and community ties. But here, it is interesting to note that some of the arguments for marriage reform in China at this time were similar in reasoning to these modernization arguments. The enormous collective effort to develop a prosperous, powerful, socialist China required that new identities, broader responsibilities, and new social values take precedence over many of the traditional family-centered values of the past.

Chinese marriage reformers argued that women, especially, needed to be freed from traditional family constraints in order to become members of a new community economically, socially and politically. They argued that women's restrictive, semislave status in the family crippled their lives, made it impossible for them to develop broader social identities and responsibilities, and greatly hindered the development of their economic potential. As a *People's Daily* editorial argued,

If this black, rotten feudal marriage system is not thoroughly done
away with, if the "family slave system" with regard to women is
not overthrown, then the slogan of equality between men and
women and a democratic and free social life cannot be realized,
nor can the development of the labor enthusiasm of the broad
masses of women be realized.[9]

Thus, if increased production and national economic construction was
a primary goal after 1949, vigorous efforts to promote family reform
and women's rights should contribute to, not hinder, that primary
goal—at least in the long run.

Yet in the short run it was undeniable that serious efforts to
popularize and implement the Marriage Law would bring to the surface
highly contentious issues, leading to family and social conflict and to
the possible disruption of village routine. Old male privileges and
control would not be relinquished easily. Nor would women themselves unanimously, quickly and fearlessly discard traditional norms
and practices which defined for them a familiar, morally sanctioned
proper place in life, a life which for millions of women had been all too
uncertain and "improper" during the years of war and disruption. But
in contrast to leaders in the earlier war years, marriage reform
advocates in the 1950s argued for a willingness to confront and accept
some level of conflict and disruption as an inevitable aspect of
progressive change for women. Reformers warned supporters, women
and young people, that they would have to engage in a prolonged,
difficult ideological and legal struggle to win their rights and to gain
public acceptance, a struggle that was both necessary and beneficial.[10]
Like land reform, marriage reform was part of the important "antifeudal democratic struggle" to destroy those oppressive, exploitative
traditional relationships which were serious obstacles to building a
more humane, egalitarian, socialist China.

Thus, between 1950 and 1953, marriage reformers advocated a series
of educational and legal campaigns to popularize and implement the
National Marriage Law promulgated in May 1950. The basic premise of
the campaigns was that it was both possible and necessary to initiate
social and cultural change by bringing forth the inherent tensions
produced by the traditional family system, and by providing subordinate family members with external legal and political support to help
them begin to adopt what was assumed to be an appealing alternative
model giving them more power and freedom. It was hoped that these
educational campaigns would set in motion a process making people
more conscious of the cultural determinants of gender inequality by
politicizing seemingly "natural," "nonpolitical" attitudes, customs,
relationships and "personal" grievances and problems.[11] While such
politicization tends to promote social conflict by mobilizing groups on

different sides of previously dormant issues, it can be a crucial step in opening up areas of social experience to change. This was precisely the result achieved during the land reform movement then in progress. Conversely, as long as customary behavior which discriminated against women remained in a realm of experience considered natural, nonpolitical or politically neutral (as accepted customs do), these areas would be better protected from politically induced change.

While some Chinese leaders (as well as a number of Western scholars)[12] would point to popular conflict and resistance to marriage reform in the 1950s as evidence of the futility of directly attempting to induce such cultural changes, marriage reformers could assert that in undertaking reforms aimed at altering basic power relationships within the family, conflict and resistance must be viewed as a predictable, necessary and normal feature of the process of change—as it is of nearly all processes of profound social change.

Public spokespersons for the Marriage Law were thus constantly at pains to argue against charges that efforts to implement the Marriage Law would lead to "chaos," counterproductive social disruption, moral degeneracy and ruination of the family. In patriarchal societies throughout the world, the prerogatives of husband and father are identified with the "unity and strength of the family" and new power for women and youth with its "disintegration."[13] In China, where norms of patriarchal authority were so thoroughly enmeshed in all aspects of religious, social, economic and political life, and were so culturally unmitigated for centuries, it is hardly surprising that reformers would be deluged with such charges from the leadership as well as from the general public, as they had been earlier in Kiangsi.

Of course the intent of giving women and the young support and encouragement to assert new rights of self-determination in marriage and social life was precisely to "disintegrate" certain features of the traditional family—specifically, its highly inegalitarian authority structure and its restrictive control over women. But the family per se (at least in its most common, monogamous form) was never publicly attacked, nor were the larger kinship structures within which the family was embedded. Structurally, the target of family reform was quite narrow—the internal gender, and to some extent age, hierarchy of individual family units. Indeed, one could argue (as I do later) that the reformers' greatest practical and theoretical weakness was that their target was too narrow and their view of the practices that needed to be altered too conservative. They failed to understand how larger kinship and marriage patterns shaped the fabric of local society and women's position within communities and individual families. Not only did they fail to take initiative in questioning patrilocal residence, they also failed to question a clause of the Marriage Law that allowed the degree of exogamy prescribed to be determined by "local customs" (see Appendix for full text of the 1950 Marriage Law). In their heavy "voluntarist" emphasis on the role of patriarchal ideology and attitudes (and specific practices these engendered—blind marriages, the sale of daughters through bride prices, mistreatment of daughters-in-law, etc.), reformers failed to strike at important links between ideology and patrilineal kinship structure.

A speech on the Marriage Law given by Teng Ying-ch'ao before a meeting of cadres and students in May 1950 was typical of the defensive stance reformers took to ward off fears and criticisms of the law, fears which had in the past led party leaders to quietly shelve actual implementation of proclaimed reforms.[14] After mentioning the critical view that the new ideas contained in the Marriage Law would cause "reckless marriage and social disorder," Teng countered that the rise in divorces and legal cases involving marriage conflicts should be blamed on the inequality and oppression of the old system, not the moral laxity of the emerging new system. The resulting "chaos" could be truly eliminated only by thoroughly implementing the new law, not by backing away from it and leaving the underlying causes of conflict unresolved. According to Teng, the ultimate goal of the law was to attain true family "unity and harmony," but she stressed that real "unity is possible only when one side has made the essential and proper struggle against the mistakes committed by the other side." Thus, Teng argued that women should no longer be discouraged from airing their family grievances for the sake of a false and repressive "unity." While warning cadres against "haste and compulsion resulting from a patronizing attitude," she also criticized the tendency to make "unprincipled concessions to the mistaken ideas of the masses" in handling marriage disputes, concessions which the leadership had previously encouraged by its silence on these issues. She therefore called on all government and Party organizations to begin a "widespread educational and propaganda campaign to transform opposition to the feudal marriage system into a broad movement of the masses."

Since the mass campaigns to popularize reform ideas would inevitably mobilize resistance forces as well as forces for change, the crucial first test for this approach to reform was whether the resistance and backlash could be managed and contained so that it did not succeed in overwhelming incipient forces for change.[15] This required a sophisticated and strong organizational capability reaching into the villages and a considerable political commitment. The Party had little experience in carrying out marriage reform and it would take much time and energy to understand and learn how to lessen public fears and to find effective ways to support and encourage change. At a minimum, the political system had to widely publicize the new law and provide reliable, accessible support and protection for those who then sought to use their new rights. Only then could new ideas and practices be expected to gain a secure foothold and momentum.

While Teng's speech in May 1950 did signal an important policy change, marriage reformers could not assume that the degree of the leadership's commitment to the policy, and its willingness to devote organizational energies to implementing it, would match the difficult task. Although the Marriage Law and the Agrarian Reform Law were among the first national reform acts of the new government and although a spate of major editorials quickly presented the task of popularizing and implementing the Marriage Law as an immediate and important duty for all Party, government and mass organizations, the marriage reform and the women's rights so closely associated with such reform were not accorded much organizational or operational priority in 1950. Marriage reform work had to vie for attention with numerous other kinds of political and economic work in the cities and, especially, in the villages. During the period from 1950 to 1953, land reform work, economic reconstruction work, the "Anti-traitor" campaign, the "Aid Korea, Resist America" campaign, the "San-Fan" (Three-Antis) and "Wu-Fan" (Five-Antis) campaigns all received as much, and in most cases far more, attention from top-level officials in their public communications sent down to lower levels. Directives on land reform tasks in particular seemed implicitly to rule out or caution against cadres trying to simultaneously carry out marriage reform work. The controversial nature of marriage reform put it at a further disadvantage in commanding attention from cadres who were swamped with other tasks and who for the most part had been allotted little, if any, time to study and understand the law themselves.

Furthermore, the top-level leaders were themselves unclear, ambiguous and seemingly divided about the amount of attention marriage reform should receive and how it should be related to other work, especially land reform. Although much editorial publicity in the major papers accompanied the promulgation of the law, the top leadership took little concrete initiative in preparing the cadres for this task or in providing guidelines for this work. The unsystematic and hapazard attention given to marriage reform contrasted sharply with the attention, preparation and learning-from-past-experience associated with the successful land reform work. It was not until 1953 that, for a brief period, the same sort of central initiative and investment was given to systematic marriage reform work.

8   Land Reform and Women's Rights

Immediately after 1949, land reform was considered the major political task in the countryside in terms of the time and energy devoted to it. Leadership ambiguity about how marriage reform should relate to other work of the period was particularly evident in the directives on land reform. In May 1950, when the Marriage Law was promulgated, 75 percent of the countryside had not yet carried out land reform. In June 1950, the government issued the Agrarian Reform Law which was to guide the land reform movement throughout the rest of the country. The close timing of the promulgation of the national marriage reform law and the land reform law has led to the impression that the two laws were supposed to be integrally related, mutually supportive, and were to be carried out simultaneously.[1] Both were "antifeudal," democratic reforms. Both indirectly attacked traditional structures of clan authority.[2] Land reform redistributed property and power in the villages; marriage reform redistributed property and power in the family. The marriage reform law gave women and children equal property rights; the land reform law gave them real property.

Yet even though the two reforms were theoretically complementary and were promulgated at the same time, land reform leaders did not appear eager to have cadres try to coordinate marriage reform educational work with land reform activity. Prior to 1949, the leadership had shown concern that marriage reform issues would undermine and complicate the class-based land reform struggles. Marriage reform issues cut across class lines and might divide class ranks. Not only did the Marriage Law raise controversy over long established moral values, but it threatened male economic positions as well: a poor male peasant might find that the gains he hoped to make through land reform would be partly or wholly cancelled out if his wife or daughter-in-law used the Marriage Law to leave his family and take her legal land share with her. No doubt many land reform authorities felt the problems of land reform were complicated enough without having to simultaneously deal with these sorts of women's issues.

Thus, even though in 1950 marriage reform was being given more attention than in the past and even though public spokespersons for marriage reform and women's rights more readily accepted the prospect of conflict over issues of gender equality, land reform authorities seem to have continued to operate on the assumption that such complicating nonclass issues should not be tackled in areas that had not yet completed land reform. Generally, the concern that marriage reform should be postponed or played down during land reform was expressed indirectly and by omission rather than taking the form of a direct prohibition.[3] Presumably local initiative could, and in some cases did, take place, but this was not encouraged.[4] Directives and articles on how to carry out land reform and how to coordinate "women's work" (meaning "political work among women") with land reform generally omitted any mention of the Marriage Law. This stood in sharp contrast to the calls being issued at the same time by others, such as Teng Ying-ch'ao, to make marriage reform work an important and immediate task, especially in doing "women's work."

This is not to say that "women's work" was ignored during land reform. Cadres were urged in other ways to integrate land reform with steps towards involving women. Land reform authorities constantly reiterated the importance of organizing women to speak up and take part in land reform along with the men.[5] This policy was an important break with the traditional practice of excluding women from important public community affairs. It was seen as a crucial step both in changing women's traditional relationship to the community and in adding strength to land reform forces. But, at this point, organizing women to participate in class struggle did not include specific, concerted efforts to educate them about or mobilize them around their new rights vis-à-vis their husbands and their families. As we have seen, this approach of organizing women for land reform while cautiously avoiding special women's issues, and avoiding the independent organization of women around these issues, was advocated during land reform in the northern liberated areas prior to 1949. After 1950 it still seemed to apply despite the new Marriage Law publicity. As one report from a model area during the final phase of the revolutionary civil war suggested,

> Concerning the forms of organization for mobilizing women at the village . . . in poor peasant leagues and new peasant associations, the women representatives should be in a certain proportion of a certain number (one-third or one-fourth) . . . women may not set up their independent organizations too early; not until after the

struggle against the landlords and the completion of apportioning their land and floating property; then we may further mobilize the women, meet their special demands and then set up independent women's representative conferences.[6]

Similarly, in a report he delivered on land reform in June 1950, Liu Shao-ch'i stressed the need to pay attention to "women's work" so as to allow and encourage women to participate in land reform, but he omitted any mention of the Marriage Law which had just been promulgated with fanfare the previous month.[7]

A directive on land reform issued by the Central Committee of the East China Region in September 1950 illustrates land reform authorities' desire to involve women in land reform and other activities, but to play down the controversial issues of marriage reform which most directly threatened traditional male prerogatives.[8] The directive dealt specifically with the need to strengthen "women's work" in preparation for land reform and the need to combat the apparently widespread tendency among cadres to adopt a "laissez-faire" (i.e., neglectful) attitude toward mobilizing women. The directive also mentioned propaganda against "feudal customs," saying that a plan should be devised of careful and patient education to explain the evil effects of feudal customs regarding women. But the approach is very cautious, stating that such work should be done only after land reform is well underway. Specific reference to the Marriage Law is conspicuous by its absence. According to the directive, the main focus of current "women's work" should be on overcoming restrictions to women's participation in production and guaranteeing that women receive an equal share of land.

Evidently there was still concern that certain kinds of reforms for women's rights would activate conflicts between the sexes and generations and that these conflicts, if not wholly illegitimate in themselves, were detrimental to the development of class goals. A speech delivered by Ch'u Ming-chiao at the first meeting of the Kwangtung Women's Federation stated the familiar, though somewhat ambiguous, restrictive conditions for "women's work":[9] to be successful "women's work" had to solve women's "special problems," but it had to avoid the tendency to become "separate" from the movement led by the (male-dominated) peasant association; it had to be carried out so as to strengthen the unity of the peasants in the struggle against the common oppressor, the landlords. Specifically, Ch'u warned that division between women and family members would provide landlords and class enemies with an opportunity to undermine the people's struggle for land reform. According to this line of argument, women and cadres who engaged in the sorts of efforts called for by Marriage Law advocates such as Teng Ying-ch'ao and the (woman) minister of justice Shih Liang might find themselves playing into the hands of counter-revolutionaries. Top-level land reform authorities, no less than "feudal-minded" lower-level cadres, seemed to prefer quiet avoidance of the issue, at least until after the resolution of land questions. Prior to the completion of land reform even earnest cadres would have probably found it very difficult to harmonize their tasks, and cadres who were personally opposed to the Marriage Law had ample excuse to ignore one central directive in order to better carry out another more important one.

There is little doubt that the Marriage Law did not fit in well with what many local cadres believed to be the central purpose of the revolution in general and land reform in particular—to provide economic security and justice to the poor, exploited, hard-working male tillers of the soil. In the absence of training on the Marriage Law and of political pressure to change, cadres' initial reactions to and interpretations of the law were, quite naturally, culturally conditioned ones. While many top leaders felt that women's rights issues had to be subordinated to other military, political or economic interests of the revolution whenever they seemed tactically in conflict, lower level cadres often assumed that women's rights as specified by the Marriage Law were supposed to be subordinated to the class interests of poor male peasants whenever these came into conflict. When women from poor families brought divorce cases, cadres often interpreted them as a means through which poor peasants "lost both their wives and their property."[10] In order to "safeguard the interests of poor peasants and hired laborers," many subdistrict and village cadres made a practice of rejecting automatically all applications for divorce by poor women. This sort of thinking indicated the extent to which poor women were not themselves seen as a part of the poor peasantry for whom the revolution was fought. In the patrilineal family idiom of the rural poor, they were, rather, the "wives of poor peasants," a status closely resembling that of family property.

In many areas during this early period when land reform authorities were so cautious about encouraging publicity on the Marriage Law, cadres had never been exposed to a questioning of these ideas. There probably were many villages in which the cadres were barely aware of the existence of the law. For example, in the fall of 1951, an investigation team in Shansi Province gave a simple test to fifteen village cadres and found that nine of these cadres, including the educational director and the vice-chair of the women's association, had no idea what the Marriage Law was. The other six had only a vague idea of the contents of the law.[11] The article reporting these findings concluded that many lower-level problems resulted from the failure of higher officials to initiate any educational efforts among lower cadres, to criticize their "feudal" notions concerning women and marriage, and to guide their handling of the numerous problems of interpreting and implementing the law. Again, in the absence of education and agitation for a new conception of women as individuals with the same basic rights as men backed by the determined and legitimate authority of the new government, male cadres would naturally tend to resolve the conflicts they were faced with by denying women the rights which familial patriarchal Chinese culture had always denied them.

Although the implementation of land reform policies clearly impeded the introductory phase of the Marriage Law in large parts of rural China, land reform by itself is considered to have made an important initial contribution to raising women's status and power. Even today in China, general discussions of the progress of women's liberation stress the important role played by land reform.[12] It is claimed that during land reform women not only became more politically conscious and active but they also took an important step toward economic equality and independence, by receiving an equal share of land along with their husbands. These general assertions deserve closer consideration, not because this brief period of land ownership had a lasting impact, but because it allows us to look at crucial issues concerning the dynamics of change for women.

In most villages, especially in the newly liberated areas of the country, land reform did provide women with their first opportunity to participate in meaningful public political activity in their communities. Even in the old liberated areas, the wartime United Front women's organizations had either been wholly production-oriented or had become more formal than real in most areas. From the time of the final revolutionary civil war, land reform struggles brought more concerted efforts than ever before to involve women in a way that symbolized a new relationship between women and community life. Although there were evident problems in getting women involved, getting them to speak up for themselves in public and getting men to allow women to participate, criticisms of cadres' failure to actively promote women's participation were repeatedly issued.[13] The peasant associations which conducted land reform were urged to attain a quota of one-fourth to one-third women members.[14] Even though these quotas may not have always been attained, large numbers of women were reported to be active participants in land reform. An article appearing in *People's Daily* on December 4, 1951, reported that in addition to comprising 30 percent of the general peasant association membership,

in the four greater administrative areas of East China, Central-South China, Southwest China and Northwest China, from ten to fifteen percent of the chairs, vice-chairs and committee members of the Peasant Association thus far established are women.[15]

It is probable that the numbers of women in the peasant association and in its leadership bodies were inflated by local cadres who were under pressure to "turn out" women and that many women did little more than register their names at meetings. But Party policy on this issue had been clear and consistent and there can be little doubt that tens of thousands of peasant women were involved in a new political experience. The best in-depth single village study of land reform, William Hinton's *Fanshen*, records how several women in Long Bow took quite an active part in the proceedings surrounding land reform and claims that each village in the county had "a few" such women. Many women activists who emerged from land reform were later recruited into local leadership posts and into the Party. During the latter stages of land reform and the period immediately following, the overall percentage of women cadres increased significantly, from 8 percent in early 1951 to 14.6 percent in 1955.[16] Most of the increase apparently occurred at the lower levels where, ever since 1949, the representation of women has tended to be higher, decreasing at each ascending level of political organization. It seems very likely that the impetus of land reform for women was a significant factor in bringing forth more women activists.

However, it is undoubtedly correct, as Margery Wolf argues, that women's public participation in political affairs during the land reform movement did not represent an overnight transformation of their personalities.[17] Rural women, especially older women, were not always the shy, submissive, withdrawn figures they were supposed to have been, just as women in the family were not as lacking in influence as male ideology and formal structures would lead one to expect. While "proper" women learned to acknowledge and accept that public community and family authority belonged to men, they nonetheless learned to assert their views and protect their interests indirectly by influencing other people and shaping the opinions of men. Thus many women possessed information, interpersonal skills and experience in influencing others which could be called forth in the service of land reform. Furthermore, during the decades of agrarian disruption that preceded land reform, there were increasing numbers of women, such as widows, women with destitute or absent husbands, and familyless lumpen women (sorcerers, prostitutes, beggars), who had already been forced to make their own way in village life.[18] Indeed, evidence suggests that these sorts of women, already accustomed to fending entirely for themselves, were among the first women to enter the reform struggle.[19] In some cases, as we have seen, the Party's failure to steadfastly support the activism of "vagrant" women (as they were sometimes referred to in Party documents) because male peasant activists considered them morally suspect may have suppressed the most readily available source of political activism among women.[20]

Still, many women certainly needed to develop a new kind of self-confidence to speak openly and directly among men and strangers. And men's resistance to openly accepting as legitimate women's public presence and women's opinions on public affairs must have been even more difficult to overcome. Thus, Party policies fostered groups where women could gain support for speaking out publicly and the Party consistently pressured and cajoled male peasant activists to accept women's participation in their meetings. The extent to which these policies succeeded in drawing women into a public forum of political importance was a significant accomplishment for the Party.

Land reform is also thought to have made an important contribution to raising women's status because it gave women property. Under land reform laws, women were supposed to be given rights to an equal share of land, with their names registered on the family deed or, if circumstances warranted, on a separate deed. One of the tasks of "women's work" during land reform was to ensure that women were allotted an equal share of land and that their legal rights to the land were registered. Giving women land changed their relationship to the means of production, at least in legal respects. Such property rights were supposed to help improve women's bargaining position inside and outside the family by increasing their potential choices and possibilities for independence and hence their power vis-à-vis men and the corporate family. The psychological impact which legal land ownership could have for women is revealed by several Shansi peasant women whose statements were recorded by William Hinton.

> Our husbands regard us as some sort of dogs who keep the house. We even despise ourselves. But that is because for a thousand years it has been, "The men go to the *hsien* [county] and the women go to the *yuan* [courtyard]." We were criticized if we even stepped out the door. After we get our share [of land] we will be masters of our own fate.

> Always before when we quarrelled my husband said, "Get out of my house." Now I can give it right back to him. I can say, "Get out of my house yourself."

> When I get my share I'll never again look for a husband. A husband is a terrible thing.[21]

Teng Ying-ch'ao stated, commenting on her work in villages during land reform, "For women, the greatest teacher [that a new era had begun] was the fact that every woman was given her own piece of land so that she had her economic independence."[22] But such an assertion is a tremendous oversimplification, as Teng herself indicated else-where.[23] There were serious practical, structural and cultural obstacles which blocked the real impact land ownership and legal equality in property rights might have on women's independence and power for self-determination. As a practical matter, not only were many women permanently crippled with bound feet, but women generally lacked the range of agricultural skills necessary to use their land independently of men. There were, of course, exceptions and during the previous decades of economic and social disruptions, such exceptions had probably grown. Poor familyless widows without adult sons, wives of indigent or poor absent husbands might, of necessity, take up the full range of field work normally considered improper for women.[24] Often, however, such women were not fortunate enough to have access to land and would be forced into even less honorable, and less secure, ways of fending for themselves. Thus even poor women were likely to lack the range of agricultural skills necessary to use their new land. Women could, of course, learn these skills and some training classes were set up for ambitious women to acquire the skills which, coupled with their land rights, would give them the potential for greater independence.

Another practical obstacle for many women was the need to find suitable and dependable childcare arrangements. As Rae Blumberg has pointed out, the major economic tasks required in extensive plow agriculture are among the least compatible with childcare responsibil-ities.[25] Rudimentary forms of daycare were begun at this time in some villages in the form of cooperative babysitting. And, of course, women could leave children with their grandmothers or other relatives on an individual basis. However, village nursery cooperatives were very rare until the late 1950s, and since men did not share domestic chores it was often difficult for younger women to shift their domestic burdens entirely to older women in the family. Lack of such social services, therefore, made it more difficult for women to develop economic independence or significantly alter the daily routine which made them dependent on men in their family for the production of staple food supplies.

Yet practical difficulties were probably less important in blunting the emancipatory impact of legal equality in property ownership than were the traditional cultural superstructure and kinship patterns which defined women as dependent and inferior appendages of male groups. There is considerable evidence to support the contention that in societies where women control important economic resources they can and do rely on this factor to increase their personal freedom and their influence in their families and communities. But neither legal property ownership nor even women's active participation in social production necessarily translate into female control over such resources.[26]

In China, simply superimposing legal equality in land ownership on centuries-old patriarchal ideology and patrilineal residential patterns was unlikely to quickly alter culturally defined social and family relationships and the noneconomic structural and normative bases of men's and the family's control over women. As Scott and Tilly find in their study of European peasants in the nineteenth century,

> Old values coexist with and are used by people to adapt to extensive structural changes. This assumes that people perceive and act on the changes they experience in terms of ideas and attitudes they already hold. . . . Behavior is less the product of new ideas than of the effects of old ideas operating in new or changing contexts.[27]

The Crooks' study of Ten Mile Inn, a village in Hopeh, revealed how patriarchal norms easily undermined the emancipatory potential of women's new right to land. As a matter of course, land reform authorities turned over women's deeds to the male family head who was still considered the family's effective "financial manager."[28] In some areas, such as Ting Hsien in the central Hopeh plain, local women's groups demanded their own deeds separate from unified family deeds to aid them in asserting their rights vis-à-vis husbands and in-laws.[29] But since central directives did not insist that this be done, only the initiative of a strong local women's group would manage to accomplish this clearer legal assertion of women's new rights. In Ten Mile Inn, wages which women earned independently through spinning coops were paid to family heads rather than to the women themselves.[30] This was done despite the fact that the women's cooperative, and hence the women themselves, presumably "owned" their means of production, paid for through their own independent labor and not from family funds. Women's labor, whether performed in the courtyard, on family fields or in a village women's coop, was considered family labor, as indeed was the labor of younger males as long as they remained in the households of their fathers. And the fruits of family labor were formally controlled by the family head, usually the eldest male of the patrilineal line. Similarly, women's land was naturally viewed as the land of patrilineally defined families.

Thus, in the village studied by the Crooks, neither property ownership nor increased participation in remunerative productive labor appears to have had the initial impact of increasing most women's actual control over the means of production or over the wealth directly produced by their own independent labor. Later national reports, although not conclusive evidence, confirm that women elsewhere had great difficulty in exercising control over their property and the wealth earned by their own labor.[31]

Social scientists sometimes use the concept of "cultural lag" to explain this sort of phenomena. The Chinese use the term "feudal ideological remnants" to express the same notion. These concepts and conceptual images imply that the "lags" and "remnants" will eventually disappear because of their developing tension and incongruity with new material and social conditions and as the influence of older generations who seek to reproduce inappropriate, old-fashioned cultural attitudes and traditions gradually diminishes and dies out. The basic assumptions of such concepts, however, oversimplify the relationship between cultural consciousness and various kinds of social and economic change. As the recent work of a number of family historians points out, the relationship is neither so direct nor immediate.[32] For example, such concepts overlook the process whereby cultural attitudes may adapt to, influence and become reintegrated with changing circumstances, shaping the process of socioeconomic change as well as being changed by it. They also overlook the possibility that human attitudes and beliefs may persist in tension with social and economic structures.

The Chinese concept of "feudal remnants" not only oversimplifies the relationship between cultural consciousness and structural change, but it also defines the structural material base of "feudal attitudes" in very narrow, economically reductionistic terms. When applied to issues of women's status, the concept of "feudal remnants" assumes that the material base for attitudes and behavior that perpetuate female subordination is a particular male-dominated private property system and the unequal exclusion of women from productive labor in the public realm. That such attitudes may have a material or structural basis aside from property relationships and participation in major spheres of productive economic activity is not considered. Party policies thus remained blind to the ways in which basic kinship structures shaped not only marriage patterns but also the social composition and organization of rooted villages. Directly and indirectly, traditional kinship provided a persistent structural basis for the subordination of women and the perpetuation of sexist attitudes despite land reform and, later, as we shall see, despite collectivization.

In the case of land reform, kinship structures and the social and residential patterns they sustained created powerful structural obstacles to the new jural rules. In this regard, as with most issues involving patrilineal and patrilocal kinship structures, young women were particularly disadvantaged. Since the question of female land rights was likely to be thought of in terms of which patrilineally defined family had rights to use and manage a women's allotment, confusion arose over how to deal with the land of young unmarried girls who would eventually be changing from their fathers' to their husbands' families.

Customs of village exogamous marriage, which meant that women were likely to be married outside their village, further complicated the issue and made it even more difficult for young women to make meaningful use of their land rights.

In the absence of detailed regulations on how to handle this common problem, one assumes that the land allotment for a girl still living at home was included in her father's family's land, even though she might have been betrothed long in advance of marriage. A report from one county indicated that the problematic issue of land for unmarried girls was settled by deciding that the land allotment of betrothed girls over seventeen years old would be included in their "mother-in-law's family's land," while the allotment of girls under seventeen, even if betrothed, would go to their natal families.[33] This formulation of the solution was probably better for women than simply including all land of betrothed girls with their fathers'. Furthermore, the wording of the formulation certainly reflects a women's perspective—that of older women who stated the terms in ways that stressed the interests of their uterine families, rather than their husbands' patrilineal families. But the wording unwittingly reveals the extent to which young women's new rights were to be settled in terms of the competing claims of family groups rather than in terms of how an individual woman might herself best choose to use her property upon marriage. It was left unclear whether the land of a girl under seventeen would remain with her natal family after her marriage. But, by omission, this seems likely. In order to derive personal benefit from her land in her natal village after marriage, a woman would need to be able to hire labor, sell, lease or trade her land. Without strong external support, few young women would be able to exercise such controversial management power over land which was considered family land. And if a woman was allowed to trade her land for some in her new husband's village, would not this be likely to figure in the bride price, so that the girl's family in effect sold her land along with the bride herself? According to one article, some villages avoided all such confusion by simply refusing to give families any land allotments for unmarried girls.[34] The notion of young women's land rights was in such contradiction to the patrilineal, patrilocal marriage system, to the entire accepted cultural matrix for young women, that similar violations undermining the spirit and letter of the land reform law must have occurred in thousands of villages.[35] Since there is little evidence of detailed guidelines issued to govern the resolution of the practical issues arising from young women's legal property rights, it is likely that patrilineal, family-oriented traditions filled the gap of interpretation.

The situation for older married women was not as problematic and their land rights may have been more meaningful, at least in intangible psychological ways. The location of a married woman's land share was not at issue. Furthermore, the fact that land reform introduced the idea that women and their children had land rights separate from their husbands' may have added strength to women and their uterine families. The uterine family that existed informally within the patrilineal family and relied on emotion and interpersonal ties to bind it together was given something of a legal economic basis through women's and children's land rights. Margery Wolf argues that Chinese women in traditional families routinely acted informally to emotionally exclude unsatisfactory husbands from their uterine groups.[36] This new economic basis might make a woman's efforts in this regard somewhat more effective and credible. Of course, fathers and husbands were not without enormous cultural, social and psychological resources of their own to shore up a legally weakened position in maintaining their patrilineal families. However emotionally distant and personally disliked a father might be, and however loyal a son was to his mother, a son would be risking ostracism from his kin group and ancestral lineage to turn his back on his father.

Further, the legal right to an equal share of land was not very likely to increase concretely the power and independence of a married woman if engrained patriarchal rights to manage family property remained intact and if she had no right to leave her husband's family with her new land and her children. As long as she and her children were "owned" by her husband and in-laws, her land in effect belonged to them and her land rights bestowed on her by the land law were only a formal matter in the face of patriarchal authority and family control over women and women's uterine families.

As a logical and practical matter, the vigorous implementation of the Marriage Law could help give concrete meaning to women's new land ownership. Only if a woman could determine the disposition of her own person could her land rights give her significantly increased leverage and power. The right of divorce, coupled with the right to keep, sell or rent her separate land share so as to support herself, gave a woman a new, feasible (even if unattractive) alternative if her married life was unbearable. More importantly, these rights—and the understanding that a woman could use them if mistreated—might also give her some leverage to improve her treatment and freedom within her family, especially if she had an equal legal claim to her young children.

This was essentially the position of the Marriage Law advocates who publicly led the efforts to make politically induced family reform an important priority at the local level. Unlike land reform authorities, they occasionally even urged specifically that such work be integrated with land reform work.[37] Although marriage reformers failed to directly address the problems posed by the larger kinship structure, they

9   The 1950 Marriage Law: Popular Resistance and Organizational Neglect

As we have seen, land reform activity hindered Marriage Law publicity and enforcement in many rural areas during the early months. Nonetheless, by focusing on urban areas, initial reports tended to emphasize the early successes attained in marriage reform. The initial publicity push in the major newspapers died down after May 1950, but for over a year occasional stories and fragmentary reports appeared which indicated that some positive changes were occurring as a result of the law.

Although this study is mainly concerned with the impact of the revolution in rural areas, it is worthwhile to discuss briefly the factors operating in urban areas which may have favored family reforms. Most modernization theories would predict that new social and economic forces were already at work in such areas, altering traditional agrarian family patterns, at least in the "modern sectors" of cities like Shanghai and Peking.[1] Although these theories exaggerate the extent to which urbanization quickly destroys traditional identities, ties and norms, there are of course aspects of urbanization which tend to weaken traditional family patterns and family control over women and youth. One of the main points at which the complex of modernizing-urbanizing-industrializing factors is thought to induce family change is where such factors begin to disrupt traditional kin patterns and to deprive the family's patriarchal elders of the ability to provide or control the economic and social role opportunities of its members.[2] At the same time, new economically viable alternatives for individual family members become available outside of the family.

Although in the countryside, the success of the revolution helped restore rooted, secure communities built around networks of male kin, thus indirectly restoring and reinforcing the basis of traditional family control for the poor,[3] early changes in the urban areas under the new

115

revolutionary government were more uniformly in the direction of supporting change away from the traditional structures and ideals. Goals and priorities in urban areas centered on strengthening, reforming and expanding precisely those new economic and social institutions which provided new opportunities and alternatives to traditional family-based security and economic survival. The cities, greatly favored by early economic priorities, would not only be the new places into which desperate people were forced, but throughout the 1950s they increasingly became places to which people—indeed, too many people—were attracted. In addition to better economic opportunities, this attraction was in part based on the greater freedom from traditional structures which urban areas offered younger individuals.[4] Urban life and work could provide greater independence, lessening the influence of family pressures and patrilineal authority structures through the greater tendency toward neolocal living patterns—a result of migration and the growth of wage labor which provides individuals with an income more independent of family control. The employment of women in wage labor, a trend which accompanied the development of textiles and other light industry in the twentieth century, is considered particularly subversive of traditional family authority structures.

The importance of such socioeconomic modernizing trends in the early 1950s should not, however, be exaggerated. While few would deny that wage labor for women provides the potential for greater independence and influence in the family, there is a great deal of evidence that this does not happen automatically or smoothly. Furthermore, while coastal cities with concentrations of light industry, such as Shanghai, had large numbers of women workers, most urban women were not engaged in regular wage-earning employment. In 1949 only 7.5 percent of "workers and employees" were women. Although both the numbers and percentage of women employees increased in the early and middle 1950s, employed women remained a minority among urban women.[5] The unemployed urban woman was likely to be as fully dependent on men and family as her traditional rural counterpart, perhaps even more so. Urbanization and the growth of wage labor tends to separate work and traditional household manufacture from the home, often making those left at home less economically productive and more dependent on wage-earners to supply cash to purchase goods and services. Thus women's work in the home may become more isolated and more "specialized" into purely nurturant, service activities which are increasingly separated from the "productive" activities of the public economy. Depending on class and other circumstances, women may also find themselves more cut off from supportive social networks such as those that often formed around women's work in villages. Because of these types of trends, many family historians, sociologists and feminists have emphasized that industrialization, with its attendant separation of work from home and rigid delineation of public and private spheres, often has a negative impact on the roles of women, especially under capitalism.[6]

Nonetheless, Chinese cities in the early 1950s clearly presented a more hospitable environment for marriage reformers, as they had in the 1920s. Urban Chinese women were less likely to live among and be controlled by social networks based on rooted male kin groups. Furthermore, urban areas, far more than most rural areas, contained the seeds of the cultural family change which marriage reformers sought to encourage. This was particularly true among the relatively small numbers of women workers, whose new remunerative work roles enhanced their potential for independence, self-determination and family power (even if these changes did not automatically change the espoused values of their families and themselves), and among students and intellectuals who had inherited the legacy of family reform ideas of the May Fourth generation.[7] Furthermore, early economic policies which favored urban industrial growth encouraged the growth of these groups, although the paramount emphasis on heavy industry, where the cultural bias against hiring women was far stronger than in light industry, hampered the growth rate of women workers. Perhaps even more important for the marriage reformers, communications were more developed and the legal apparatus more accessible to women and young people in urban areas. Women near urban areas and towns were therefore more likely to learn about and to be able to use the Marriage Law than women in more remote rural areas. And nonagrarian areas, of course, were not preoccupied with land reform.

Thus, it is not surprising that early reports emphasizing successes in implementing the Marriage Law provided fragmentary statistics coming mostly (though not entirely) from cities and towns. These reports indicated that both free-choice marriages and divorce suits, brought mostly by women, were increasing, showing that people were finding it possible to use the Marriage Law to free themselves from traditional restraints. For example, justice ministry statistics on court cases of matrimonial disputes for twenty-one large and medium cities (unspecified) showed that there were 9,300 such cases between January and April 1950, a period during which one of the earlier reform laws was presumably in effect but without much, if any, publicity. During May through August, the first four months after the promulgation of the new Marriage Law and the order to publicize and implement it, there were 17,763 cases, an increase of 91 percent. For ten major county towns the figures were 986 and 1,982 respectively for the two time periods, showing an increase of over 100 percent. In Hupei, the average number of cases per court each month increased from 13.7 in February to 23.9 in July.[8]

The significance of divorce as an "antifeudal," or more accurately, antipatriarchal, reform was clearly underlined by the fact that the vast majority of divorce cases were filed by women. This fact was emphasized in numerous reports and was used by marriage reform advocates to defend the rising divorce rate.[9] For example, it was reported that during the first year of the law in Shanghai, 75 percent of the 13,349 court cases were brought by women alone; in thirty-two cities and thirty-four county-seat towns nearly 77 percent of the 21,433 cases were brought by women; in three counties in Shansi, 92 percent of the divorce cases were filed by women.[10]

Throughout the 1950 to 1953 period, spokespersons for the Marriage Law consistently defended the rising divorce rate as a necessary consequence of liberation from traditional bondage despite the obviously controversial nature of this trend. To be sure, leaders such as Teng Ying-ch'ao, Shih Liang, Ch'en Shao-yu (Wang Wing), Liu Ching-fan and others who frequently commented on marriage reform, warned against "taking divorce lightly." A mediation clause in the Marriage Law was supposed to prevent "hasty" and "unnecessary" divorces such as those asked for in a "fit of anger." Furthermore, after 1951 a noticeably increasing emphasis was placed on reforming "feudal families" rather than dissolving them. The primary purpose of the marriage reform was to improve women's freedom and status within a more egalitarian family, not to take them out of it. Nonetheless, it was a unique feature of this period that the general and frequently expressed official view of divorce was positive and supportive, stressing that one of the major problems in family relationships was the traditional lack of freedom for women and young people.

Early reports on the implementation of the Marriage Law also reported an increase in free-choice marriages in some areas. Claims about the rise in free-choice marriages and the decline in arranged, blind, "buying and selling" marriages are more difficult to evaluate than those made about divorces. Not only is the information provided far more fragmentary and usually specific to small areas, but it is unclear how free-choice marriage was defined and how investigators determined whether a marriage was "free" or traditionally arranged. Some of the figures seem so extraordinarily high that one must assume that a very loose definition was used. For example, it was reported that in 178 villages in a county of Chahar Province, about 80 percent of the 400 marriages which took place during the first ten months of the Marriage Law were free-choice marriages.[11] This percentage seems unbelievably high in light of earlier demographic surveys and village studies which indicate that self-determined marriages—even "compromise" arranged marriages in which the couple were first consulted—were virtually unheard of in rural areas.[12] The 80 percent figure for a rural area, attained after only ten months, seems especially high given the necessity that meaningful free-choice marriage practices be supported by new, more extensive and freer patterns of social interaction among village youth, providing them with courtship opportunities. As Teng Ying-ch'ao had commented in May 1950, greater social freedom between the sexes still scandalized even educated, presumably more progressive cadres and Party members. She criticized the existence of an "unhealthy attitude" against the freedom of young men and women to fall in love, saying that usually "rumors run wild when a man and woman comrade become friendly."[13] But various published discussions imply that at this early date, any marriage, even if arranged, in which the parties involved were given the prior opportunity to agree or disagree and in which compulsion was not used might be classified as a free-choice marriage.[14] Cadres were responsible for ascertaining prior to registration whether both parties were marrying of their own free will. To the extent that this was actually being done, the free-choice marriage figures from the villages in Chahar seemed to indicate that marriage reform work there at least decreased compulsion and increased the role of the couple themselves in sanctioning the marriage by giving them some opportunity to give or withhold consent.

Most other reports were more modest in their claims, indicating one-third to one-half of the marriages in a particular locality were free, or providing free-choice figures without reference to the number of traditionally arranged or "buying and selling" marriages for the same area.[15] Deviations from the traditional norm, ranging from the couple simply giving a formal consent at the time of registration to the more radical occurrence when the couple actually made their own "love match" independent of parental control, seemed to be more frequent. In some cases, reference to a struggle between parents and children over the marriage indicated that this latter, more meaningful kind of free marriage was occurring, encouraged and supported by local marriage reform work.

Reports of people's experiences with the new law illustrated the kinds of difficulties sometimes involved. One example is the experience of Yen Ts'ai-nu, a nineteen-year-old Shanghai textile worker whose father and paternal grandmother arranged her marriage in the traditional manner without her knowledge. When Yen learned of the arranged marriage on the day of the wedding, she demanded it be called off, but her father refused and beat her. To avoid going through with the wedding, Yen escaped to her deceased mother's relatives for refuge but was soon discovered by her father and grandmother who tried to take her back. After a fight involving relatives, neighbors and the local women's association, Yen took her case to the local court, which supported her right to break the betrothal and forced her father to abide by the ruling.[16]

Such stories showed that women had to be brave, defiant, persistent and willing to confront some sort of intergenerational or interpersonal struggle if they wished to use their new rights, otherwise their lives would go on as before despite the new law. Significantly, this young woman's access to her maternal relatives and their community also seems to have been important. Simply going to a court to apply for a divorce was portrayed as a "bold" act, as indeed it often was.[17] The significance of these reported stories was not that they were representative, but that they held up rebellious young women as positive models. Such women were engaged in a personal rebellion against social and family norms, against Confucian ethics of female propriety, subservience and respectful obedience of elders and male authority. Again, the frequent emphasis on examples of struggle and personal rebellion sets this marriage reform period apart from later periods when the new socialist woman is rarely portrayed in situations of intense conflict over new family rights. Rather, she assumes her new rights in an atmosphere of relative harmony, which allows her to be both a new liberated woman and respectful, helpful daughter, daughter-in-law and wife.[18] In the early 1950s the serious tensions and lack of consensus involved in social and cultural change in the area of women's rights were more clearly recognized and realistically portrayed.

The early stories on marriage reform had another common theme: because of the strength of the forces they had to confront, the women involved in defying old customs in most cases ultimately needed to, and were able to, rely on strong external political and legal support to tip the heavily weighted scales in their favor. Women needed to be able to mobilize new sources of supportive power such as neighborhood committees, local courts or Party branches to give them leverage in their interpersonal relationships. It was the combination of the emergence of a new consciousness among women with the development of new, reliable institutional and political supports that was crucial to the success of marriage reform. The early reports on the course of marriage reform didactically tended to stress cases in which both these factors operated together.

But by late 1951 the tone and intensity of marriage reform reports had clearly changed. Increasingly, reports began to appear which stressed the problems being encountered in carrying out reform. The problems discussed were of two general sorts, those relating to the difficulty of breaking through the traditional consciousness of "feudal ideology'' of the masses, and those relating to the failure of political and legal organizations to support the reforms.

Implicitly, and sometimes explicitly, many of the reports revealed the cool, even hostile, reception of the Marriage Law in many villages. Frequent references were made to the tendency for people to ''misunderstand'' and ''misinterpret'' the intention and likely consequences of the law, leading to fear and resistance. In many areas, rumor had it that the law required that all marriages arranged in the traditional manner be dissolved and that those who had previously participated in traditional practices which were now illegal be punished.[19] In some areas, anti-Communist Kuomintang propaganda fed fears that the Communists ultimately aimed to destroy the family and ''communize'' all women. Poor official communications in many areas and a mostly illiterate population meant that many people had to rely on such distorted word-of-mouth rumors. These problems tended to complicate and reinforce an apparently widespread predisposition to defend the traditional distribution of power and privilege in the family against new principles and practices. Evidence of open resistance to the Marriage Law appeared in numerous reports. Several articles recounted instances of public antireform forces mobilizing to oppose official application of the Marriage Law in their villages and to halt such norm-breaking behavior as the application for divorce by women, young people's efforts to court and arrange their own marriages, and women's participation in new social and political activities.[20]

This kind of situation raised a classic dilemma for the reformer committed to popular, grass-roots change. The reformers had to serve as catalysts and supporters of changes which were likely to be unpopular and threatening to many people. Yet, at the same time, they had to avoid alienating and isolating themselves from those whom they hoped ultimately to win over or at least neutralize. Teng Ying-ch'ao in one of her first major speeches on the Marriage Law had underscored this dilemma.[21] In the long run, she said, the thorough reform of the marriage system depended on the consciousness of the masses. Cadres therefore had to avoid ''haste and compulsion resulting from a subjective and patronizing attitude.'' Yet Teng also warned cadres against the tendency to make ''unprincipled concessions to the mistaken ideas of the masses.''

Similarly, an early directive from the Hunan Women's Association warned cadres that they had to be more careful not to alienate the ''sympathy of the masses'' and ''isolate'' themselves.[22] Yet the major critical thrust of the directive was that cadres also had to be far more bold and active in protecting and building up the ranks of those women and young people who were struggling for their rights. In practice it might be very difficult for a cadre to support a justified divorce or annulment of a betrothal without earning the distrust and antipathy of a large proportion of villagers who saw such developments as an immoral and threatening trend.[23] The marriage reformers' task was thus a difficult one, having to support what was at the outset likely to be, from the perspective of "decent" village opinion, a radical minority position at best.

This dilemma is probably far more pronounced for Chinese revolutionaries who have insisted (in theory, if not so often in practice) on mass participatory change than for more elitist, "Leninist" approaches, which are less ambivalent about conceiving of change emanating, and if necessary being imposed, entirely from above by a vanguard elite. Yet the simultaneous emphasis on the role of consciousness and the optimistic belief that consciousness can be transformed through mass political struggle and education has infused Chinese Marxism with its well-known, characteristic radicalism and its emphasis on continual political confrontation and agitation for change.[24] If the motor of change is conflict, which gives rise to political struggle, and if political struggle is the process whereby a progressive, "correct" minority may establish itself and grow, the process entails at least a temporary willingness to confront the polarizing consequences, even among one's coalition of supporters. Understandably, marriage reformers emphasized this latter radical thrust of Chinese revolutionary thinking to counteract the conservative implications of the stiff resistance that was evident in many villages. Thus, their injunctions to avoid "isolation" and "seek the sympathy of the masses" were not the same as the earlier calls to maintain "unity," calls which were clearly a coded way of asking cadres to back off from the issues. Rather, marriage reformers were asking cadres for more. They instructed cadres that their purpose was to transform, not simply suppress, resistance; that marriage reform was "an ideological struggle among the people," not a struggle to destroy a class enemy; and that the Party must therefore educate, persuade and win over the opposition while simultaneously supporting those seeking changes in their own lives. Given the widespread resistance, progress in marriage reform depended heavily on the ability (and willingness) of cadres to perform these difficult tasks.

These tasks were all the more difficult because popular resistance cut across gender as well as class lines. Male resistance to reforms which challenged the normative basis of their traditional family power and privileges was predictable and well documented in articles published during this period. Somewhat less well documented, but clearly evident, was the fact that many women, especially older women, also often resisted the introduction of the new marriage and family practices. Reformers of many kinds have been confronted with the disconcerting phenomena of the beneficiaries of their reforms, the victims of a system of subordination and discrimination which the reformers seek to change, actually forming part of the resistance to those reforms. One model woman cadre discussed the discouraging popular reaction to her initial efforts to publicize the Marriage Law, noting that older women were particularly fearful of and opposed to the moral implications of the new law.[25] The woman cadre was particularly discouraged because their reaction contrasted so sharply with her own excited enthusiasm for a law which, she felt, would greatly alleviate the suffering of all women. Many marriage reformers might expect the restrictive subordinate family roles of females—roles which, as we have seen, created enormous, often unbearable, psychological stresses and tensions at certain points of their life cycles—to motivate most women to rebel in some way when given the opportunity. Yet for many women these were the institutional norms within which they had learned to operate, define and defend themselves. The prospect of leaving that familiar, if narrow world, was threatening.

As discussed earlier, a number of scholars as well as a variety of reformers, have noted the conservative psychology of oppressed, subordinated groups in situations of change, arguing that pervasive social and cultural conditioning imposed by powerful institutions may lead to an almost total internalization, and even active defense, of self-denigrating images, identities and norms. Certainly, the conditions and stability of institutions which severely subordinate one group to another require a significant degree of penetration of the subordinate group's self-identity. Revolutionaries who believe that oppressive institutions are maintained primarily by the use or threat of coercion, and that the impact on the oppressed is no more than skin deep, gravely underestimate the power of those institutions to shape and deform below the surface. Nonetheless, neither notions of "false consciousness" nor the engrained "psychology of the oppressed" provides adequate explanations for the apparent conservatism of Chinese women in the face of a marriage reform movement aimed at raising the status of women. In this regard, it is more useful to recall the world which Chinese women traditionally *created for themselves* within the patrilineal Chinese family and to consider the immediate historical experiences of many rural Chinese women at the time of marriage reform.

The conservative attachment of many women to traditional norms and practices must be interpreted in light of the experience of millions of rural women during the preceding chaotic decades of war and disruption when the inability to attain and hold on to stable, "proper" family relationships caused much suffering and economic insecurity. Women were left particularly vulnerable to the ravages of poverty when families were disrupted because they were heavily dependent upon the strength of interpersonal relationships within their families and villages for influence and survival.

An old South China woman speaking twenty-five years after the revolution about how that revolution had changed her life told a story similar to many others recounted in village studies and visitor accounts.[26] Speaking about the most meaningful changes in her own life since 1949, she did not focus on the return of social order, the more equitable economic redistribution, or the extension of political rights and legal equality. These things were important only indirectly. Rather, she spoke of how changes after 1949 made it possible for her son to stay under her roof, get married and give her grandchildren, whose pictures she proudly displayed. During the 1940s her greatest fear, she said, had been that her son would be forced to leave his landless parents and ancestral village to fend for himself and be forever a bachelor, forever lost to his mother, because they could not afford a bride, a wedding or an additional mouth to feed. Like so many others, this poor peasant woman experienced and evaluated the revolution in terms of how it allowed her to reknit secure family relationships. Certainly women's traditional view of the family was not synonomous with the dominant, male-centered Confucian ideal; this peasant woman's view clearly placed the relationships of her own uterine family, built upon mother-son bonds, at the center of her vision of the family. Nonetheless, women's ideal of the uterine family was shaped by the traditional ideals and norms of the patriarchal Confucian family within whose structures it existed. Thus, for many women living in the aftermath of decades of war and disruption, the marriage reformers' attack on old ideals and the reformers' desire to rebuild family life on a new reformed basis must have appeared as a threat, coming precisely at a time when many women hoped to be able to reconsolidate their uterine families.

The tendency among poor women to identify security and well-being with traditional family ideals, an identification confirmed and heightened for many by recent experience, was backed by a number of specific, hard-headed, self-protecting reasons for older women to resist new family practices. Women who had had no voice in their own marriage, who had adapted to the traditional lowly status of new stranger-bride and daughter-in-law, expected in their older years to have a voice in their children's marriages, especially in the matter of acquiring a daughter-in-law. This was one area of family life where accepted traditional practice gave an older woman important power, power which could help her influence relationships that were crucial in her daily life and to her future security within a patriarchal, patrilineal family system. By custom, a mother-in-law exercised legitimate authority as well as informal power over her daughter-in-law, who was expected to take over a major share of the daily domestic work under the mother-in-law's supervision. An obedient, hard-working daughter-in-law who accepted her traditional role could greatly ease the burden on her mother-in-law, while a rebellious, independent or "modern-minded" young woman (such as the kind who would dare to take a hand in her own marriage) would be far more likely to violate such expectations. Most importantly, an arranged blind marriage and the traditional daughter-in-law's lowly status helped protect the crucial mother-son bond from the potential threat of a strong husband-wife bond or a strong-willed daughter-in-law striving to establish her own independent uterine family. In this way, the traditional family system pitted women against each other and created generational cleavages which cut across a gender-defined underclass. The Marriage Law threatened not only patriarchal power but, inadvertently, older women's uterine families as well.[27]

For many older women the Marriage Law and the principles it represented, especially those emphasizing free-choice marriage and the elevation of the conjugal bond vis-à-vis parent-child relationships, not only created new insecurities, but offered very little in return. For an older woman who had lived through the isolation and powerlessness of entering an alien family and village as a young bride, and who had already built her own uterine family and social networks among women in the village, the right of divorce was no longer as meaningful as it might have been earlier in her life. She would be approaching a stage of life where her husband and surviving in-laws, even if hated, were increasingly less relevant to her and her aspirations. Both the emotional quality of her life and her future security depended far more on her relationship with her children, especially her sons. Traditional norms encouraged, indeed demanded, that the conjugal relationship be an emotionally distant and secondary one. While this increased the loneliness and powerlessness of young married women, older women had far less need for a close conjugal relationship once they had older children. Indeed, these norms made it easier for an older woman to effectively exclude an unsatisfactory husband from her life. She could, in effect, obtain a type of de facto divorce. Furthermore, the emotional distance of the husband-father in the traditional family may have actually helped a woman enhance the strength of her relationship with her children. Most older peasant women had long since built their lives, aspirations and hopes for the future around these cultural realities.

On the other hand, the real divorce made possible by the Marriage Law might very well threaten or even destroy a woman's more crucial relationship with her children, especially sons. By custom, even if no longer by law, male children belonged to her husband's family and patrilineage exclusively. Even if the letter of the law was followed (which was too often not the case), a mother was guaranteed only the custody of nursing infants. None of this is to assert that there were no older women desperate and embittered enough to seek divorce. There were. But older women generally had more to lose and less to gain from this new right than younger women. In many ways, older women were trapped between two worlds. Having lived out their younger lives in a powerless status, they were being asked to accept changes which seemed to threaten the basis of the influence and security they had managed to build out of interpersonal relationships shaped by the norms and structures of the traditional patriarchal family.

Many mothers-in-law may have also feared that they, not their more powerful menfolk, would become major targets of criticism and attack during a marriage reform campaign. While traditional-minded men, including many cadres, were likely to disparage them as women, marriage reformers often looked down on them for their mother-in-law role, frequently characterized in traditional literature, popular culture and myth as cruel, hateful and fearful. The formal structures and normative ideals of the traditional family did accord more authority to older women by virtue of generational age. But the gender hierarchy limited this authority and at times contradicted it (as in the formally prescribed injunction that widows should obey adult sons), making older women's authority ambiguous. While women's real influence and informal power frequently exceeded the limits of their formal authority, the exercise of that influence always carried greater risk of being viewed as illegitimate, petty or cruel. Further, an older woman's need to act to protect her bond with her son against the potential threat of a daughter-in-law, and her frequent role as the most immediate, daily enforcer of restrictive norms on younger female family members, may indeed have made her more vulnerable to attack than men. Men, precisely because of their superior, more secure position, could stand above the fray. As the holders of formally legitimate positions of authority, they would appear less petty than those who had to actively garner and continually defend their influence and informal power. Furthermore, men, because of their political representation and their greater prestige and power in rural communities built around patrilineal kinship networks, were in a much better position to defend themselves against public criticism.

Whether authoritarian mothers-in-law were consistently singled out as perpetrators of mistreatment and the suppression of others' rights more often than similarly offending men is not clear. But there is evidence that mothers-in-law often bore the brunt of the attack on the old family system. For example, in Wu An County, Honan Province, the county administration decided to make its first determined stand against the traditional family system and the forms of mistreatment this system bred by sentencing a mother-in-law to death.[28] The woman's harsh actions were held responsible for driving her daughter-in-law to suicide. The suicide victim's husband was apparently not brought into the case at all. The case was then publicized throughout the county as an object lesson, not against a family system built on male supremacy, but against "the traditional tyranny of the mother-in-law."[29] Such lessons suggest that it was the traditional mother-centered uterine family which might come under most direct attack rather than the patrilineally defined, patriarchal family that encompassed it, and indeed made it necessary. Obviously the vulnerability of women occupying the traditional role of mother-in-law, and a patriarchal, patrilocal family system which cast women in the role of both victim and participant, greatly complicated efforts to unify, organize, educate and mobilize women in support of family reform.

For the most part, marriage reformers and others writing about marriage reform did not show much understanding of the complex dynamics and interests which might lie behind women's reactions. Resistance tended to be understood almost entirely in terms of "remnant feudal ideology" and "false consciousness"—supposed fear and ignorance left over from years of cultural conditioning. Yet, while failing to see the complexities, marriage reformers were not insensitive to the problems of resistance.

By early 1953, national leaders in charge of overseeing marriage reform efforts began to lay greater stress on the use of more moderate, less individually threatening methods of carrying out reform, apparently trying to lessen the fears and moral objections of conservative older women and men. Cadres were cautioned against the use of public struggle tactics against specific individuals except in extreme cases of mistreatment. It seems that most reform leaders came to believe that although public demonstrations of struggle against offending family members sometimes broke through some women's fearful silence, giving them courage to speak out about their own repressed griev-ances, the fear and alienation such public struggle methods caused in others could outweigh the benefits. Instead, reliance on "democratic persuasion" was urged. A nationally distributed propaganda manual instructed cadres to stress the intended benefits of reform to all family members and to the health of the family as a whole. In the long run, it advised, reform would create greater harmony and cooperation be-tween the generations and sexes.[30] It emphasized that divorce would be necessary in only a tiny minority of unreconcilable cases and put increased emphasis on reforming poor relations between husband and wife, daughter-in-law and parents-in-law. With respect to the security concerns of older women (and elderly men) who were dependent on the family for survival and a decent old age, it was stressed that the law and the new morality envisioned upheld the filial obligations of adult children to support and care for their parents. Thus, as the campaigns wore on and included feedback about popular reactions, marriage reform leaders increasingly sought to promote reforms by trying to identify their intended goals with certain popularly held aspirations for the family. The ideal reformed family was portrayed as one which embodied many of the benefits and the security of the idealized traditional family, but did so without violating the rights of women and young people.

However reasonable and politically important it may have been for reformers to emphasize and legally sanction traditional family-based means of security in old age, as long as patrilocal marriage patterns (especially village exogamous patrilocal patterns) remained unchanged, the consequences contradicted marriage reformers' goals of promoting equality for males and females within the family. As long as sons remained with (or nearby) the family and daughters left at marriage, as long as patrilineal ties and obligations predominated and superceded matrilineal ties, security in old age and the family's future well-being had to be based on sons, not daughters. Women's uterine families, as well, would have to continue to be centered around mother-son bonds and potential conflict between older and younger women would be perpetuated. Patterns of discrimination would be reinforced and perpetuated regardless of whether or not women's productive capabilities were made equal to men's. In many ways, marriage reformers were unwittingly trapped by their failure to comprehend and deal with larger kinship and marriage patterns and the family structure these created. This failure made it impossible for them to deal with the obviously legitimate concerns of older women and men without simultaneously reinforcing the discriminatory implications of patrilocality. Neither the Marxist-Engelsian nor Maoist theory provided insights that might have helped alert reformers to their cultural blinders in this respect. The 1950s Marriage Law campaigns addressed the status of women within their husband's family, implicitly accepting the patrilineal context.

Indeed, the blindness of marriage reformers to the implications of patrilocality and patrilineally defined community and family structures led marriage reformers to miss an opportunity during the early 1950s to draw attention to and build upon the one traditional custom which could have served as a starting point for breaking down preferred patrilocal marriage patterns. That custom was the practice of "adopting a son-in-law" (*chui-fu*) and other varieties of matrilocal marriage aimed at providing male progeny for the wife's parents when they had no sons of their own. Although these sorts of marriage arrangements were traditionally viewed as less desirable and the men who married this way were likely to be looked down upon, they were an accepted last resort for obtaining male progeny. There is also reason to believe that in some places prior to 1949 conditions of social disruption were leading to an increase of such practices by depriving families of adult sons and creating larger numbers of uprooted young men who would be willing to enter such marriages.[31] The demobilization of soldiers after more than twenty years of war and revolution must have contributed further to these conditions, at least temporarily. Yet there is no evidence that marriage reformers ever attempted to elevate the status of matrilocal marriage or encourage it as a legitimate, progressive alternative to the major form of marriage under normal circumstances. Indeed, there is evidence of cases where cadres interpreted the law as proscribing this custom because it was "feudal."[32] Thus a relatively favorable historical moment for beginning to dislodge the unquestioned cultural preference for patrilocality was missed. After the mid 1950s, as a result of the return of social stability, land reform, collectivization and a variety of government policies that made it very difficult for males to move from their natal villages, the incidence of matrilocal marriages very probably decreased, or even died out, in most areas.[33]

Although popular resistance was obviously a problem during the early 1950s, the more frequent reports of serious difficulties in the fall of 1951 did not dwell on popular apprehension and resistance as the primary obstacle to progress. It was generally assumed, implicitly or explicitly, that popular consciousness would be undeveloped on issues of women's rights and that there would be resistance to the new law. Indeed, the need for the campaigns was predicated on this assumption. Rather, the main focus of criticism was the failure of the political and legal apparatus at various levels to respond to the central directive concerning the Marriage Law. According to various central and regional investigation teams dispatched during the summer and fall of 1951, this failure was the main problem hindering progress. Publicity and educational work were being neglected so that in some places even minimal knowledge of the existence of the legal reforms was absent.[34] Even more serious was the finding that women and young people who dared to assert their new rights were often unable to obtain political support and legal protection, at times with tragic, even fatal, consequences.[35] When women were left vulnerable to retribution and punishment for their offending actions, others were discouraged from even trying to assert their new rights or adopting new modes of behavior. Fear and intimidation of women by family members and other villagers could be a serious obstacle to getting women together to discuss family reform even if cadres were supportive. Without the reliable support of local officials, open support of the Marriage Law or efforts to use it became forbiddingly dangerous.

The earliest investigative reports on these problems to received publicity came from the Central-South region where the Military Government Council, the Party Bureau and the Women's Federation each published reports in August 1951. Other regional investigations followed, and in October the Central Government Administrative Council headed by Teng Ying-ch'ao's husband, Chou En-lai, gave Minister of Justice Shih Liang the authority to dispatch several central investigation teams throughout the country.

The Central-South reports, apparently indicative of the national situation, placed a large part of the blame for lack of progress on the region's cadres.[36] Cadres continued to hold and act upon traditional conceptions about women, they neglected to promote women's rights and some used their power to actively suppress those women who, even without their support, dared to struggle to obtain their rights. According to the Party Bureau,

> In recent times, owing to the development of land reform and oth-
> er social movements, the struggle of the women for their funda-
> mental rights has become sharper by the day. But owing to the
> fact that the comrades at various levels of the Party have not at-
> tached importance to this and have failed to exercise leadership in
> this matter and that the bulk of the masses and cadres are still un-
> der the influence of feudal thought, this struggle has not yet been
> reasonably led, with the result that women still commit suicide and
> are maltreated with fatal results.

All cadres were urged to "overcome their feudal thought such as the suppression of women's reasonable demands, the neglect of their immediate sufferings and the fear of mobilizing them."

This latter concern, the cadres' fear of mobilizing women, recalls the problem that all organizers of women since the Northern Expedition had in the villages. The very act of getting women together at meetings to discuss their problems and learn of their rights created fears of men's "losing control" over their actions. As long as cadres were under little pressure from above to take action on such issues, it was always easier to back off from the conflict, especially if cadres shared the view that women should stay in their traditional place. Thus, over a year and a half after organizational and educational work on women's rights and the Marriage Law was supposed to have begun as "an important and regular task," many cadres had not yet undertaken even the first step.

The report of the Central-South Democratic Women's Federation emphasized even more strongly that many cadres, from the village up to the county level, actively opposed those who promoted family reform. According to the report:

> The abuse of authority by cadres of the township (*hsiang*) and village (*tsun*) levels who still entertain feudal conceptions on marriage for the protection of "male rights" constitutes the major obstruction to the thorough implementation of the Marriage Law. Many women have been heard to say: "To get a divorce, three obstacles must be surmounted—the obstacle of the husband, the obstacle of the mother-in-law, and the obstacle of the cadres. The last is the most difficult to overcome."
>
> There have also been cadres of the county (*hsien*) and district (*ch'u*) level who have . . . looked upon women as the private property of men. They consider that when a peasant is divorced, he loses his wife in the same way that he loses his cattle and other chattels. They even consider this to be the proper class standpoint. They refuse to give publicity to the Marriage Law. They deal leniently with acts of oppression of women. They persist in various fallacious statements which have been exploded such as "Freedom in marriage will lead to general confusion" and "The granting of divorce to women will deprive peasants of wives."[37]

The report criticized judicial cadres for passing light sentences for crimes committed against women, for procrastinating on women's cases, for refusing legitimate divorce requests and colluding with husbands to force women into submission. According to the report, sometimes even polygamous arrangements were ordered maintained against the demands of the women involved.

The Women's Federation also criticized itself for failing to carry out its responsibilities in organizing women to fight persecution. Other reports indicated that even active women cadres in some places acted to support old family norms. Although the Central-South Women's Federation report does not specifically make this charge against its own cadres, it does make an interesting observation about the psychological underpinnings and social pressures which led even politically active (hence traditionally deviant) women to shun women's rights issues. According to the report, one of the organization's problems was that "some women cadres still retain the feudal conception of taking a conservative stand lest their enthusiasm be considered too 'prominent.' " Unlike men cadres, women cadres were vulnerable to accusations against their moral character simply because they were engaged in new public social roles long considered unsuitable for decent women. This was especially true if their work brought them into contact with men.[38] Under such circumstances many women cadres would be understandably reluctant to associate themselves too closely with women's rights issues. Politically active women were already too vulnerable to take the lead in marriage reform unless they were first sure of a reliable local official following.

The very real danger to the lives of women who did take the lead was one of the major points the Central-South Women's Federation used to underscore the urgency of improving marriage reform work and protecting women struggling for their new rights. According to the report, "the struggle of large numbers of women for freedom in marriage has resulted in cruel persecution and many cases of bloodshed." Within the Central-South region, an estimated 10,000 were "killed or driven to suicide during the previous year as a result of marriage complications." It is impossible to know for sure whether this state of affairs simply represented a continuation of the situation prior to the introduction of marriage reform. In the past, wife beating and female suicide to escape a dreaded marriage or family situation were certainly legendary. Ethnographers have generally believed that, traditionally, physical mistreatment was not uncommon and female suicides were relatively high, especially for younger women.[39] But the Central-South Women's Federation was asserting more than this—that the tragic loss of life was related not only to an intolerable traditional situation which had not yet been sufficiently changed, but also to the unsupported struggles waged by increasing numbers of women to change that situation. Because women were not receiving adequate political support and protection, their new efforts and aspirations, which the central government and its Marriage Law had encouraged, actually increased their frustrations and the danger to their lives.

Other reports made similar arguments and confirmed the contention of the Central-South Women's Federation that significant numbers of young and "progressive" women were being persecuted and dying because of their unsupported struggles against traditional norms.[40] Numerous stories, often told in shocking detail, recounted examples of women who were tortured and murdered. Examples were given of women who were beaten, sometimes fatally, by husbands, in-laws or local militia-turned-vigilantes because they sought a divorce, refused a betrothal, courted a lover in public, attended political meetings or organized women.[41] Some women were driven to suicide after unsuccessful efforts to obtain a divorce or a betrothal cancellation from local political and legal officials, thus being forced to return to angry and abusive family members. In 1953, the Ministry of Justice estimated that, nationally, 70,000 to 80,000 women had "been murdered or forced into suicide" each year since 1950 as a result of family problems and mistreatment.[42]

These disturbing facts became a central part of the marriage reform advocates' argument that work concerning the Marriage Law needed to receive far more nationwide attention than it had yet been accorded.

The initial central directives on implementation and the occasional reminders had proven insufficient to mobilize forces in most areas. The lack of a centrally initiated organizational effort for marriage reform and the higher priority problems of land reform and local political consolidation had contributed to a pattern of avoidance and inattention to the difficult, potentially coalition-disrupting issues of family reform. Although in late 1951 the central leadership was apparently not yet prepared to mount a major organizational and political effort on behalf of marriage reform, it did act to increase the pressure on regional and provincial authorities to investigate conditions in their areas, to check up on their cadres and to increase cadre training. In late September, Chou En-lai, as head of the Government Administrative Council, issued a directive ordering all authorities at the regional and provincial levels to initiate local investigations to uncover cases which had been mishandled in the past, to "deal appropriately" with cadres who persisted in serious violations of the law and to promote training and educational work, especially among cadres.[43]

In October, Shih Liang dispatched central government investigative work teams to various regions. Their summary final report provided the most definitive, though highly general, assessment of the national situation regarding marriage reform.[44] The report classified investigated areas into three groups: relatively good, mediocre and bad. It was found that there were often wide variations within areas, even within the same county or between neighboring villages. Therefore, with a few exceptions, broad generalizations about large areas were not possible. This pattern seemed to indicate that fairly specific local factors were important in determining the degree of success. The contention of Shih Liang's central inspection teams, like that of the Central-South Women's Federation, was that the crucial variable was the quality of local cadres and how conscientious they were in carrying out marriage reform work. The only clear exception is noteworthy. Almost the entire Northwest, where traditional restrictions on women's behavior and freedom of movement were particularly strong, where footbinding was prevalent and persisted into the 1940s, where women's nondomestic economic participation was particularly weak, and where bride prices relative to dowries were highest in the country, showed uniformly poor results.[45] Furthermore, the length of time an area had been liberated (hence, presumably living under marriage reform laws) was not necessarily a reliable indicator. Although examples of better areas were found in older liberated areas, so were examples of the worst, as in the Northwest, the site of the Party's formative Yenan experience.

Areas that fell into the "relatively good" category constituted a small minority. The main examples were from some of the villages in the anti-Japanese base areas in Shansi (in Wu-hsiang County) and Shantung (Wen-teng County). The report also cited villages in Lu Shan County, Honan, an area which was liberated in 1948. In these areas, according to the report, a good foundation had been laid for family reform. Notable progress already had been made in abolishing arranged "buying and selling" marriages, women were able to exercise their legal rights of divorce and remarriage, and where betrothals had already been arranged by parents, the couple were often allowed to meet and decide themselves whether or not they wished to marry. While this "choice" may not have been very significant where social and parental pressure to accept the marriage was strong, it helped guard against extremes of compulsion which in the past had driven young women to suicide, and it helped to establish the importance of the couple's own will in entering a marriage. The report concluded that under the influence of new emerging marriage practices, "progressive thought" was beginning to take hold. Additionally, the report pointedly observed that production flourished at the same time. This latter observation was obviously made to counter the argument frequently made by cadres, and probably not a few top-level leaders, that concerted efforts to carry out marriage reform work caused confusion, led to social instability, diverted attention from other work and hence indirectly hindered production. The report stressed that where reform work had been done well this did not occur, implying that this argument should not be an excuse for neglecting important social reforms. The report stressed that in all of these "good" areas, the determining factor was that the government and Party organs had given considerable time and great consideration to carrying out marriage reform work.

The places that fell into the "mediocre" or "medium" level category were far more numerous. There were many places in Central-South and East China that fell into this category. Here "a part of the masses" had stopped practicing blind "buying and selling" arrangements. But child and arranged marriages were still frequent and, for the most part, women were not free to exercise their rights of divorce and remarriage. Marriage reform work had not received much attention in most of these areas, but some areas began to pay more attention to such educational and organizational work during the 1951 check-up investigations—in other words, when some upper-level pressure was applied.

There were also many areas in the third and worst category. A county in Shansi was given as a specific example. Almost all of the Northwest region (including the old Shen-Kan-Ning Anti-Japanese Base Area), the newly liberated areas in Chekiang and Shantung, and parts of Kwangtung were mentioned in this category. In these places, little if any marriage reform work had been carried out and the situation remained virtually unchanged. Arranged and early marriages and the taking of "foster daughters-in-law" continued as before. In some places in Kwangtung, the practices of buying young girls as servants or slaves and of taking concubines were still allowed to continue.

The various investigation reports argued that the most serious immediate problem for reformers was the need to make it at least possible for "deviant," convention-breaking individuals to safely break away from traditional practices and norms. As long as local cadres were negligent toward or intentionally acted to violate the new reform law, the cost of change for individuals who were dissatisfied with traditional practices and who desired greater freedom and self-determination was often forbiddingly high. In addition to the suicides and deaths which were partly blamed on negligence and the lack of active official support for the victims, the following sorts of cadre harrassment were apparently not uncommon in the villages.

> In Ta Tung *hsiang* in Chin Tang *hsien*, Szechuan, during the past year cadres forcibly separated more than 30 couples (seeking free-choice marriages) who loved each other. In Po Ai *hsien*, Honan, from January to March 1952, there were 82 cases in which cadres interfered with free choice marriages. In a certain *hsiang*, in Yen-cheng *hsien*, Honan, cadres forced young men and women who were in love with each other to put wine containers and broken shoes [A "broken shoe" is a colloquial term for a prostitute.] over their bodies and parade through the streets.[46]

It was not surprising that lack of responsiveness to the central reforms within the political apparatus was most noticeable at the bottom of the hierarchy where the predominantly male cadres were least trained and most representative of and tied to the traditional-minded male peasant and male defined kinship networks. The revolution envisioned by the rural cadre, like that hoped for by the peasant supporter, was more likely to be one that restored traditional family security and patriarchal privileges to poor men than one that embodied the ideals of family reform. Creating local political and legal support for those who sought to use the Marriage Law would not be easy.

But the investigative reports indicated that reformers also were meeting indifference and resistance from high-placed authorities. The reports clearly argued that the Party and government had far from exhausted their available energies and resources in trying to help train, educate, guide and discipline its cadres on marriage reform. Indeed many middle- and upper-level officials had done virtually nothing to enforce the central reforms. The central investigation teams had found that "administrative problems," neglect and inaction by superiors at the county level and above had contributed significantly to the failure of lower cadres. Overburdened with work, inexperienced and un-trained lower cadres had been left on their own to deal with the complex and contentious tasks of marriage reform if and when they had the time and inclination. Their superiors had failed to provide any guidance or initiative in this difficult work. Other reports gave similar findings. Lower-level cadres were neither encouraged, trained, assist-ed, criticized or disciplined by upper-level branches, and above the county level, provincial and regional leadership levels had done little on behalf of promoting reform.[47] The inescapable conclusion was that at many levels and in many areas marriage reform work had suffered from being shuffled to the bottom of the pile of official priority work. Organizational neglect was rife.

Those urging a more active approach by the leadership accused unnamed persons of hiding their indifference or hostility to marriage reform behind a mechanical view of change for women and the family. According to one article, such people put forward the view that "since the feudal marriage system is built on the foundation of feudal economy it will disintegrate automatically along with the disintegration of feudal economy following the completion of the land reform program. Thus they need not do anything to improve the marriage system."[48] The author argued that these views were a manifestation of "bureaucra-tism" and "right opportunism" and were put forward as an excuse for a neglectful work style and the desire to avoid having to deal with women's rights issues.

Shih Liang and other marriage reform advocates apparently hoped and believed that if the Party applied itself more fully, if the central leadership stressed the priority of marriage reform work, they could at least narrow the cruel gap between official national-level encourage-ment of youth and women to rebel against restrictive family tradition and the practice of local officials who used their power to stifle and punish such rebellion. After all, cadres in Lu Shan County, Honan, in Wen Teng County, Shantung, in eight counties of Shansi, and several other scattered places had apparently succeeded through continuous conscientious work in doing just that.[49] If marriage reform was an effort to impose a new alien morality on a monolithically resistant traditional peasantry, as some authors have portrayed it, probably no amount of organizational skill, determination and discipline could have much success. But evidence showed that the rigidity of the traditional marriage system and its morality had bred sufficient tensions for some village women and young people to try to break away from old norms even without much support and at considerable risk to themselves. The Party certainly could do far more to crack down on vigilante-like behavior among its own cadres and to create some local legal and political support for those who wanted reform, to lessen their danger and increase their numbers. From this perspective, success in marriage reform work was not so much a matter of fundamentally transforming the values of the vast majority in a short period of time. Given the widespread nature of traditional attitudes, marriage reformers knew by 1952 that this was an unrealistic expectation. Rather, marriage reform was a matter of finding ways to support a minority, encourage incipiently rebellious groups and gradually enlarge their ranks through education about their new rights while easing some of the fears of the more traditional-minded peasants who foresaw "social chaos" in new marriage practices.[50]

Although the justice minister's central inspection team's final report recommended that family reform work immediately be designated a central and regular task for a long time to come, the Central Committee and the Government Administrative Council did not act to endorse the report's recommendations at the time. In fact, the report, which was written in April, does not appear to have been published until July and it then appeared without editorial comment. Publicity on the Marriage Law and its problems died down again. But reform advocates continued to press their case until they finally gained enough attention and support at the top to promote a serious national campaign to implement the Marriage Law in the spring of 1953.

10 The 1953 Marriage Law Campaign

The lull in publicity and the lack of noticeable top-level attention to marriage reform lasted from early spring until late 1952. According to an article on reform in Shansi Province, the situation there had improved during the period of the national check-up, but backsliding occurred during 1952 because of the "preoccupation of leadership cadres with the San-Fan [Three-Antis] campaign and other central tasks."[1] Like others who found signs of backsliding when upper-level pressure was removed,[2] the author argued that this tendency showed that "the slightest slackening of efforts on the part of leadership elements tends to revive feudal practices and that the campaign against the old marriage system involves an extremely difficult and intricate process." Indeed, the tendency for a wide variety of traditional familial, religious and superstitious practices deemed "backward" to tenaciously reassert themselves during periods of relaxation was noted by Chinese analysts throughout the 1960s and 1970s.[3] In the early 1950s marriage reform advocates understandably argued that, even in areas where some progress had been made, it was far too soon for the center to abandon pressure for marriage reform and to allow local reform efforts to take their own course.

The 1952 lull did not in fact signal the end of national reform efforts, even though the highly defensive stance of articles supporting a major reform campaign suggests serious disagreement over the scope of the campaign. By late summer, there were signs of preparations for a systematic, nationwide educational campaign on the Marriage Law. It was later announced that after each area completed preparations, the campaign would culminate in the spring of 1953 when the local leadership in all areas was to make intensive marriage reform educational work their top political task for one month.[4] Because land reform and other major campaigns had inhibited marriage reform activity, the campaign was timed to coincide with the virtual completion of land reform and the waning of various other campaigns. The few areas that had not yet completed land reform, as well as all of the national minority areas, were explicitly excluded from the campaign.

The 1953 Marriage Law campaign differed significantly from previous efforts to propagate the law. It was more extensive, more coordinated, better directed and better prepared for. In these respects, the long-standing rhetorical commitment to marriage reform and women's rights issues was for the first time being accorded some of the organizational attention and energy which had been invested in problems and goals which the leadership considered important to the revolution and construction. While the first two years of marriage reform efforts had suffered from organizational neglect and an almost total lack of preparation, the 1953 campaign was preceded by thousands of "keypoint" experiments in selected villages and counties throughout the country and by prescribed cadre training classes.[5] These experiments helped familiarize leadership cadres with the sorts of problems and conflicts that were likely to arise and helped provide an experiential basis for evaluating and correcting the methods of carrying out the campaign.[6] Given the complicated nature of the problems and social conflicts that surrounded marriage reform, this kind of preparation was particularly important.

Furthermore, special marriage reform committees, made up of representatives of Party, government and mass organizations, were set up outside of the regular Party and administrative apparatus at various levels from the region down to the county (in some cases lower) to plan, coordinate, and supervise the preparations and campaign activities.[7] The National Committee for the Thorough Implementation of the Marriage Law, with Chief Justice Shen Chun-ju as chairperson and Teng Ying-ch'ao, Shih Liang and Ho Hsiang-ning, among others, as vice-chairs, was established at the national level.[8] The National Committee was charged with the task of coordinating preparations for the campaign, monitoring its progress, drawing up educational materials for cadre study and generally keeping the campaign on course.[9] Although major debates and decisions concerning the nature and scope of the campaign almost certainly took place within the Central Committee and the Government Administrative Council, the National Committee exercised control over the daily development of the campaign. To help evaluate keypoint experiments and the adequacy of cadre training, the National Committee frequently dispatched check-up work teams to various districts.[10] These check-up work teams were the primary means of supervision, control and political pressure which the National Committee had at its disposal and, along with the special marriage reform committees, signalled the leadership's determination to tighten discipline on the issue.

Of course, the marriage reform committees, especially those at lower levels, were likely to be subject to some of the same pressures from conservative forces and the same tendencies to accommodate these pressures as the regular Party organs had been. Furthermore, the cooperation, or at least the acquiescence, of the regular leadership organs would still be of paramount importance to the committees' assigned work. But the special marriage reform committees, which were presumably to be packed with Party members and mass activists who supported marriage reform, might help provide new initiative, focus support and create political pressure which had previously been lacking in carrying out marriage reform work. Such organizational measures could not in themselves guarantee adequate responsiveness to central reforms. But, along with outside work teams, they could improve the situation and help provide a new source of support for reform forces and dissatisfied individuals who desperately needed it.

Several other measures were taken in late 1952 to help make the implementing apparatus more responsive to the center. During 1952, the courts underwent a general rectification to retrain, discipline or replace judicial personnel, many of whom had been retained from the previous court system.[11] This effort was aimed at rooting out "old legal views" which violated the new government's principles and at making local courts more responsive to Party policy.

The All-China Democratic Women's Federation (later the All-China Women's Federation) was also reorganized in late 1952. In an effort to strengthen central organizational control and the effective outreach of the formally large but amorphous federation, permanent work committees were established at the regional level.[12] These committees, acting as the operational arm of the Women's Federation Central Executive, were responsible for setting up and supervising local women's associations and for increasing the recruitment and training of new cadres. On one hand, this reorganization effort was probably expected to help promote local activities in support of the upcoming marriage reform campaign. On the other hand, the desire to strengthen central control, emphasizing the federation's subordination to the Party, and to the Party-dominated Women's Federation Executive, seems to reflect the long-standing concern that the activities of local women's groups not become separate from Party control or go beyond centrally formulated Party policy in pressing their demands. While criticism of feminist tendencies had not been pronounced in the early 1950s, central directives immediately preceding the 1953 campaign again indicated concern among some leaders that leftist or feminist deviations were likely to develop during the campaign and that they had to be moderated and controlled. Thus, even though the major aim of the Women's Federation reorganization appears to have been to strengthen reform forces against traditionalist resistance to change, there is also evidence of the desire to increase central control over these strengthened forces to prevent them from "going too far."

Although all of these various preparatory organizational efforts indicate that a serious leadership commitment had been made to this campaign, there is evidence of continuing controversy among the leadership over the proper nature, scope and methods of the campaign. The defensive tone of the articles advocating strong and continuing marriage reform efforts implies that they were still presenting one side of an ongoing debate. Three somewhat conflicting and increasingly cautious Central Committee and Government Administrative Council directives on the campaign issued during the first six weeks of 1953 also suggest controversy within those bodies. Although the second two directives were presented as elaborations and clarifications of the first, they in fact represent fairly significant modifications in approach and methods, becoming increasingly cautious and concerned about maintaining Party control over the conduct of the campaign.

The first central directive initiating nationwide campaign preparations was issued by the Central Committee on December 26. Although this directive appears to have been widely disseminated among cadres and acted upon by some, it was never published.[13] Its general tone, therefore, can only be surmised from two later directives made public and from the changes which many cadres perceived and reacted to in the later directives. Not until February, when the Government Administrative Council (GAC) passed a resolution announcing the outlines of the upcoming campaign, was a central directive on the issue publicly announced.[14] The GAC directive indicated that the proposed campaign and preparation for it were to be more extensive and thorough than previous efforts to popularize the Marriage Law. The focus of the campaign was first on rectifying cadre behavior and then on propagandizing for marriage reform among the general population. The directive stressed the need to avoid punitive or coercive "class struggle" methods. Except in cases of serious injury or death (in which case a carefully monitored educative public trial might be held), violators of the law, including cadres, were to be patiently criticized and educated to change, not punished or disciplined. Similarly, rather than dissolving unsatisfactory marriages, persuasion, education, and democratic family criticism meetings were recommended to reform "feudal families" into more harmonious, democratic ones. Only in the "small minority" of cases where reconcilation was impossible was divorce to be considered an appropriate solution. While none of these points were new, they received greater emphasis in the GAC directive than previously.

The relatively cautious tone of this public directive, certain to have been noticed by cadres, appears to have been in part an effort to assuage people's fears that a marriage reform campaign would destroy their families, threaten their security and lead to social chaos. This caution also reflected concern to conduct the campaign in a way that would minimize social conflict and disrupt Party control and village routine as little as possible. The polarizing social conflict which sometimes erupted over marriage reform issues would make it more difficult for the Party to control local social forces and could even interfere with local economic production. The GAC sought to mount an extensive but relatively moderate campaign which would avoid these politically costly consequences.

Yet two weeks after the second directive, the Central Committee found it necessary to issue a third directive.[15] The Central Committee's supplementary directive, which superceded both the December 26 Central Committee directive and the GAC directive, went even further in warning against tendencies which could be termed "leftist." It is impossible to know precisely how the Central Committee's supplementary directive differed from its initial directive. Nonetheless, it is clear that some cadres perceived it as greatly moderating the tone and fundamentally narrowing the scope of the campaign. Some cadres even interpreted it as a basic reversal of policy, believing that the Party was prepared to abandon any serious efforts to implement reform.[16]

According to the vice-chairperson of the National Committee for the Thorough Implementation of the Marriage Law, Liu Ching-fan, those cadres who had not liked the idea of the campaign in the first place interpreted the supplementary directive as a license to virtually call off the campaign, reducing their task to merely reading a public report at a mass meeting during the designated month.[17] Such cadres recalled personnel from training courses and halted preparations. This sort of reaction to what was perceived as a weakening of central leadership pressure was predictable in light of past trends. More interesting, and revealing about the apparent new strength of marriage reform supporters among cadres, was Liu's comment that some "impatient" cadres who had been enthusiastic about the campaign were disheartened by the supplementary directive and considered it a serious blow to their efforts to carry out meaningful reform. Some cadres reportedly disparaged the Central Committee's campaign proposals as a lot of "thunder which would not produce any rain" and complained that the leadership was out of touch with local conditions.[18] These cadres who supported women's rights and family reform and who were dissatisfied with the government's efforts were no doubt a minority. Yet, as in Yenan, they were numerous enough and vocal enough that their views warranted comment and refutation by a major leader.

Thus, although then it was presented as merely an elaboration of the earlier directives and although Liu Ching-fan refuted those who interpreted it as a call to lessen campaign efforts, the directive represented more clearly than before leadership concerns to conduct the campaign in a manner that would minimize social conflict, protect the local power base of the Party and government and better protect cadres from demoralization and severe public criticism. The supplementary directive was much more forceful in its criticism of leftist ",errors" than the GAC directive had been. It also spelled out the limited scope and tactics of the campaign much more clearly. The supplementary directive complained that not only were there cadres who still resisted the law, but that there was now also a "portion of cadres" who, in their impatience to carry out reform, erroneously employed methods such as "struggle meetings, frank confession meetings, investigations house by house, comparisons of family with family, the demarcation of fronts and the appointment of watches in homes." According to the directive, the "policy of education" adopted for the current campaign explicitly excluded such tactics.

Earlier in the campaign preparations, however, some of these methods had been sanctioned and portrayed as successful in the published accounts of model cadres and model areas. Model cadre Wang Kuei-ying of Lu Shan County, Honan Province, for example, had organized women cadres to go house to house to talk to the women and investigate for cases of mistreatment.[19] In Lu Shan this sort of cadre initiative and activism had been credited with helping to protect women and furthering reform goals. Similarly, in Cheng Kung County, Yunnan Province, another keypoint area designated a model during the National Committee's campaign preparations, villagewide "struggle meetings for airing grievances against the feudal marriage system" had been portrayed as successful in breaking through women's acceptance of mistreatment and fear of standing up for their rights.[20] Less intrusive and less personally threatening ways of promoting reform might lessen resistance among men and parents and induce more villagers to remain open to the basic message of the movement for marriage reform. Nonetheless, some cadres obviously felt that the blanket exclusion of such activities as struggle meetings and investigations cut them off from potentially powerful and successful methods of promoting change and of demonstrating firm support for women's rights. Whether or not such methods were necessary and could be successful obviously depended on local circumstances. Hence the complaint by some cadres that the leadership was "out of touch" with the local problems they faced.

The supplementary directive specifically prohibited investigations of past illegal activities and of "general family relations" among the public and cautioned against singling out individual offenders unless their offense involved serious injury or death. Rather, progressive families and individuals were to be identified and publicly praised as good husbands, in-laws, parents or couples and held up as models to be emulated. In this way the Central Committee obviously hoped to avoid bringing interpersonal and male-female tensions to the surface while providing positive educational publicity for the Marriage Law.

The supplementary directive also made criticism and self-criticism of erring cadres a matter to be taken care of among cadres, not in public. Keeping this process confined to official channels afforded greater protection to cadres' reputations and spared them public embarrassment. Furthermore, disciplinary action was to be taken only against those cadres who, after receiving training and internal criticism, intentionally persisted in subverting the law. For most cadres, past illegal behavior would not be taken as a basis for punishment or disciplinary action unless their violations involved murder or injury of women. Cadres' "personal marriage and sexual relationships" were also excluded from investigation and criticism. Only official public behavior was subject to review. All of these limitations could be expected to have the effect of lessening cadre apprehension about the campaign and helping to protect the base of the Party and government from the possibly disruptive consequences of the campaign. This approach virtually ensured that the campaign would not result in any significant purge of local officials from their positions of power and it signalled that a cadre's attitude toward women's rights and marriage reform should not be made a major criteria in judging his fitness for leadership or Party membership.

Finally, the supplementary directive permitted local cadres to suspend or sharply limit the campaign under certain conditions. If serious "confusion and deviations" occurred during the campaign, the campaign could be halted. This presumably referred to the outbreak of major incidents of social conflict, the disruption of production or the improper conduct of the campaign by local cadres. Also, in areas short of labor power the scope of the campaign could be limited so as not to interfere with production. Because some areas would be approaching the busy spring planting season, there was probably pressure to restrict their obligations in carrying out marriage reform work. The Central Committee's directive clearly reflected these concerns even though marriage reformers had previously argued that reform work need not interfere with production if cadres were conscientious and willing to make the effort.

While pressures for toning down the proposed 1953 campaign no doubt resulted primarily from the reassertion of more conservative political forces who all along had placed a low priority on the pursuit of marriage reform, even some ardent supporters of marriage reform apparently had come to believe that a cautious approach would be more effective in promoting reform goals. According to Liu Ching-fan, who had been a fairly active public supporter of marriage reform since 1950, many of the keypoint experiments had shown that when reform activities turned into a sharp struggle in which parents, in-laws or husbands were treated as "enemies," as "conscienceless and inhuman old fools," a counterproductive atmosphere of general "fear and confusion" was often created.[21] Even cases of suicide had resulted from the reformer's attacks. According to Liu, when sharp struggle and punishment was meted out only to the "absolutely small number of serious criminals" it could help to further the primary objective of raising people's consciousness. But, Liu argued, among the general public where the practice of "feudal" customs was still widespread, the use of struggle and punitive measures would not succeed in transforming people's ideology and consciousness, but would heighten resistance out of fear. Rather, the "Outline for Propaganda" issued by the National Committee for the Thorough Implementation of the Marriage Law in February 1953 attempted to present democratic marriage reform primarily as a means to "revive" the traditional but previously elusive ideals of the harmonious, secure, multigenerational family.[22]

In support of the Central Committee's supplementary directive, Liu thus argued that a less ambitious, more cautious, essentially less participatory approach presented less danger of provoking resistance and isolating reform supporters. Such an approach, it was argued, was also more appropriate and realistic given the inherently limited possibilities of any single campaign for altering personal attitudes and behavior. Accordingly, Liu and others on the National Committee increasingly stressed the long-term nature of building a new marriage and family system, pointing out that this campaign could do no more than lay the foundation for continuing efforts. The goals of the campaign had become essentially informational, trying to eradicate popular fears and misconceptions about the Marriage Law while making the new legal rights of women and youth better known to them and better enforced by the courts and local cadres when people sought to use them. If some cadres were disappointed and felt that a more ambitious, dramatic and dynamic approach was needed to break through old patterns of authority and subordination, they must have been partially appeased because the central authorities were at last putting greater organizational energy into carrying out an extensive nationwide campaign.

Because there were relatively few investigative reports published after mid-1953, it is difficult to evaluate the course and results of the spring 1953 campaign. But, judging from the nature of the preparations and the official reports which did appear, the campaign was undoubtedly the most extensive propaganda effort ever carried out on behalf of marriage reform. Even though the publicity month did not get off on schedule in many areas,[23] more people learned about, studied and discussed the Marriage Law than at any time since the law was passed. Summing up information gathered throughout the country, Liu Ching-fan estimated that 70 percent of the nation's population had been reached in some way through various mediums of education and publicity during the month.[24] Not only does it seem that millions became more clearly aware of the major issues of marriage reform and women's rights, but people also became more aware of some degree of government determination in supporting such changes—something which, given the past behavior of local officials, may not have been understood in many areas prior to the 1953 campaign.

Articles in the press further indicated that the extensive publicity had, in some places at least, prompted an increase in free-choice marriages. These claims had, of course, been made earlier in 1950 and 1951 and were later shown to be highly unrepresentative. While such trends were still clearly not representative—perhaps they were not even trends but temporary increases more or less dependent upon the supportive campaign atmosphere itself—they showed that the campaign had succeeded in helping to encourage or make possible greater self-determination for women and young people in some places. Couples who had previously been prevented from marrying because of family resistance and general social pressure were finally able to find the political support they needed during the campaign to get married.[25]

Claims were also made that, as a result of the campaign, tens of thousands of families began to solve conflicts and reform "feudal relationships" through the efforts of mediating teams and the popularization of family group discussions which introduced principles of "family democracy." In many areas, mistreatment of women and cases of murder and suicide were reported to be successfully reduced and public opinion against serious mistreatment of women increased. A few articles reported that in some areas the publicity for women's rights and gender equality had a favorable impact on areas of life outside the family, for example, increasing women's participation in literacy classes and public meetings. In one village, it was reported that criticism of the traditional concept of male superiority led to a successful attack on the accepted practice of automatically paying women less than men for the same work. As a result, the number of women participating in labor production of various kinds increased from 12 to 72 percent.[26]

Significantly, the impact of the publicity month and cadre rectification efforts on divorce rates was not stressed as in earlier years. Divorce appears to have been the most controversial and threatening aspect of the Marriage Law, as it had been for women's rights advocates since the mid-1920s when Ho Hsiang-ning, then head of the KMT-CCP Central Women's Department, declared that divorce was "the most difficult and complicated question in China." Clearly divorce was still widely perceived as immoral, probably even by some of the leadership. It also threatened to disrupt the exchange of women upon which patrilineal families and rural communities were based. When a woman got a divorce, she was divorcing a family as much as a husband and the family was threatened with the loss of its bride price investment. The thrust of the 1953 marriage reform campaign was precisely to emphasize that the democratic reform of the family could be carried out without undermining basic, traditional aspirations for a secure family life. Therefore the disruptive incidence of divorce was downplayed.

Nontheless, statistics published later indicated that divorces in fact did rise sharply and reach a peak in 1953 as a result of the campaign and the government's efforts to make the legal and political apparatus more responsive in upholding the law at the local level.[27]

While the articles that reported on the campaign claimed important successes, most accounts also mentioned continuing difficulties and pointed out that only a minority of areas had attained truly satisfactory results. As we have seen, since late 1951 this sort of candid admission of difficulties had been accompanied by urgent arguments for greater resolve and for greater efforts to help support minority reform forces. But after the 1953 campaign, the sobering discussion of continuing problems in bringing about change was not accompanied by a sense of political urgency, nor did it underline a prescription for continuing political action except at a very low level. Indeed, some articles strongly suggested that persistent problems, such as the well-documented traditionalist resistance to change still very evident in rural areas, showed the futility of persisting with political agitation for family reform. In short, it was increasingly suggested that it was unrealistic to expect the situation to improve except with the passage of time and with the gradual development of other socioeconomic changes. Similarly the failure of the political-legal apparatus to fully support and cultivate reform forces was no longer treated as a primary obstacle to further progress. Rather, the stubborn traditional consciousness of a majority of the populace was seen as the main obstacle to further progress at the moment, an obstacle which was not, it was suggested, very amenable to direct political pressure for change.

This was essentially the message of an authoritative *People's Daily* editorial which summed up the campaign of 1953.[28] Although the editorial voiced a need for some level of political action, it stated, quoting from Lenin,

"In uniting with the masses of laboring peasants and in marching forward with them, the speed will be so slow that it will be even slower than our most conservative estimate. But nonetheless, the masses as a whole shall march along with us." . . . If we do not do things merely on subjective enthusiasm but on the basis of reality, if we do not want to be divorced from the masses but desire that the whole of the masses march along with us, we must assuredly adopt the measure of marching forward with steady steps.

The editorial added that a policy of taking "steady steps" and a "policy of persistence on education," should not be construed to mean simply "letting the movement take its own course." "Positive action" should be taken to foster and expand the influence of model democratic families. But it was clear from the major thrust of the editorial that a decision had been made to at least temporarily shelve marriage reform, and the sorts of women's rights issues associated with family reform, as national issues. Highly visible, nationally organized, politically activist efforts prodded on by top-level pressure and investigations would in the future be replaced with lower-level "regular activities" which were unspecified and left, again, to local initiative.

The National Committee for the Thorough Implementation of the Marriage Law's final summary report, delivered by Liu Ching-fan, contained many of the same views as the *People's Daily* editorial, accepting at least a partial retreat from family reform efforts.[29] But the committee still argued the need for maintaining, on a long-term basis, a more active approach, including periodic national propaganda campaigns and, in some areas, the early renewal of a campaign on the scale of the 1953 campaign.

In the view of the committee, only a beginning had been made in laying a foundation upon which a new consciousness and moral code would develop. According to Liu, the campaign had achieved extremely varied results, ranging from very good to nothing. As in earlier investigations, these wide variations were found even within single counties. In the committee's evaluation, creditably good efforts and results had been made in about 15 percent of the country. In these areas, cadres had been well trained and had actively supported the campaign, and from 80 to 90 percent of the adult population had been reached through educational activities. In such areas, "the new moral code of democratic and harmonious families had begun to be established," preparing the ground for more thorough implementation in the future. In a second type of area, comprising about 60 percent of the country, 60 to 70 percent of the adults received education during the movement and "a portion of the population" was beginning to make improvements in attitudes and relationships. But many still entertained "doubts and anxieties" over free marriage and gender equality. The maltreatment and even deaths of women persisted, though reportedly to a lesser degree, at least during the months immediately following the campaign. In about 25 percent of the country, the cadres as well as the masses had at best "a flimsy understanding" of the Marriage Law. In these areas essentially no improvement was made and the campaign had not been developed at all.

As in the *People's Daily* editorial, these very uneven and probably disappointing results were seen as reflecting the general "cultural and economic backwardness" of China. This position assumed general limits to politically induced change in the family system until broader changes began to alter the socioeconomic context of the family more substantially. A sobering emphasis was therefore placed on the need for patience and for understanding that political will and activism could not work miracles. But the report did not imply that direct political efforts should now be disparaged or put aside, only that the hoped for improvements would be slow and would require considerable long-term effort. The committee's recommendations therefore reflected a moderate, multifaceted approach which would lower the national political visibility of family reform as an urgent priority, but which aimed at preventing the issues from being totally eclipsed by other tasks at both the national and local levels. The recommendations included increased, regularly scheduled training in implementing reform for local cadres, village "mediation teams" and teachers, and the inclusion of family reform policy in the regular curriculum of the middle schools and peasant night schools. Model families and couples should be selected, praised and used as a vehicle for publicity and education. General propaganda on the Marriage Law and gender equality should be included in or coordinated with other central tasks such as production and the upcoming National People's Congress elections when the election of women should be encouraged. To help ensure that this sort of regularized work was carried out at the local level, the committee recommended that regular periods of inspection be carried out by administrative, judicial, cultural and educational departments at all levels within their organizations. The committee also hoped that, in addition to regular periods of inspection, national campaigns would be mounted periodically to help keep attention on the issues. In the 25 percent of the country where the March campaign had been the most slipshod and ineffective, they recommended that the large-scale campaign be launched again as soon as possible. The committee also recommended another nationwide propaganda campaign to be carried out around the time of the 1954 Spring Festival.

Thus the committee reflected the leadership's new, more conservative approach and the pressures to demote marriage reform as a national priority. But, as advocates of reform goals concerned that marriage reform efforts not be allowed to disappear, they also included recommendations aimed at keeping the issues alive in local and national politics and they continued to stress the need for upper-level measures to ensure that the local legal and political apparatus upheld the law for women and youth. Yet even these moderate recommendations argued for a higher level of involvement than the dominant leadership views would sustain. While many of the committee's recommendations may have been carried out quietly in some local areas, they were given little national publicity and there were no publicly issued central directives backing these measures. There is little evidence of even a small-scale national publicity campaign being carried out during the Spring Festival period as the committee had anticipated.

In areas like the model county of Lu Shan, Honan, the early support and initiative which local cadres had demonstrated prior to 1953 indicated that local support for marriage reform activities might continue at a lower level even without a high level of national prodding. But the central leadership certainly knew that putting marriage reform aside as a national issue while decentralizing it as a "regular" local task was likely to renew the pattern of neglect and inaction in most areas. But, whether resulting from a new understanding of social change or from a desire to provide a justification for a politically expedient policy, the new emphasis on "cultural and economic backwardness," rather than cadre malfeasance or organizational laxity, as the main obstacle to change implied that it would be futile to press for politically induced reform activity any longer. Thus political mobilization for change was again replaced by the view that changes in the socioeconomic environment surrounding the family, mainly involving changes in women's economic activities, would indirectly promote the desired changes in family authority structures, customs and personal attitudes. The Party in fact never returned to another large scale marriage reform effort.

At the same time, as will be discussed in the following chapters, Party leaders were becoming more aware of the value of traditional family and community solidarity for various socioeconomic goals as they turned their attention to economic development and socialist construction in the countryside. In the mid-1950s, when the state was confronting the problems of financing the First Five Year Plan, debates over welfare policies began to emphasize more strongly the need to rely on traditional corporate family forms of welfare, especially in the countryside, in order to release state and, later, collective funds for productive investment.[30] Furthermore, the cooperative socialist structures developing in the countryside in the mid-1950s were built on and in many ways drew strength from traditional community solidarities based on networks of patrilineal families and male kin. Efforts to control excessive rural-to-urban migration in the 1950s similarly could benefit from shoring up the traditional ties and obligations that bound people to rural families and communities. Thus the state began to develop a real, if indirect and barely acknowledged, stake in the maintenance of the rooted, traditional patrilineal bonds that reinforced and strengthened the stability of the rural family and community.

The Marriage Law, on the other hand, was essentially a democratic conjugal family law, a form whose development has been historically associated with the loosening of the larger traditional bonds of the extended family and the kinship basis of community. Although the Marriage Law contained a clause affirming the obligations of children to support elderly parents, many of the law's provisions were aimed precisely at creating a greater sphere of personal freedom for youth and women from traditional group obligations and control within the family. While marriage reformers in the early 1950s viewed this positively as liberation from "feudal" authority and oppressive restrictions on the individual rights of women and youth, others soon voiced concern over how the Marriage Law encouraged selfish, irresponsible "individualism" associated with the development of "bourgeois" society and culture.

In a debate over the problems of youth and marriage which was publicly aired in 1956–57 in a number of publications, certain intended consequences of family reform (liberalized attitudes toward marriage, divorce and relations between the sexes) were related to an allegedly growing danger of such "individualism" and decadent "bourgeois" attitudes toward love and family.[31] Those who held this position argued, somewhat ingenuously, that this trend had superceded those earlier problems of "feudal" restrictions on women and youth that had concerned marriage reformers prior to 1953. Despite the fact that the number of divorces granted by the courts had dropped precipitously after 1953,[32] these problems were blamed in part on courts that still granted divorces too lightly, thereby creating a permissive atmosphere in which youth failed to develop a serious and moral attitude toward marriage. Such views did not go entirely unchallenged; others pointed to evidence that "feudal" marriage arrangements that violated the rights of women and youth were still the major problems in most areas, not that youth "abused" their rights.[33] But these views were given greater credence than before and, most important, they were supported implicitly by an increasingly restrictive official policy on granting divorce after 1953.

Ambivalence over the "bourgeois" implications of the democratic ideology of the conjugal family which bolstered May Fourth youth in their attacks against Confucianism (an ambivalence compounded by the Western source of inspiration for such ideas) can be traced back to the early years of the Party. Such ambivalence was implicit in the views of those Party leaders who put forth the classic Marxist and Leninist critique of the urban women's rights movement as "bourgeois" in the 1920s. It was also clear in the accusations in Kiangsi against "petit bourgeois" women cadres who focused too much on marriage problems and in the criticisms of the Yenan feminists in the 1940s.

The antibourgeois ideology of the Maoist left in China has not infrequently, if unwittingly, dovetailed with the interest of conservative social forces in shoring up traditional norms and structures on issues related to women, youth and the family. Just as notions of individualism were considered alien and a threat to traditional Chinese culture with its emphasis on familism and patrilineal group obligations, so too were they easily considered alien and a threat to the development of socialism, both ideologically and practically in terms of the socialist development strategies emerging in the mid- and late fifties. On issues of family reform, one sees glimpses in the mid-1950s of an implicit, tenuous joining of the interests and views of traditionalist forces seeking to maintain control over women and youth in the family and village with a left socialist critique of "bourgeois" tendencies in Chinese society. Of course, when such views did merge, they were always masked in proper socialist rhetoric. But the joining of the two strains is nonetheless clear.

The tensions created by pursuing a far-from-complete "antifeudal" cultural revolution in the context of the "antibourgeois" concerns of left socialist leaders has indeed marked the development of Chinese socialism in a variety of ways. Especially since the early 1950s, the historic tensions between the anti-Confucian heritage of revolutionary intellectuals and the traditionalist aspirations of the peasant base have interacted with and in some ways been cross-cut by tensions within socialist elite thinking over the "foreign" and "bourgeois" ideology that has informed the antifeudal thrust of cultural revolution in China since the early twentieth century. As we shall see in Part 4, these tensions explode in the Cultural Revolution and are played out in a variety of confusing and contradictory ways, some of which link traditionalist and nativist sentiment with left Maoist thinking against the May Fourth heritage, including outright attacks against surviving May Fourth figures who spearheaded the original "antifeudal" cultural revolution among youth.

4 Women, the Family and the Chinese Road to Socialism, 1955–80

Since the early 1950s, the reform of women's family position has been left to occur indirectly as a result of other general social and economic transformations undertaken by the government in pursuit of economic development and "building socialism." Indeed, with a few exceptions, issues of gender equality in general have been raised only when the leadership has felt they bore a direct relation to the success of campaigns and central efforts aimed at other priorities. The remaining chapters review the impact on rural women's roles of some of the most relevant major developments and campaigns since the mid-1950s and assess their significance in promoting change toward gender equality and, particularly, toward the original egalitarian goals of family reform for women, reform central to women's position in other areas of society. Three major developments will be considered: the collectivization drives of the 1950s, the Cultural Revolution from 1966–70, and the period surrounding the Anti-Confucian campaign in the early and mid-1970s. Finally, the increasingly urgent family planning and population control efforts since the mid-1970s, and their relationship to gender equality and family reform, will also be considered more briefly in the conclusion.

11 Collectivization and the Mobilization of Female Labor

After the conclusion of the 1953 Marriage Law campaign, the Party returned to the general approach to gender equality and family reform that had been espoused in the days of Yenan—that women would gain equality in the family and society at large as a consequence of being brought into productive labor outside of the family. The abolition of private property and the socialization of the means of production were supposed to lessen the family's role as the economic unit of production. Simultaneously, this would provide an organizational framework which would facilitate the mobilization of women's labor outside the private domestic realm alongside men. Thus Engels's two-pronged policy prescriptions (abolish private property and bring women into public production), as spelled out in *The Origins of the Family, Private Property and the State*, became central to the Party's official view of how to build a socialist society with equality for men and women. Engels himself has been frequently quoted by Party officials:

> The emancipation of women and their equality with men are impossible and must remain so as long as women are excluded from socially productive work and restricted to housework, which is private. The emancipation of women becomes possible only when women are enabled to take part in production on a large, social scale, and when domestic duties require their attention to a minor degree.[1]

As in Yenan, the dominant view also condemned as unnecessary and ineffective political, legal and propaganda efforts aimed directly at aiding changes in family practices and attitudes toward women. Similarly, the official view in most periods has carried with it the implication that women who struggle directly in the family for their rights or greater power are engaging in efforts that are not only

157

fruitless, but disruptive. Even the Maoist Cultural Revolution left, known for its emphasis on struggle, conflict, and a willingness to promote disruptive politics, tended to accept the Engelsian paradigm's implications for the depoliticization of the private realm of family relations, at least on women's issues.

Lu Yu-lan, a Central Committee member and National Labor Heroine from Hopei, expressed in 1972 the view which has been dominant among the leadership since 1953:

> Women's emancipation is not easy. A wrong idea was that women win their freedom simply by seizing control in the family, and this wrong idea led to a lot of fruitless quarreling among husband, wife and in-laws. Lack of understanding on the relationship between raising women's position in the family and taking part in class struggle in society at large disrupted family harmony and failed to win public sympathy and achieve its aim.
> Then the Party organized the women to study what Chairman Mao says about women's emancipation: "Genuine equality between man and woman can be realized only in the process of socialist transformation of society as a whole." Women began taking a broader view, to understand that to achieve their own emancipation they must look at things in terms of the entire society, to see the family as a basic social unit, as changing with the transformation of society as a whole. It was realized that after women take their position in society, changes in family relations follow, and men and women can be equal.[2]

Throughout most of the period since the end of the marriage reform campaigns, the main policies claimed by the government to promote gender equality have centered on the collective organization of the economy and the mobilization of women's labor into the collective economy. The Cultural Revolution era added to this approach a greater emphasis on the need to promote women's participation in political activity and organizations outside the home (even while it destroyed the only national organization of women, the All-China Women's Federation), but did not fundamentally alter it.

Thus after the Marriage Law campaigns, the Party's "women's work" in the countryside centered almost exclusively on the utilization of female labor in the agrarian economy alongside efforts to promote collectivization. The major collectivization drives of the 1950s were accompanied by increased efforts to mobilize female labor. Indeed, economically, the fuller utilization of female labor was central to the logic of collectivization. Collectivization was to provide an organizational framework for production that would permit more efficient use of land and labor and a diversification of the agrarian economy. Given the relatively low investment rates for agriculture, increasing agricultural production was more or less dependent on changing the organization of production and significantly increasing the use of labor. As in the Yenan production war, the Party's earliest experience with cooperative, labor-intensive development strategies, women's "underutilized" labor was considered a major source of new labor. Also, as in Yenan, these efforts were portrayed as striking at the heart of the causes of women's inequality in family and society. A major *People's Daily* editorial in November 1955, at the beginning of the high tide of agricultural cooperativization, spelled out the Party's official view of the relationship between collectivization, women's labor and the realization of women's equality. According to the editorial, entitled "Mobilize Women to Join the Cooperativization Movement,"

> The development and victory of [the cooperativization] movement
> . . . signifies the complete emancipation of the broad masses of rural women constituting half the rural population.
>   Through the agrarian reform and other democratic reforms, the broad masses of rural women in our country have politically and economically acquired a [formal] status of complete equality with men. . . . However, as small peasant economy based on private property still occupies a dominant position in our country, the majority of rural women are still completely bound to dispersed and fragmentary house labor, economically not being independent and intellectually being unable to develop their intelligence and talents. Their status in family and society cannot be made equal to that of men. Where is the way for women to achieve their complete emancipation? On this question, Engels said in his *Origin of the Family, Property and the State*: "The first prerequisite for the emancipation of women is that all women participate again in social labor; to achieve this, individual families are required to be no longer units of the social economy."[3]

Cooperativization removed control over the organization of labor from the single family. It also removed control, and eventually all ownership, of the means of production from the family. It was argued that these developments would reduce patriarchal economic power in the family by depriving the traditional family head of the ability to manage and control family labor and resources. While land reform had presumably removed these rights from the patriarch, it was now implicitly acknowledged that the customary powers of husband and father had continued to operate nonetheless. Cooperativization was also expected to provide the structural basis for breaking down the public/private sexual division of family labor, which, in the Marxist view, lies at the heart of female subordination. Eliminating the family as the main unit of production would provide women with new opportunities for labor in remunerated collective endeavors and provide a cooperative framework for progressively lessening women's private labor.

In its earliest efforts at promoting cooperativization the Party was quite cautious in calling for new patterns for women's labor—for example, not including in the first Mutual Aid Teams (the earliest form of cooperativization) the sideline activities which women traditionally performed individually in the home.[4] But as cooperativization progressed, the Party mounted increasing efforts to raise women's participation in labor outside the home. The high tide of cooperativization in late 1955 and 1956 was accompanied by a major campaign in this direction. As most of the countryside rapidly moved from the formation of Lower Agricultural Producer Cooperatives (APCs) (ranging from 20 to 50 households) to Higher Agricultural Producer Cooperatives (ranging from 100 to 350 households, constituting a small village or a section of a large village), women were reported to be joining cooperative labor in large numbers. By late 1956, various provinces claimed that 80 percent or more of the women of working age were participating in agriculture.[5] Furthermore, the Draft National Agrarian Program in 1956 set a minimum of 120 work days per year (compared to 250 for men) as the goal for each woman working in agriculture.[6] While press reports almost certainly exaggerated the levels of women's participation in collective agricultural labor it is clear that the central mobilization push increased the number and percentage of rural women working in agriculture in most parts of the country, as well as the average number of days worked per woman. Both central pressure and the structural reorganization of production (which allowed for more intensive farming, some degree of diversification, and the launching of capital construction projects) called for increased labor, thereby increasing the demand for female labor.

In 1957 there was a fall-off from the high rates of participation of rural women, perhaps due to a pulling back from the expansion of capital construction. In urban areas, a slight economic slump, coupled with fairly substantial rural-urban migration and the relatively slow rate at which new industrial jobs were being created under the capital-intensive, heavy industry-centered First Five Year Plan, caused rather severe unemployment. In China, as in all patriarchal societies, it is politically easier to push women from the labor force back into the domestic sphere than to confront high unemployment among men, the preferred breadwinners. Women's family roles and social subordination to men make them a "flexible labor force" that both socialist and capitalist economic systems can manipulate to help adjust to economic fluctuations. Thus in 1957 there were efforts to pull some women out of the urban labor force accompanied by a propaganda campaign concentrating on the positive role of the housewife.[7]

Yet the downturn in female participation in urban and rural production was rapidly and dramatically reversed in 1958 with the Great Leap Forward, as the leadership turned to a new type of development strategy which called for yet another, more total reorganization of production, especially outside the state-owned industrial sector. In the countryside, the Great Leap called for the formation of much larger collective units by amalgamating the existing Higher Agricultural Producer Cooperatives into People's Communes. The goal of the reorganization was again to increase and diversify production by drastically increasing labor inputs and the scale of production. With the simultaneous launching of massive construction projects, rural industries and agricultural sidelines, labor shortages quickly emerged. As before, women were considered to be the greatest single source of available underutilized labor. The most massive efforts ever made to mobilize rural female labor were mounted as part of the Great Leap.

Although the campaign of 1956 had succeeded in drawing more women into the agricultural labor force, it had also shown that it was extremely difficult to get many women to meet even the minimal goal set in 1956 of 120 work days a year because of family demands on their private domestic labor. While some facilities, primarily nurseries and kindergartens, had been set up before and during the 1956 drive, most only operated during the busy season and were in any case hardly sufficient in number. The reorganization of the Great Leap eventually had to include efforts to socialize some of women's traditional private labor in order to release more women for collective labor for more days per year. Creches, year-round nurseries and kindergartens, communal dining halls and collective sewing groups were set up on a larger scale.

Thus in 1958 and 1959 large numbers of women were mobilized to fill the increased demand for labor in the collective rural sector. More women were needed in field work as men were drawn into capital construction projects, local industries and other new economic activities. Tens of millions of women were also mobilized to work on water conservation and afforestation projects. Several millions took jobs in communal dining halls and nearly all of the six to seven million workers in daycare centers were women.[8] In late 1958 it was reported at an All-China Women's Work Conference that in most places 90 percent of the women were participating in collective labor. Some model areas reported 100 percent.[9] The average number of work days also was reported to have increased greatly in 1958 and 1959. It was later reported that women worked an average of 250 days in 1959 as compared to 166 in 1957.[10]

Again, while these reports were exaggerated (as were almost all such reports in the Great Leap), there is little question that the pressures created by the Great Leap produced extremely high levels of female participation in collective labor outside the home, surpassing the previous high levels of 1956. Marina Thorborg estimates that while the percentage of rural women participating in collective labor in 1956 was within the range of 60 percent to 75 percent, in 1958–59 the range was probably between 80 percent and 90 percent of able-bodied women of working age (15 to 59).[11] Basing her estimates on the data of John Buck, she calculates that the comparable figures for 1930 were in the range of 30 percent to 50 percent, with the higher range including those engaged in rural subsidiary occupations. These subsidiary occupations had actually shrunk by the late 1950s due to state centralization of textile production and the restriction of free markets in rural areas. As mentioned earlier, Buck's figures, which probably underestimate women's contribution, indicate that before 1949 Chinese women had higher rates of participation in many areas than the traditional stereotype suggested. Indeed, most poor peasant women in most parts of China probably worked in agriculture and subsidiary occupations fairly regularly. Certainly the notion of using female labor in nondomestic work when necessary for family survival was not new to most peasants. Nonetheless the 1956 and especially the 1958–59 period witnessed a significant increase in the percentage of women who worked in agriculture and in the amount of time they engaged in this work. In a sense, what in many areas was once, out of necessity, a practice of the poor (i.e., women doing year-round field work and heavy physical labor) was now to become a general, expected norm which the Party insisted should carry honor and status for women.

These dramatic changes during the Great Leap Forward were accompanied by a renewed flurry of articles discussing the issue of family reform, though in a very different vein than those of the 1950–1953 period. A number of highly theoretical articles appeared which argued that, while the democratic reforms of the early fifties, including the marriage reform, had established formally equal treatment for men and women in family and society, the structural economic changes of the Great Leap would bring true and actual equality to women in the family.[12] Unlike propaganda in the early fifties, these articles did not encourage women to stand up for their rights in the family, nor was the Marriage Law emphasized as a point of reference. Indeed, in the atmosphere of the "communist wind" that accompanied the Great Leap at its height, the Marriage Law seemed somewhat tainted as a document of "bourgeois democratic rights," no longer relevant as China made a rapid transition toward a communist future. China was to skip a capitalist stage in family matters as in the economy. The spirit of individualism which often fueled notions of a democratic family and women's rights was just as readily seen by left Maoists as the enemy of advanced socialism as the enemy of "feudalism" and the traditional patriarchal control of women. It is perhaps significant that encouragement of women and youth to struggle for their new rights in the family against "feudal" authority was at its height during what was seen by Maoists as the bourgeois democratic period of recovery prior to the major drives to build socialism.

For the most part, discussions of the family during the Great Leap were orthodox, straightforward explications of Engels' major theoretical points, minus his hint of uncertainty about the endurance of the monogamous family under communism. Indeed, like the marriage reformers of the early fifties, writers now were at pains to explain as groundless the apparently widespread fears that socialization of female labor and many family functions in the communes meant that "the family was going to disappear." Following Engels' materialist analysis, they argued that the abolition of private property, coupled with the large-scale socialization of household labor and large-scale participation of women in social labor, would end the family's status as a socioeconomic unit and bring about the final destruction of patriarchy. No longer based on relations of economic control and dependency, family relations would be based on equality and mutuality in the interests of all. Divorces would become increasingly unnecessary and unlikely because the family would be established on a firmer and more harmonious basis than ever before.

In many ways this approach depoliticized many of the specific issues surrounding family reform, while affirming that the goals would be attained through other means—changing the organization of the society and economy outside of the family. To be sure these means were quite drastic, entailing a profound restructuring of social and economic life outside of the family which if sustained would have a profound impact on the family as well. But the issues and political activism were focused outside of the family and its interpersonal relationships and away from the specific issues of marriage and family reform (bride prices, free-choice marriage, women's divorce rights, even, to a great extent, the right of women to control and dispose of their own income). In contrast to the marriage reform period of the early fifties, there was not much emphasis on the need for ideological struggle and education of other family members. The May Fourth ethos of individual rebellion and struggle against traditional authority by women and youth was replaced by an ethos of collective struggle to increase production and socialize the economy and society. Women's legal rights, and the role of the courts or local cadres in safeguarding these, were hardly, if ever, mentioned in discussions of family life.

In many ways the Great Leap's approach both to economic development and women was a logical, if extreme, extension of the approach which had emerged from the Party's base areas experience. The Yenan production war provided a model experience, in embryonic form, of a socialist development strategy suited to a desperately poor, undercapitalized peasant society forced by external circumstances to deal self-reliantly with its poverty. In Yenan, the Party had argued that this development strategy also simultaneously and adequately addressed the major traditional causes of gender inequality, including the subordination of women in the family.

This politically conservative position on gender equality, supported and rationalized by Engelsian theoretical assumptions, allowed the Party to silence feminist critics who complained that it was ignoring women's family rights and male chauvinist attitudes; "unnecessary," direct confrontation with male peasant supporters over issues of women and the family could be avoided, except when absolutely necessary to obtain female labor from the family; and the Party leaders could concentrate on economic and political priorities, assured that they were not abandoning a principled commitment to the goal of gender equality. In fact, as long as the demand for female labor was not too great, the Party did not need to push very hard against the traditional family roles and duties of women. In the base areas, by emphasizing the expansion of cottage industries and home production (once traditional work for middle peasant women in this area), the family and women's position within it had been disturbed as little as possible while still greatly increasing women's production for wartime needs.

But the Great Leap's version of the earlier narrow economic approach to women had a far from conservative impact on the functions and routine of women and the family. The Great Leap was not conceived or carried out in the earlier spirit of coalition politics that kept a careful eye on the cultural, social and political sensibilities of peasant supporters, though it allegedly was carried out in their interests and with their initial support. Both its design and incredibly ambitious economic goals, as shaped by Mao's radical and impatient social and economic visions, created enormously disruptive demands on rural communities and families. Whereas the Party leadership had been hesitant to cause conflict or press too hard for changes in family practices and relationships for the sake of marriage reform and women's rights in the family, in pursuit of the labor for the Great Leap's utopian economic goals, Maoist Party leaders were willing to move hard and precipitously against the features of the family and community that held women's rates of labor participation below what was needed. The "socialization of housework" emerged as the ad hoc solution for mobilizing enough female labor to keep both new projects and agricultural production afloat.

As soon as these measures began to take shape, they were hailed as the creation of the embryonic forms of the communist society of the future and as the measures which would bring about the final realization of complete gender equality. Engelsian theory again explained how and why this was so. The full range of policy prescriptions flowing from the theoretical assumptions were being enacted within the communes: the abolition of private property, the large-scale introduction of women into public social labor and the socialization of private domestic labor. The communes represented a great leap into the future for women and the world historical defeat of patriarchy was at hand.

It might seem somewhat ironic that a movement which has been characterized as the Maoist leaderships' most utopian and radically voluntarist social and economic experiment drew so heavily for its vision of women's emancipation from the theory and policy prescriptions of Engels, known for his mechanistic expressions of the most materialist and determinist side of Marxist theory. Of course, it is less ironic when one realizes that Maoists were less in search of an architect or vision of gender equality than they were for a rapid means to release needed female labor from competing demands. This is not to argue that the Maoist leadership was not concerned with the social consequences of the Great Leap Forward and the communes. It is undoubtedly true, as Maurice Meisner has argued, that to assume the Great Leap was conceived merely as a crash program for "modernization" obscures its meaning and history.[13] In the highly charged ideological atmosphere at the height of the Great Leap, the Maoist leadership's economic goals became inextricably intertwined with the pursuit of utopian social goals and the expectation that the new social forms would call forth a communist consciousness among the masses. In this context, the presumption that the ad hoc measures within the communes to socialize housework and massively mobilize female labor would quickly bring liberation should perhaps be taken seriously as part of the utopian Maoist visions of the day.

What was radically Maoist about the version of Engels' narrowly economistic view of women's emancipation prevalent during the Great Leap Forward was that the Great Leap presumed to implement the social designs (at least in embryonic form) of complete female liberation in the communist society long before the advanced development of production and material conditions deemed necessary by Engels. Indeed, the Maoist assumption here as elsewhere was that the development of advanced social relations and relations of production was more a precondition for the development of productive forces than the result of such forces. The social forms of the communist future were to be set up in a technologically primitive, desperately poor peasant society.

But aside from this distinctively voluntarist Maoist use of Engels, the Great Leap was quite orthodox and offered little creative thought on issues of women's equality for the distinctive Chinese context. A number of feminist scholars have argued that the entire body of Marxist literature is remarkably narrow and uncreative on issues of women's equality.[14] Mao continued in this tradition, though in theory (if not in practice) he rose above the confines of narrow orthodoxy on a host of other issues, such as the revolutionary role of the peasantry, the problems of bureaucracy and the problems of building socialism in a peasant society. The Maoist treatment of the "women's question" is particularly striking when one contrasts its materialist orthodoxy with the more innovative and radical utopian conceptions and approaches to eliminating other social inequalities that were put forward, at least in theory, during the Great Leap.

For example, besides being heavily economistic, the Engelsian prescription for gender equality adopted by Maoists implies an "assimilationist" approach for women, an approach which fails to raise questions about the importance of mutually redefining male-female roles. Women become equal to the extent that they can join men in social production, that is, to the extent that they enter the traditionally male public domain on the same basis as men. While both Marx and Engels accepted as natural some sexual division of labor, the theory implies that women must become "more like men" if they are to become equal. Men have little reciprocal responsibility to end their alienation from the nurturant, service-oriented roles which history consigned to women alone. There is also little emphasis on the need to revalue the general social worth of women's traditional work aside from bringing it into the public realm. Although in the communist society all work is supposed to be for use and of equal social value, the entire Marxist view of history disparages the kinds of work and functions associated with women and the "feminine." For Marx, civilization and human progress spring forth from work in the public realm, from which women and women's work have been excluded; although shaped by the forces of history and by the public realm, women have, since the creation of private property, stood passively outside of history, culture and the creation of value. Thus in some ways, the entire Marxist historical view reinforces the traditional social denigration of women and their traditional work, while accepting that some degree of this division of labor by sex, in terms of function, is "natural."

In contrast to the Maoist acceptance of an assimilationist approach to gender equality is the utopian Maoist vision of the "all-around person" (to-mien-shou), a vision which can also be glimpsed in Marx. This utopian vision imagined the elimination of status distinctions between mental and manual labor, between intellectual and peasant, through an ultimate fusion of roles which would end the alienation of both from their essential unity. Thus in the future, it was proclaimed during the Great Leap, "everyone will be a mental laborer and at the same time a physical laborer; everyone can be a philosopher, scientist, writer and artist."[15] Moreover, Maoism claimed in theory that efforts to eliminate these status distinctions should not be consigned entirely to a distant future. Maoist ideology, in extolling the virtues and wisdom of the poor peasantry and exhorting urban intellectuals and cadres to go to the countryside to "learn from the peasant masses" (a practice accelerated in the Great Leap), insisted on a re-evaluation of both mental and manual labor. During the Great Leap and later in the Cultural Revolution, Maoists claimed this vision was also supposed to be manifested in practice in such policies as the "three-in-one combinations" and the "two participations" in the factories.[16] Under these policies, technicians and managers were supposed to take part in manual factory labor and workers were to learn to participate in management, in making technical decisions and in contributing to technical innovations.

Yet Maoist Party leaders never thought to apply such concepts even in theory to male-female role and status distinctions. Never was it suggested, even in the most utopian movements, that men should learn from women or that men should be sent down to the laundry or nursery to learn the value of, and how to perform, the nurturant human services relegated to women. Never did Maoists insist that women's traditional work be given greater respect and value; indeed the opposite was the case. Rather, the Maoist approach is epitomized by the quotation popular in the Cultural Revolution: "Times have changed. Whatever men comrades can do, women comrades can do too."

While at least a segment of the leadership continued over the next decades to be influenced by the social and economic visions of the Great Leap, serious problems quickly forced a general retreat. Not only did the frenetic pace and pressure of the Great Leap and commune movement break with the careful, localized experimentation called for by "mass line" politics, but the size and forms of organization exceeded and violated peasant notions of community and social life far more drastically than any previous movement. The seeds of early cooperativization in Yenan and in the Mutual Aid Teams of the early fifties had been carefully nurtured and expanded from traditional forms of seasonal peasant cooperation among neighbors and relatives.[17] The Agricultural Producer Cooperatives had also been built on existing neighborhoods and villages, without expanding much beyond the reach of social ties in rooted rural communities. The commune movement, however, called for the amalgamation of a number of APCs into a single accounting unit that far exceeded, and in some cases cut across, even the more distant existing social boundaries, such as natural marketing areas, within which trust and cooperation could be built.[18] In a situation where everyone had to work hard in order to inch above the level of bare subsistence, peasants were precipitously asked to tie their means of livelihood and survival to the honesty and hard work of strangers. Furthermore, the abrupt attempt at collectivization of women's domestic labor and some of the functions of the family created a serious disruption of family routine, even if it did not (and could not) "liberate" women.

The demands placed on labor were enormous, reportedly up to sixteen hours a day in some places. These demands must have been particularly difficult for women, many of whom were unaccustomed to the type of field and construction labor they now performed at breakneck pace and most of whom in fact still had domestic chores awaiting them when they returned home at night. Most of the population, both men and women, was physically and emotionally exhausted within a matter of months. The serious economic problems arising from the local mismanagement and misallocation of resources and labor that was inevitable, given the central policy demands, must have created widespread disillusionment among an overworked peasantry. If the Great Leap was in part an attempt to transform social life and norms, including those of the family, certainly it was a far more disruptive approach to family change than the legal and political activist approach suggested by even the most radical family reformers. It was also, no doubt, far more politically costly.

Within a matter of months, the leadership took its first step back, lowering the accounting unit to the old Higher APCs (now called production brigades) and trying to put checks on the "communist wind," which it had stirred up, by calling for the return of private possessions (such as houses and furniture), small family private plots, small domestic animals and farm implements wherever these had been communized.[19] Later the accounting unit was lowered even further, back to the production team, which in many cases more closely approximated the unit of the Lower APCs. By the early 1960s the commune remained a unit of account only for some rural industry, functioning primarily as an administrative unit to coordinate the activities of the teams and brigades.

Labor participation rates for women apparently remained high throughout 1959 and, to a slightly lesser degree, through 1960. But the serious economic difficulties, coupled with the unpopularity of the hastily and haphazardly constructed socialized services led to a cutback in most of the services that were supposed to lighten some of women's domestic tasks, leaving in only a few places daycare that was seasonal and rudimentary at best. Under such circumstances, it was impossible to maintain the rates of female labor participation for long. Cutbacks in capital construction, the end of the abortive "backyard steel furnace" projects, and a decline in other small-scale industries due to the need to stem the plummeting production of grain also meant a return of many men to field work and a greatly lessened demand for female labor. The organization of production and rural life returned more or less to pre-Leap conditions and the rate of women's labor participation in collective work also fell back to pre-Leap levels. It has been estimated that, during the early 1960s, from 50 percent to 60 percent of working-age women took part in collective agricultural labor, down from the highs of 80 percent to 95 percent in 1958–59.[20]

The idea that the communes would soon bring about the complete emancipation of women and abolition of the patriarchal family institution gave way to the less optimistic view that, while enormous strides had been made, the "material conditions" for women's emancipation were not yet ripe and would only gradually develop over time.[21] However, the goals of family reform were still to be accomplished through gradually increasing women's "social labor" while increasing and improving services to relieve them of their domestic labor.

From the mid-1960s on, the percentage of women working in collective labor and their number of labor days did begin gradually to increase again as the economy recovered. Various policies re-emphasized small-scale rural industrialization, labor-intensive collective agriculture and rural capital construction. Along with this, nurseries and some other collective services such as grain-processing stations began to reappear on a small scale. By the early seventies, it is estimated the 70 percent of working age women worked in collective labor, probably around one-third of whom were "full labor power," providing 250 or more labor days per year, as compared with two-thirds of the male labor force working 250 days or more per year in collective agriculture and sidelines.[22] In at least some places, evidence suggests participation increased further in the mid-1970s.[23]

Statistics on women's collective labor participation, however, tend to underrate the amount of time women spend in agricultural labor and income-earning activities. In most areas, both women and men put in time working on private plots whose produce is used primarily, though not entirely, for private consumption. Small privately owned animals raised near the home are frequently tended exclusively by women. These private activities provide a major portion of the nongrain foods consumed by the family, and the domestic pig raised by the woman may provide the main cash income for the family. During times when free rural markets have been allowed to flourish, as in the early 1960s and following 1978, women have also engaged in private income-earning activities by producing handicrafts or prepared foodstuffs for the market. Women may in fact be more highly (and more directly) remunerated for these latter kinds of activities than they are for their collective labor, in part because of persistent wage discrimination in the collective sector. There is virtually no systematic data on the amount of time women spend in such productive activities outside the collective sector, although probably it varies considerably by locale and ethnic group.[24] Nonetheless, it is clear that women's rates of participation in agricultural labor and sideline activities are higher than the estimates derived merely from collective figures. Moreover, decline in those figures, as in the early sixties, may partially be taken up by other kinds of "productive" and even more highly remunerated private labor as well as by nonremunerated "nonproductive" domestic labor.

Whatever the regional variations and fluctuations over time, it appears that policies since 1949 have in fact mobilized a significantly higher percentage of women into the agrarian labor force, and since the early sixties, this has been done on a relatively permanent, stable basis. In part this must be attributed to the general outlines of a development strategy which has emphasized labor-intensive organization of the rural economy through intensive farming, decentralized small-scale industrialization and diversification. While the Maoists' political mobilization approach and many other important aspects of policy have been matters of serious leadership dispute (such as the type of collective sidelines and rural industries that should be pursued, the role of the free market and private sidelines, and state procurement and pricing policies), these general outlines for agrarian development have been pursued more or less continually since the 1956 Draft National Agrarian Program. It could be argued that by utilizing rural labor more fully than many other developing economies, Chinese economic policies have been able to enlarge rural women's economic roles, rather than merely maintaining or shrinking women's involvement as has happened in some underdeveloped countries (such as parts of India) where development has been more capital-intensive and rural unemployment has been higher.[25]

But, the picture is not unmixed on the issue of rural women's economic roles. The state more or less finished the destruction of an important source of rural employment for women—textile handicrafts—begun by foreign economic forces in the early twentieth century through the nationalization of textiles in the 1950s. Furthermore, other nonagricultural sidelines, handicrafts and home manufacture which women traditionally did in some areas, have been severely limited or closed down due to the centralization of commerce and tight restrictions on free rural markets. This has been particularly true during leftist periods when such nonagricultural activities have been condemmed as "capitalist," whether organized privately or as collective sidelines.[26] Although policies since the late 1970s appear to be reviving some of these activities, only women's field labor has been clearly expanded in the last thirty years, and some portion of this represents a narrowing and shift away from traditional nonagricultural work for rural women.

Moreover, this "liberation through labor" approach to gender equality, and the way it has been implemented, clearly has imposed heavy burdens on women. One of the major consequences has been the creation of a classic double burden for women. This burden often has been exacerbated further by the priorities of male political authorities at the top and by the way policies have been implemented and controlled by male political authority at the bottom. This double burden results, of course, from adding collective labor duties without proportionally diminishing domestic responsibilities. The labor mobilization campaigns of the 1950s were probably the most difficult in these terms, with the precipitous demands for female labor far outstripping the provision of services to help women meet the demands of their expected traditional responsibilities. Although an estimated 60 to 75 percent of women participated in agriculture in 1956 (official reports claimed rates of 80 percent or more) childcare facilities were sufficient for only a small percentage of young children, probably no more than 5 percent of the children of working mothers.[27] In addition to childcare, cooking, cleaning, laundering and mending, women were responsible for processing and manufacturing nearly all goods and foodstuffs consumed by the family (including grain, blankets, clothes, shoes and often yarn and cloth). In the 1950s there were no other services available and few, if any, consumer goods to ease some of this burden.

Not surprisingly, during the busy season of 1956 there were numerous reports of women being overworked. There were also alarming complaints that no consideration was given in assigning tasks and hours to women who were pregnant or had recently given birth.[28] Numerous cases of miscarriage and hemmorhaging were reported to have resulted from the way cooperatives used female labor. Although it is commonly believed by both Chinese medical authorities and popular folk medicine that it is hazardous to a woman's health to work in cold water or in cold damp places during menses, in many places it was reported that women were routinely assigned such work regardless of whether or not they were menstruating. Some reports indicated that, in an atmosphere extolling "superwomen" as the appropriate models pointing the way to liberation, some women overworked themselves and endangered their health because they felt they had to "prove themselves" and not complain to male cadres when they found the work too heavy or were exhausted from their double workload.[29]

Most of these problems were attributed to the ignorance, lack of concern and, occasionally, active hostility of local male cadres who were responsible for organizing production. Equal blame certainly could have been placed on the rapidly building pressure from the top leadership to mobilize female labor without prior regard for the lack of local facilities and without providing any concrete state aid or incentives to create them. Thus, in addition to undertaking a second job by entering the labor force, women also found themselves entering a man's world organized and dominated by male political power that frequently neglected women's needs and still considered them inferior.

Given traditional attitudes about the value of female labor and given the male-dominated local power structures that organized labor in the cooperatives, it is not surprising that women were also paid poorly for their efforts. Discrimination in pay was clearly rife throughout the 1950s. In 1956, women leaders used the national Women's Federation conference and Party Congress to complain about this state of affairs and pressed for fair remuneration practices in the countryside.[30] It was argued then, as later, that providing women with "equal pay for equal work" was not only just, but was necessary to induce more women to join the labor force.

Most of these problems continued in the Great Leap Forward, although when the severe labor shortage became evident and women were more fully mobilized into collective labor, the collectives were forced to pay more attention to setting up collective services to lighten women's domestic burdens. Thorborg has estimated that from 50 percent to over 70 percent of the children of working mothers were in some sort of collective childcare in 1958 and 1959.[31] The most advanced communes also provided services such as laundering, clothes making and mending in addition to the more generally available canteens, nurseries and kindergartens. There was also a somewhat greater effort to provide central guidance for women's labor protection and general health care.[32] Nonetheless, overall demands on most women's time no doubt greatly increased; even in the most advanced communes, women still faced a considerable amount of domestic work after returning from a day's work of often very heavy field or construction work. The assumption that housework and child-tending were entirely women's responsibility remained unquestioned by official propaganda throughout this period. Furthermore, the frenetic pace of the period led to continued violation of women's labor protection despite the publication of central regulations.[33] The priority was production, and the demands to reach unreasonably high quotas predictably led to a tendency to push aside labor regulations and a reluctance to invest more than a minimum in services such as canteens and nurseries.

These services, most of which were hastily constructed and poorly run, were, predictably, the first cut back in the economic crises years of the early 1960s. Working women were left almost entirely to make private arrangements for childcare and other help for themselves, either with mothers-in-law or nonworking neighbors. Over the years, as women's collective labor gradually increased again, seasonal child-care and sometimes year-round nurseries and kindergartens began to re-emerge in many teams and brigades, probably on a sounder but much less widespread basis. The general improvement in the availability of consumer goods, increased electrification and the mechanization and collectivization of grain processing in some brigades no doubt helped to ease women's domestic burden, at least in wealthier areas. In the early 1960s, the official media also began to raise the idea that men should be willing to "help out" at home, although with the possible exception of the 1974 Anti-Confucian campaign there has never been any real propaganda effort to promote this.

Despite gradual improvements and the attainment of relatively high and stable rates of women's participation in collective agricultural labor, basic services have remained extremely inadequate through the late 1970s. Although visitors, who usually see advanced and model rural units, gain the impression that various forms of daycare are generally available, many rural areas still do not provide daycare on a regular basis. In rural Kwangtung, where women's participation rates remain among the highest in the country, probably only slightly less than men's, Parish and Whyte found in the fifty-one teams and brigades for which they had data, only 19 percent had regular year-round nurseries or kindergartens in the mid-1970s.[34] In 1978, leaders of the Hopeh Women's Federation reported that after unusually active efforts on their part since 1973–74, 36 percent of the brigades in the province had regular nurseries, while 60 percent had kindergartens and 80 percent had set up cooperative sewing groups.[35] There may have been improvements in other places around the country in 1973–74 as well as a result of the re-establishment of provincial branches of the Women's Federation after their destruction during the Cultural Revolution and as a result of the Anti-Confucian campaign. But Hopeh is considered to be relatively good in this regard and its figures are probably better than average.

Like women in almost all societies, capitalist or socialist, where there is a clear separation of production from the domestic sphere and where women work outside the home, women in rural China still must deal with most of their domestic responsibilities as "private" problems, even when there is limited outside support.[36] This has consequences for older women who no longer work much outside the home as well. Younger able-bodied women must obtain at least some help with domestic responsibilities from family or neighbors. Although a number of family members may do more as a result, it seems most common that the largest share of the shifted burden goes to other females in the family, particularly grandmothers (mothers-in-law), who live in the same household or nearby. Parish and Whyte found that fathers-husbands were the least likely to help out, while mothers-in-law tended to pick up the greatest amount of additional work in childcare and domestic chores.[37] My own observations in a Hopeh village confirm this impression, especially for childcare. Chinese literature and articles extolling harmonious cooperative family relationships often have stressed a mutual aid relationship between working daughters-in-law and mothers-in-law in dealing with housework and childcare.[38]

Thus the mobilization of women into collective labor has resulted in a redistribution of some domestic labor from younger women to older women. This probably represents a gain in the status and independence of daughters-in-law vis-à-vis mothers-in-law in recognition of the value to the family of younger women's remunerated labor outside the home. But just as the provisions of the Marriage Law seemed to encroach upon the authority and informal power of older women over their uterine families, this change in labor patterns means a greater burden for older women at a time when older women in economically stable families traditionally expected their domestic burden to be lightened by daughters-in-law. Not only do younger women have less time, but their labor is organized outside the home and no longer as readily influenced by the authority of a mother-in-law. The double burden for working women means more work and probably less influence for older women. Relationships and the distribution of duties between men and women seem to have been affected least of all.

The patterns of collective and traditional private labor for women also mean that women, by working extra long hours, indirectly provide necessary, but unremunerated and largely hidden, services to the collective, services which the collective therefore need not supply. Contemporary Marxist critics of capitalism have analyzed the ways in which the continuation of patriarchy and the subordination of women in family and society is functional and beneficial to capitalism, contrary to Marx's own expectation that advanced capitalism would sweep away all traditional forms of inequality, such as patriarchy, leaving only an undifferentiated and equally exploitable proletariat impoverished by capital.[39] Such critiques argue that the maintenance of the structural subordination of women to men in the family is functional for capitalism and for the creation of surplus value in at least two ways. First, women's traditional functions in the family provide valuable, unpaid services which are necessary for the reproduction of labor and which capital therefore need not provide. Secondly, women in the home provide a relatively cheap, flexible, "reserve" labor force that can be called forth when needed, but can also be pushed back into the family during economic downturns without political repercussions because patriarchal social norms assert that women's primary place remains in the home as wife and mother.[40]

The same arguments, however, could be made about the situation of women in socialist rural China. Women in China have experienced the same pull and push, in and out of the labor market according to economic booms and busts, and women remain a flexible labor force available for accommodating seasonal fluctuations. Furthermore, the continuation of a sizeable part of women's traditional domestic burden even while they are supplying an important part of the public labor force has helped maintain collective members' standard of living by providing necessary nurturant and manufacturing services that improve living conditions at no collective expense. This in turn has aided in maintaining higher rates of accumulation through the funds thereby saved by the collective.[41] Not only are women not remunerated for their extra contributions in the domestic sphere, but the social value to collective wealth of this female labor (in terms of funds saved from investment in daycare, use value created and money saved by manufacturing clothes, necessary services provided to the health and care of labor, etc.) is largely unrecognized and unacknowledged, for it springs forth from traditional, "natural" obligations of women that patriarchal society always denigrated.

This is not to argue that the subordination and exploitation of women is necessary for greater collective wealth. Indeed, because most women at least partially reduce their contribution to collective labor in order to meet domestic obligations, especially childcare obligations of young mothers, one would imagine a variety of circumstances where it would be profitable for the collective to invest more funds in daycare so as to obtain more collective labor directly from these women. This, indeed, seems to be happening gradually in some areas as diversification of the local economy into relatively profitable nonagricultural sidelines proceeds and peasants begin to receive higher state prices for their produce. As birth rates decline and facilities improve, the discrepancy between daycare needs and availability also should decline.[42] Yet since a significant portion of women's domestic labor is not performed in lieu of collective labor, but in addition to it the decision to invest in services is a decision to provide women with the same amount of leisure and rest which men enjoy.[43] Male-dominated local political structures are not likely to make that decision unprodded. As long as traditional norms and expectations that make it possible to impose this extra unremunerated burden on women persist, the collective economy in general and men in particular will benefit from these traditional family norms and the consequent exploitation of female labor. Truly reforming these family norms would mean that men would have to increase their own burden or decide that men and women together find collective solutions for their mutually shared benefit.

For their "liberation through labor," women have born a significantly unequal burden. Even in theory, this burden is inherent in the Engelsian approach during the transitional stages, since the theory posits that women must take up social production first, and then and only then will changes in attitudes and expectations concerning women's traditional roles in the family naturally follow. In practice, of course, the burden is perpetuated. Shulamith Firestone's observation that as a result of the Russian Revolution "women's roles have been enlarged rather than redefined" applies as well to China, and to most other socialist and capitalist nations where women work in significant numbers outside the home.[44]

It is clear from this review of women's role in the collective labor force since the mid-1950s that a singular emphasis on a materialist, Engelsian approach to women's liberation fails to deal adequately with women's subordination in the family, a subordination which has a number of noneconomic structural and psychosocial bases. Certainly the Chinese and other experiences show that women's large-scale participation in social labor does not lead to a commensurate redefinition of women's traditional obligations and roles in the family. On the contrary, those traditional obligations and subordinate roles condition women's entry into social production on fundamentally unequal terms with men and shape an inferior structural position for women in the labor force. Women's traditional family burdens necessarily create pressures to adjust outside work to family work, and their accepted primary social identity as wife and mother helps perpetuate traditional attitudes concerning women's inferiority as workers in social production and make women a flexible, cheap labor force. At the same time, women find themselves bearing a heavy double burden.

The resulting situation for women is double-edged as well. While women are denigrated in their public roles as workers, because they are seen primarily as wives and mothers, they are simultaneously at risk of coming under criticism and pressure for falling short in their traditional domestic roles because they are working. In 1943 Ting Ling raised the problem of the double bind women faced in trying to mediate the contradictions between the new demands placed on them and the traditional ones for which they continued to be held responsible. At the time, she criticized the Party for its failure to sympathize with and give attention to women's situation. Ting Ling was herself criticized for expressing these views in 1943 and was finally purged in 1957. Yet her criticism, voiced almost forty years ago, continues to ring true.

12 The Cultural Revolution

Although women's issues, and especially family reform issues have generally been thought of even by Maoist leaders in basically materialist, economistic terms, leadership groups have not always tied the promotion of gender equality entirely to women's labor roles. During the politically conflict-ridden period of the Cultural Revolution (1966–70), all issues, including some involving women's roles, were subjected to voluntarist Maoist assumptions asserting the leading role of politics and ideology as the motor of change. Deriving in part from a critical understanding of what had become of the Russian Revolution, Maoist leaders came to believe that the mere abolition of private property and collectivization of the major means of production after the seizure of political power by a Leninist Communist Party were not sufficient conditions for guaranteeing the development of a socialist society. Such conditions did not, in and of themselves, transform social relations. "Putting politics in command," revolutionizing people's thought and culture were understood by left Maoists to be the means through which the revolution would be kept alive and further progress made toward socialist goals and socialist economic development.

While the actual impact of the Cultural Revolution on rural women and the family was far less than the rhetoric and tenor of the times suggested, one can identify in the way "women's issues" were presented in the media three general themes which were indicative of the left Maoist leadership's thinking during this period.[1] First of all, a much greater stress was placed on "revolutionizing ideology" as the primary means for overcoming obstacles to women's equality. While in the early 1960s the primary obstacle was said to be "insufficient material conditions," as the Cultural Revolution approached, it was increasingly asserted that "bourgeois ideology" and to a lesser extent "remnant feudal ideas" among both men and women were creating the major obstacles to further progress toward gender equality and the redefinition of women's roles. Second, in line with the Cultural Revolution's call to "put politics in command," a greater emphasis than before was placed on promoting public political images and roles for women as well as expanded economic roles in the collective sector. Finally, and most importantly, issues of class were strongly reasserted as the primary categories for understanding social problems, including the problems of women.

On the surface, at least, the Cultural Revolution seemed initially to call forth the spirit and some of the ideas about promoting change that had characterized marriage reformers' approach to family reform in the early 1950s—the May Fourth spirit of youthful rebellion against traditional authority, faith in the liberating power of ideas and a conviction that building a new society required a thoroughgoing cultural revolution. Yet the Cultural Revolution of the 1960s maintained neither the "antifeudal" cultural terms nor the spirit of enlightenment which had fueled the original youth movement and inspired the marriage reformers' approach. While some of the early rhetoric of the Cultural Revolution suggested an attempt to mobilize youth to reform "feudal" culture and the "four olds," this was in fact a minor current among the left Maoist leaders who attempted to shape and propel events. In practice, this current seemed to be guided and played out mainly in the scapegoating of the children of former landlords, the repudiation of tradition in the arts and a period of spontaneous, largely uncontrolled vandalism against cultural relics. The main targets of attack were identified as "bourgeois" culture and the forces of "capitalist restoration." Indeed, many of the ideas that had inspired the original "antifeudal" cultural revolution of the teens became targets of attack as manifestations of "bourgeois ideology."

Thus, the Great Proletarian Cultural Revolution, waged in the name of socialism, purported to attack "bourgeois culture" and the restoration of capitalism in a largely peasant society that remained steeped in unreformed "feudal" ideas and social relations, a society which had in fact never experienced a real capitalist economic or social transformation. It is not surprising, then, that the Cultural Revolution created strange bedfellows, repeating in more exaggerated ways a pattern seen before. That pattern was a coming together of socialist and barely veiled traditional "feudal" mentality, of left Maoist and traditional nativist sentiment against manifestations of "bourgeois" notions of individualism and personal social freedom supposed to be the enemy of both. It was also not surprising that the Cultural Revolution, like other left Maoist periods in which "bourgeois democratic" rights have been particularly suspect, tended to submerge many of the original issues of marriage reform and women's rights as if these had already been transcended.

Indeed, the Cultural Revolution's reassertion of issues of class and class struggle as the primary categories for understanding all social problems led to a denial of gender as a significant social category. In the same vein, the emphasis on fighting bourgeois culture and capitalist restoration led to a reactivation of the hostility which Marxist revolutionaries, in China as elsewhere, have often expressed toward feminism as a manifestation of "bourgeois" thinking.

This latter trend was foreshadowed in an article entitled "How to Look at the Women Question" which appeared in the Party's theoretical journal *Red Flag* in October 1964.[2] The article was a thinly veiled attack on the Women's Federation journal *Women of China* and the way the journal attempted to deal with women's issues and the "special problems" women confronted in their new roles in society. The *Red Flag* article specifically attacked a 1963 series of featured articles and letters in *Women of China* titled "What Do Women Live For?" which explored the conflicts that arose from women's double burden.[3] The *Red Flag* article asserted that it was impossible to abstract "women's problems" and a "women's point of view" which transcended class, that indeed the problems under discussion were issues of "class viewpoint" and that to raise them as "women's issues" was to adopt a "bourgeois viewpoint." The article claimed (in materialist fashion) that socialist society had "ended the history of the previous periods of discrimination and oppression of women" by abolishing private property and removing the family as the economic unit of society. Thus, "the open or hidden position of women as slaves in the home and in society has changed." On the other hand, the article asserted (in nonmaterialist fashion) a basic proposition of the Cultural Revolution that "in socialist society, class, class contradictions, and class struggle have remained in existence."

With singular insensitivity to the structural and cultural factors which continued to define women's lives and to the double bind women faced in expanding their roles without having their old roles redefined, the article asserted that the issues surrounding women's double burden were entirely a matter of whether or not a woman had "true revolutionary proletarian consciousness." If she did, she would be able to handle all of her responsibilities without complaint. In short, women themselves were to be blamed. According to *Red Flag*:

> A woman comrade with true proletarian revolutionary consciousness will invariably display the revolutionary spirit in both her performance of duty and in the necessary household chores, and will always make correct arrangements in accordance with

revolutionary principles. Conversely, if she does not solve the question of proletarian revolutionary consciousness, then, she may either slight the necessary household labor and abandon the responsibility for educating children, in order to engage in . . . selfish pursuits; or she will waste a great deal of thought in the narrow-minded pursuit of so-called "family happiness" for the pleasure of self-satisfaction. The question in this respect is, therefore, one of whether there is the resolute will and determination in the individual to devote herself to the cause of proletarian revolution.

. . . It is unthinkable that there is a revolutionary woman cadre who does not know for what she is living, and who is confused all day long over whether she should place her husband, children, and home in the first position, or her revolutionary work in foremost position.[4]

Not only did the article, in the name of "putting politics in command," make women's double burden and their culturally imposed subordinate family roles personal problems to be resolved by women adopting a "proper attitude," but, quoting Lenin, it also warned against making such personal and presumably bourgeois issues as marriage and romance suitable for public discussion among women and young people. It warned that questions of "family happiness" were used by bourgeois forces to "divert women's attention, sabotage the socialist ideology of working women, harm their revolutionary determination, and push their downfall along the directions of capitalism and revisionism."

Two years later, amidst such charges, the editor of *Women of China*, Tung Pien, was openly attacked and the magazine finally ceased publication.[5] Soon thereafter the Women's Federation was disbanded. The reasons commonly given for the destruction of the Women's Federation and its local branches illustrate the antifeminist potential of the ideology of the Cultural Revolution left, with their singular emphasis on class struggle and the development of "proletarian consciousness" as the primary means to apprehend and transform the world. Not only was it claimed that the federation had been infiltrated by bourgeois ideas, leading it to dwell on "narrow" family and welfare issues and to ignore the "class education" of women, but this ultra-left line also claimed that under the dictatorship of the proletariat, women had no special interests, only common class interests with men. Therefore women did not need a separate organization, which in any case only served to divide the proletariat.[6]

At the same time, in line with the ultra-left's views, the Cultural Revolution vigorously promoted public images of women that were almost entirely purged of family roles as well as of "bourgeois" notions of female sexuality.[7] The media showed women wholly defined by public roles as proletarian fighters on the fronts of socialist production and politics. The Cultural Revolution also witnessed the most vigorous affirmative action efforts since 1949 to recruit larger numbers of women into political organizations, even as it created stronger pressures against the newly recruited women representing "women's point of view."[8]

Initially such images and political trends undoubtedly held an exciting appeal to many young, unmarried women who joined the Red Guard movement and thereby asserted greater independence from their families. Married women, however, already burdened with children and family responsibilities (which of course continued despite the media image that denied their existence), must have experienced yet additional demands on their time and energy. In effect, they were asked to expand their public roles even further without any fundamental alleviation of their existing responsibilities, as all people were under pressure to prove their "redness" in public by participating in an explosion of political meetings and political study groups. Furthermore, the Cultural Revolution's emphasis on the adoption of "proletarian consciousness" as the key to the solution to all problems, carried with it strong implications of "blaming the victim" for the problems women faced, as clearly illustrated in the *Red Flag* article. Rather than focusing on real cultural and structural reforms that could help equalize women's position with men in the private realm and make the terms of their public participation more equal, the Cultural Revolution insisted that the tensions women faced could be solved or overcome once women adopted a self-sacrificing proletarian attitude and devotion to their public duties. Thus, the Cultural Revolution, like earlier periods, tried to "leapfrog" the reform of persisting traditional family structures and norms, placing the main responsibility on women to deal with their "private problems" and get on with the expansion of their public responsibilities without complaint.

Furthermore, the extraordinary puritanism behind the view that raising topics about problems of "marriage and romance" was a reflection of "bourgeois decadence" dovetailed with traditional conservative views about the immorality of romantic love between young people. Such views were traditionally used to prevent free-choice marriages, uphold patriarchal control and keep women in their place in patrilineally defined families. In the mid-1950s, the view that "bourgeois mentality" was a more serious and pervasive problem than "feudal mentality" in matters of marriage and the family was used to argue for a more restrictive interpretation of marriage law freedoms. The Cultural Revolution similarly illustrated how the ultra-left's anti-bourgeois ideology, with its suspicion of individual social freedoms, joined with and derived support from traditionalist social forces attempting to maintain social control over youth and women.

Young people who participated in the Red Guard movement report that they initially experienced an unprecedented degree of freedom from parental control and adult authority in their social relations as well as in their political activities.[9] Once the Red Guard movement was brought under some control, however, many of these youth found that the social and political atmosphere became more stringent than ever, no doubt partly reflecting a backlash against the chaos Red Guards created in the early, heady months of the Cultural Revolution as well as the imposition of the strict left Maoists' version of proletarian morality. People felt compelled to guard against the slightest sign of "bourgeois decadence" in their personal behavior, which included "talking of love." When the Red Guard movement culminated in urban young people being sent to the countryside, they often found themselves under even greater restrictions as the traditionally conservative village morality of their peasant hosts was coupled with the stringent ultra-leftist outlook. Some of these "sent-down youth" reported that during their entire stay in the countryside they were afraid to talk in public with members of the opposite sex unless their work required it.[10] Others got into trouble with villagers for not being sufficiently circumspect. In one village, the local militia arrested a group of "sent-down youth" during their first weeks in the countryside when they found the young men and women talking together in one of their rooms late at night.[11]

Officially propagated socialist morality for youth has always shown the influence of traditional puritanical attitudes concerning relations between young men and women.[12] Indeed, an increasingly vigorous campaign since the early 1960s to promote late marriages while maintaining strict norms of premarital chastity as part of the effort to control population growth has to a large extent relied upon traditional norms prohibiting intimacy between unmarried women and men. As we have seen repeatedly, accusations of profligate "bourgeois" behavior among youth have often seemed to mask a traditional "feudal" reaction against the development of the freer social interactions between young people which are necessary if true free-choice marriages are to become the norm.[13] But during earlier periods, official writings were also periodically critical of "feudal" attitudes and restrictions which prevented "normal," "healthy" interactions among young people, attitudes which prevented the development of free-choice marriage and often prevented young women from participating freely in public activities.[14] Yet even though the renewed call to young people to fight old customs and attitudes during the Socialist Education movement had been a prelude to the Cultural Revolution,[15] and even though the Cultural Revolution had led off with an appeal to "fight the four olds," the Cultural Revolution eventually took the puritanism of socialist morality to new heights. Traditional "feudal" attitudes easily masked themselves in the extreme, ascetic antibourgeois idiom of the period, leading in some ways to a contraction of the sphere of personal social freedom for youth. Similarly, women who complained about burdens in their families, or discrimination in collective labor, were easily charged with having selfish, individualistic "bourgeois attitudes," and "putting material rewards in command."[16]

Interestingly, after the death of Mao and the fall of the "Gang of Four" (accused of being the main ring-leaders of the ultra-left) in 1976, Chinese critics of the Cultural Revolution suggested that Mao and the ultra-left had partially fueled the Cultural Revolution, especially the Cult of Mao, by calling forth and playing upon the "feudal mentality" remaining in Chinese society. The strange merging of the left with traditionalist forces seems to weave its way through a number of trends of the era. (Not surprisingly this view of the Cultural Revolution was suggested to me by a group of prominent intellectuals who saw themselves in the intellectual tradition of May Fourth. They also were ardent admirers of the anti-Confucian writer and critic of the traditional family, Pa Chin, who was much maligned by the left in the Cultural Revolution.) Any examination of women's rights and family reform in the Chinese Revolution must take account of the way Maoism and other political forces of the revolutionary coalition merge with as well as diverge from, build on as well as fight against, the traditionalist aspirations of a deeply wounded peasant society in crisis.

The actual impact of the Cultural Revolution on women and the family in the countryside was varied and uneven. It was primarily an urban movement, in part by default, for the initial appeal which Mao had made to his old class base of "poor and lower-middle peasants" during the Socialist Education movement had failed. It was not until at least some of its initial excesses had been checked and the influence of more moderate political forces, such as Chou En-lai, began to re-emerge in 1968–69 that the Cultural Revolution had much impact on many areas of the countryside.

At this point there was some new impetus for increasing rural women's participation in collective labor which had been gradually growing since the cutbacks of the early 1960s. An increase in capital construction and a re-emphasis on expanding collective sidelines and developing small-scale industry to serve agriculture led to a greater need for labor in some areas. While in order to mobilize more labor, the greatest stress was placed on using political education to exhort women to become more strongly committed to "serving the revolution," by 1969 some articles on rural women also criticized cadres for looking down on women and discussed the need to lighten household chores for women.[17] There was also greater stress on the political recruitment of women into local political organizations than in previous years. After the initial stage of the Cultural Revolution when Revolutionary Committees were being established at all levels and Party committees were being reconstituted, local authorities were directed from the top to increase the number of women on these bodies. Membership lists of new committees submitted to higher levels for approval were supposed to be rejected if they did not include a "reasonable proportion" of women.[18] Although apparently no specific national quotas were set and local targets appear to have been very modest, there does seem to have been a definite overall increase in the number of females at various levels throughout the country, including an overall increase in the percentage of female Party members.[19]

During the earlier part of the Cultural Revolution, articles stressing the importance of recruiting more women into political organizations tended to emphasize that it was women's duty to participate and that women needed to be educated to abandon their "selfish" attitude of caring more about the happiness of their "small family" than about the affairs of state. Thus, a woman cadre in Liu Ling told Jan Myrdal in 1970 that before the Cultural Revolution she had not been an active member of the brigade management committee to which she belonged because she was "selfishly" preoccupied with her household responsibilities.

> I was selfish. I had my household and my children to look after. I thought of my own private interests and was not an active member of the board. . . . But after studying Chairman Mao I realized what a mistake I'd been making, to sit silent at the meetings . . . thinking of my own household instead of the affairs of state. Before the Cultural Revolution women were too tied to their own homes. . . . Now we women are studying Chairman Mao. We read newspapers and discuss things. . . . Before the Cultural Revolution, I never spoke in meetings. . . . Sometimes I didn't even attend them. But now I take part in all discussions.[20]

In Liu Ling some measures to relieve some of the household burdens of women reportedly facilitated this greater participation. Men were criticized for refusing to watch the children so that women could sometimes attend meetings. The women also set up a small sewing group from funds they earned on a collective plot and they obtained brigade funds to purchase a mill to process grain.

But in most places, the demand that women play a more active role in political organizations and general meetings in addition to collective labor and household responsibilities meant that women were again expected to expand their working day. One young woman who was a cadre in charge of women's work in a commune in Chung-shan County, Kwangtung, claimed that many women resented the increased pressure to attend the growing number of meetings during the Cultural Revolution years because they were already overworked. Most of them had to bring their mending or other work with them to the meetings in order to avoid having to stay up too late to finish their work.[21] Under the circumstances, the woman cadre felt that the women's attendance was merely pro forma, to meet the outward requirements of the local male leadership. While the women in fact had grievances and complaints about political matters (primarily their unequal pay), they never spoke their minds at the public meetings, fearing that they would be laughed at or criticized for "putting material rewards in command" and feeling that in any event the male cadres would not listen or change anything.

Whatever the weaknesses of the Cultural Revolution's approach for strengthening the representation of women's concerns and grievances, its emphasis on women's political roles did signal a recognition that the economic materialist assumptions of the productive labor theory were incorrect. Just as the increase in women's participation in collective remunerative labor outside the home did not bring about an automatic redefinition of their family roles and status, women's public political participation and status did not automatically increase along with increases in their labor participation. It appears that after the early 1950s, when there was an effort to ensure some female representation as various governing bodies were first being established, female political participation at most levels did not increase significantly up to the late 1960s, even though there was an increase in women's collective economic participation. In 1956, it was reported that women comprised about 10 percent of the Party membership and it appears that this proportion did not change until the early years of the Cultural Revolution, over ten years later.[22] Significantly, twenty years earlier at the beginning of the Yenan period it was estimated that women were about 15 percent of the Party's membership in the base areas.[23] The same lack of momentum appears to have characterized other forms of participation and leadership as well. In the early stages of coop formation, many coops (under central urging) adopted the practice of selecting a woman to be a deputy chair in charge of women's mobilization and electing women leaders of women's work groups.[24] But beyond this initial representation of those charged with "women's work," only a very small percentage of women gained other posts in rural political organizations, and there seems to have been little increase through the next decade.

The issue of promoting women's political participation and political influence may be particularly important for the pursuit of greater gender equality in China given the organization of rural China. Cross-cultural comparisons indicate that there is in fact no simple relationship between women's power in society or family and their rate of participation in the economy.[25] However, a number of studies suggest that a high level of economic participation does seem to contribute to greater freedom, status and influence for women when the particular conditions of that participation give women control over important economic resources, such as the production and marketing of an important crop.[26] This can occur even when women are barred from exercising formal political power in societies where economic power is partially separate from political power.[27]

In China, however, this is not possible. Even where women are important producers or where women are almost entirely responsible for an important crop (such as cotton), the means of production, the sale and distribution of the product and the level of remuneration paid to producers are controlled by organs of political power. In other words, the organization of production and political power effectively severs economic participation from any control over production. Decisions about quotas, work assignments, levels of remuneration, investments and distribution of income are all made by team, brigade and commune Party and management committees in conjunction with central guidelines. Thus to have greater economic power, to translate higher levels of participation in production into greater public influence, women must gain access to political power and have influence in the groups that make the crucial decisions about who gets what, when and how.

The Cultural Revolution seemed to make some progress in terms of numbers of women representatives. Yet even the percentages still remained low and it is likely that much of this increase was token. There is some indication that even the modest increase may have since declined.[28] The Cultural Revolution's call to turn out higher numbers of women does not seem to have tapped any strong groups capable of pushing forward and sustaining women's representatives in the face of local male power structure.

The analysis I have presented would suggest that the Cultural Revolution indeed failed to attack the basic obstacles to the development of stronger female participation; in a sense it merely tried to override them with the necessarily temporary mobilizational force of the movement. At the beginning of this chapter, Lu Yu-lan, a Hopeh woman peasant who rose to prominence in the Cultural Revolution, was quoted expressing the dominant view that women would gain equality in the home once they took up their place in society, including politics. Yet, just as unreformed family structures have placed women in a structurally inferior position in the labor force, the unreformed nature of the family also creates obstacles to women's equal political participation which exhortations to participation cannot easily overcome.

Most obviously, one major factor is the double burden which women experience due to the maintenance of much of their traditional family burden while they expand their roles in production. The call to women to adopt a proletarian consciousness, abandon their narrow preoccupation with their "small family" and become involved in public politics alongside men imposed a third burden, particularly on married women. Even in places that made some adjustments to ease women's domestic burden, after their family expectations and collective work obligations were met, most women had very little time and energy for meaningful political participation and formal political responsibility. The propaganda of the later stages of the Cultural Revolution did not entirely ignore the need to alter these family expectations. But it did not make them a major target for reform and indeed still expected that a responsible woman would find less time-consuming ways to meet these responsibilities. The major emphasis remained on using "political education" to strengthen women's identification with, and sense of responsibility to, collective affairs above family affairs. The Cultural Revolution terms for increasing women's political participation demanded that they be "superwomen."

The continuation of traditional moral and proprietary attitudes presented other obstacles to women's political participation. Many people continued to feel that it was immoral for women to engage in activities that brought them into contact with men outside the family. A few articles during the Socialist Education movement complained that such "feudal" attitudes continued to lead parents to prevent daughters from attending village youth meetings in the evenings.[29] The pressures on young married women against having contact with men were apparently even stronger in some places, and rumors of "loose moral behavior" could be spread against women cadres simply because of their dealing with male cadres through their work.[30] While the Cultural Revolution propaganda occasionally criticized people for looking down on the abilities of women, it barely touched on the highly restrictive moral attitudes related to women's sexuality, due to the general socialist puritanism pervading the movement even in the cities.

In addition to the practical problems created by women's traditional family roles and double burden, and the ideological problems created by traditional attitudes that disdained women's participation in public affairs and restricted women's public activities for the sake of propriety, there were even more serious obstacles stemming from women's position as an outsider within the unreformed patrilineal kinship system. Evidence suggests that patrilocal and village exogamous marriage patterns remain common in most parts of rural China.[31] Thus most women continue to enter new communities as strangers when they marry, and groups of men continue to form the rooted ongoing bonds upon which the solidarity of rural communities is built.

Since the 1950s, the general outlines of the government's agrarian development strategy has reinforced and ensured the continuation of this situation by virtually freezing the male population of villages. It is extremely difficult for households or individuals to move from their natal villages except through marriage, which means, given patrilocal customs, becoming a bride. Given the strict control of labor, enforced through household registration and the rationing of food staples, sons are perhaps more likely than ever to live out their lives in the natal village of their fathers. In rooted, parochial rural communities where outsiders are distrusted, where lineal descent into the community is a criterion of belonging and "membership," village exogamous patrilocality "naturally" and structurally disadvantages females in seeking positions of political leadership in the village community.

In 1962 and again in 1969, the villagers of Liu Ling in their interviews with Jan Myrdal tended to refer to married women as the "wife of so-and-so" or the "mother of so-and-so," inevitably a male. Daughters on the other hand were more likely to have names.[32] Such naming practices for women, common in the past,[33] are more than crude, unconscious, sexist holdovers from engrained habits. Married women continue to gain a relationship to a community only through relationship to a male who is rooted there. Daughters are temporary members, but they are natives who have a patrilineal family membership and a given name or nickname known to their friends, relatives and neighbors. Natives are more likely to gain political posts, unless the posts are appointed by the state apparatus. Significantly, from the days of Yenan through the Cultural Revolution it appears that unmarried women have been more likely to be active in politics and gain political posts than married women.[34] This is no doubt in part because unmarried women are less burdened with family duties (daughters-in-law come under heavier pressures from in-laws even before bearing children than natural parents place on their own adult daughters). But it also appears to be related to the native status of these women.

Norma Diamond observed in her interviews in 1973 that women with village political leadership positions tended to have been born or raised in the village.[35] Often they had been "foster daughters-in-law" and had therefore come to the village as young children. Similarly, information I gathered with three colleagues in a large, multilineage, model village in Hopeh in 1978 showed that a disproportionate percentage of married women with village and work-team leadership positions were drawn from the minority of married women who were village natives. The only woman on the powerful brigade (village) Party committee was a veteran cadre who was a native of the village, the elder sister of a vice-chair of the brigade and a member of one of the most prominent political families in the village since the Anti-Japanese War.

Certainly young women today have more opportunity than in the past to develop social networks within their natal villages through school, the Youth League, the militia and work groups. This may provide an improved basis for women to gain public status in their villages, yet they lose this political and social capital when they move out at marriage. Once married in a new village, not only must they start again, but they have fewer opportunities to build villagewide networks except through their work groups. In fact, Parish and Whyte's interviews suggest that because of the heavy double burden of married women and the way work is organized in the villages, the women's community that often developed around married women in their husbands' villages in the past has become weaker, as have ties with maternal kin.[36] Women (unlike men) have little time to spend together socially. Furthermore, work groups, which could, and in some areas probably do, provide a good forum for the development of such networks, may shift around too often to form the basis for solidarity networks on their own.

Thus the same structural features of traditional kinship patterns which block female equality within the family also block women's equal participation in public community life. The Cultural Revolution's ideological approach to change did little to address this problem. Indeed there is little evidence that the problems which village exogamous patrilocal marriage practices posed for the goals of women's participation in politics were even considered until the early 1970s, just as the implications of these patterns for marriage reform had been unrecognized earlier.

That patrilocal marriage patterns did place women at a political disadvantage and did indirectly create obstacles to the leadership's efforts to recruit more women cadres was implied in a report from a commune in Kwangtung published in *People's Daily* in September 1971.[37] The report concerned the need for the Party to make greater efforts to recruit female cadres and it criticized the various "reasons" given by "some cadres" as to why village women could not or should not be cultivated as leaders. Among those reasons criticized was that "no matter how well we train women, they will be taken away [at marriage]." The report did not, however, question the requirement that women marry into another family and village, while men were never expected to do so. Instead the report suggested, in the vein of the

Maoist ideology of the Cultural Revolution, that adopting a larger view of the collective interests of the revolution would solve this problem: "As long as we can train outstanding female party members, they will help make the Party strong even when they are married away to another village. How can we say 'it doesn't pay'?"

Another set of obstacles to women's increased participation in politics no doubt has involved the attitudes of women themselves. Implicit in the Cultural Revolution's emphasis on ideological education among women was the assumption that women were in large part held back from involvement in public roles because of their own acceptance of traditional values and definitions of themselves in traditional family roles. Indeed, it was asserted in the earlier years of the Cultural Revolution that this was the primary hurdle that needed to be overcome, although by the early seventies it was more fully understood that women faced a host of other obstacles as well. During the Socialist Education movement, numerous articles suggested that older women were among the staunchest defenders of old customs and beliefs, those most likely to insist on proper weddings, the maintenance of rituals, and pious filial behavior from children.[38]

One need not unsympathetically "blame the victim" to give credence to the evidence that women themselves have been in many ways primary carriers of traditional values about women and their identities and that these values continue to be a factor which hinder women in striving for public roles and direct political power. Most sympathetic observers of Chinese women have in fact concluded that a major obstacle on the road to furthering gender equality in China remains the task of overcoming women's long engrained "sense of inferiority" in their new roles and their acceptance of subordination in light of a thousand years of cultural conditioning.[39]

It is probably true that self-deprecating attitudes of women and the conservative traditional outlook these reinforce, particularly on issues of public authority, continue to be pervasive and need to be overcome. Yet we need again to consider the complex nature of "female conservatism" in light of the dynamics of female behavior created by the persistent features of the Chinese family and community. To some extent, women's conservatism in holding on to their traditional family roles, and the continuing tendency for women to identify these roles as more central than the new public roles which they have been encouraged to put first, must be understood in the context of the same dynamics of family structure and female behavior that created a conservative reaction among many older women to the marriage reform campaigns. While women traditionally understood and had little choice but to accept that the public world and public authority belonged to men, they were able to build family and even community influence informally through the emotional ties they created within their own uterine family. Women were also able to use certain patriarchal norms and customs to secure and protect these crucial bonds. As in other patrilocal, patrilineal family systems the strength of the mother-centered uterine family was women's central means for overcoming the disadvantages and lack of authority which they faced as outsiders in their husbands' male-dominated families and communities.

To a large extent, the structural family features that create this strategy among women continue to exist in rural Chinese communities. Women's attachment to their traditional family roles as mother and primary nurturer of a uterine family group reflects their continuing needs and their understanding of the influence they gain from this role. Feminists and Marxist revolutionaries may believe that the primary source of women's subordination lies in the fact that women, rather than being centrally involved in public productive roles, are absorbed in narrow and dependent traditional roles that tie them to the private realm of the family; Chinese peasant women, however, may remain understandably attached to these roles precisely because they have been their primary source of influence and control in a society that provides them with few channels for attaining influence. While it is perhaps true that other sources of influence and status are becoming available to women, there remains little doubt that the public world continues to be organized and controlled primarily by men. For women to have followed the Cultural Revolution's urgings to abandon the centrality of private family roles as mothers in favor of a primary identity as a devoted collective member and producer in a public world still dominated by men and male interests would have meant abandoning a major source of traditional influence in return for a role as an acknowledged inferior on male turf. Given the choices, women themselves have good reasons to prefer retaining a strong claim to their traditional roles even at the expense of bearing an extremely heavy double burden.

Clearly the conditions that will allow a redefinition of women's and men's roles to give women greater equality in public life require far more than developing "material conditions" or solving practical problems with sewing groups and nurseries; they also require far more than "raising women's consciousness." Changes which fundamentally alter the basic family structure and women's relationship to family and community seem essential to end women's need to rely on their centrality in a uterine family and on their bonds with adult sons to obtain influence and security in their husband's families and communities. If women as a group did not have to leave their own communities at marriage in order to join other communities based on ongoing rooted male lineages, they would be far more likely and more able to develop and invest in public roles and identities which, in rural China today, remain built on long-standing social ties to neighbors, friends and kin. If, to the Cultural Revolution left, women's commitment to the collective seemed too weak and their investment in their "small families" too great and suffocating to women's potential, it was in large part due to the fact that most women continued to be outsiders in the ancient, rooted, and (by government policy) frozen communities on which the collectives are built.

Finally, long-standing Party policies toward village women's groups must be considered in understanding the apparent lack of sufficiently strong social forces in the villages for promoting women's representatives into public office. Since the late 1920s, periodic warnings to women cadres and groups that they must "avoid separating the women's movement from the movement as a whole" and "maintain the unity of the workers and peasants" have signalled the Party's consistent desire to avoid the divisiveness that strong, autonomous women's groups might create and to check any potential for local women acting on issues not defined and timed for them by the Party. Toward this end, Party policy has consistently subordinated these groups to those male power structures which represent the Party's local base. Although the late Cultural Revolution and post-Cultural Revolution period brought efforts to increase the political recruitment of women, women were to join the mostly male groups as individuals. While their purpose was usually to do political work among women, they were recruited as "representatives of the poor and lower-middle peasants," not as representatives of women. Only rarely was it even suggested that a reason to recruit more women into Party and management committees was to provide a distinctively woman's voice on issues.[40]

Given the long-neglected structural obstacles embedded in rural family and community patterns, and given Party policies that have discouraged and undercut whatever potential has existed for the development of strong, autonomous local women's groups, it is hardly surprising that a leadership call for local male leaders to recruit more women as individuals to "represent the interests of poor and lower-middle peasants" failed to have a more significant impact.

13 The Anti-Confucian Campaign

In a variety of ways we have seen how traditional attitudes and practices arising from unreformed aspects of the family have continued to hinder the promotion of changes for women in political and economic roles outside the family. Neither the efforts that accompanied the collectivization drives of the 1950s nor the voluntarist approach of the Cultural Revolution truly addressed these issues. Both of these approaches attempted to leapfrog or by-pass the need to reform the family by emphasizing the expansion of women's public roles, even though the nature of the family profoundly affects the ways women can assume these roles. In this respect both approaches shared a basic premise of the Engelsian approach that has been generally dominant since the days of Yenan: that women's subordination within the family will change as a natural result of expanding women's roles outside of the family.

In the mid-1970s, some of the issues surrounding persisting patriarchal attitudes and family and marriage practices were finally addressed in the context of the Anti-Lin Piao, Anti-Confucian campaign. In the early 1970s, there already had appeared the beginnings of a broader and more sympathetic concern for the obstacles which women faced in trying to become the fully equal revolutionary fighters propagated as the ideal by the Cultural Revolution media.[1] This greater concern coincided with the recruitment of more women into the reconstituted party and political organs in the wake of the Cultural Revolution. More importantly, it also coincided with efforts by moderate political forces to rehabilitate some of the cadres criticized in the Cultural Revolution and with moves to rehabilitate the structures and some of the personnel of the Women's Federation.

In 1972 the widow of Sun Yat-sen, Soong Ching-ling, a venerated United Front figure, early women's rights activist and head of the

Hankow Women's Training Center under the KMT-CCP Women's Department in the 1920s, wrote an article arguing that, despite the progress women had made, a "Women's Liberation Movement" was still necessary in China because of the discrimination fostered by a persisting "feudal-patriarchal ideology."[2] Soong implicitly rejected the view that had been dominant in the class struggle analysis of the Cultural Revolution—that women had only class interests and not interests defined by their gender. She mentioned a number of unresolved issues which plagued rural areas, none of which had been major concerns in the Cultural Revolution: the failure to implement equal pay for equal work, the continuation of bride prices and impediments to freedom in marriage, and the tendency for parents to prefer sons and to provide them with a better education because they felt that "girls will eventually enter another family." This list of problems confronting women drew attention back to "feudal-patriarchal" forces as the primary problem for women's work, rather than the struggle against the "restoration of capitalism."

During 1972 and early 1973, the Women's Federation was re-established up to the provincial level throughout most of the country. The Women's Federation had never acted as a powerful interest group for women; it had always been under strictures not to "separate its work from socialist development as a whole" and it lacked effective autonomy from Party control. But it was the only national forum for women and when Party politics allowed, it had provided a public forum for certain problems confronting women.[3] Thus the re-establishment of the Women's Federation within the provinces seemed to signal that attention to "women's work" was to be revived as a part of the Party's agenda at local levels.

The final, national-level reconstitution of the Women's Federation which was supposed to culminate the process was unexpectedly postponed until 1978, reportedly due to political struggles and animosities involving veteran Women's Federation leaders such as Teng Ying-ch'ao and Chiang Ch'ing and her followers.[4] Nonetheless a number of issues concerning discrimination against women in the family and society gained national attention as part of the Anti-Lin Piao, Anti-Confucian campaign.

The original authors, targets and purposes of the campaign remain obscure. Certainly they were more concerned with upper-level power struggles emerging from the Cultural Revolution than with purging Chinese culture of its stubborn Confucian heritage, the incomplete task of the New Culture-May Fourth movement fifty years earlier. Growing out of the criticism of the late defense minister Lin Piao and his military followers who plotted to assassinate Mao Tse-tung and seize power in 1971, the Anti-Lin Piao, Anti-Confucian campaign appears to have been used in its early stages as a vehicle of the top leaders of the Cultural Revolution left (later known as the "Gang of Four") to attack Party moderates. Premier Chou En-lai appeared to be, in veiled historical analogy, Confucius.[5] This struggle may indeed have been more than tangentially related to the failure to reconstitute the national Women's Federation; the struggle between Chou and the Gang of Four was probably reflected in the inability of the likes of Teng Ying-ch'ao, Chou's wife and long-time federation vice-chair, to come to terms with Chiang Ch'ing loyalists over issues of leadership in the new federation. Yet eventually the campaign did take on the character of a real anti-Confucian culture campaign, perhaps partly because Chou was able to deflect the attack on him into channels of genuine cultural questioning. It is also possible that the left, and especially Chiang Ch'ing, attempted to turn the campaign into an appeal to youth and women in order to gain support for their position in the power struggle going on in the capital. If the latter is the case, it is ironic that in many ways the campaign began to build upon the criticisms voiced by such "bourgeois democratic" women leaders as Soong Ching-ling as well as issues long associated with Teng Ying-ch'ao. Chiang Ch'ing, in fact, had been cultivating her own national "model village" (Hsiaochinchuang, near Tientsin) which came to exemplify some of the Anti-Confucian campaign's women's issues in "revolutionizing the superstructure."[6]

Whatever the origins and byzantine political background of the campaign, it became the occasion for the most nationally visible attack on feudal-patriarchal ideology since 1953. The campaign certainly suffered from its ambiguous and shifting nature and from the consequent failure of the leadership to mobilize concerted organizational energies at various levels in pursuit of specific goals related to women's family and social status. But as a propaganda campaign, it focused attention on important long-neglected problems related to the reform of attitudes and practices embedded in the culture. As such, it provided a forum and at least some support for the newly organized Women's Federation groups and the increased number of local women cadres to undertake efforts to further women's issues or address local women's grievances, something which the ideology of the Cultural Revolution had discouraged.

The main message of the campaign for women was that the traditional ethical code derived from the teachings of Confucius and Mencius and based on ideas of "respecting men and despising women" still existed and needed to be abolished for the success of the revolution. Throughout the country in 1974, groups of women were organized to study and criticize the Confucian ethical code for women and the classic "Book on Virtuous Womanhood" (*Nuer-ching*), which advocated the "three obediences" and "four virtues" for guiding women's behavior. For example, speakers at a meeting of 1,300 women workers and peasants of the Lanchow region of Kansu Province reportedly denounced the "Book on Virtuous Womanhood" for

> advertising reactionary absurdities such as "loyalty," "filial piety," "chastity" and "righteousness" and demanding that women behave as "dutiful wives" devoting their time and energy to their husbands. . . . The "Book on Virtuous Womanhood" is a strong rope binding the working women.[7]

Thus, the private attitudes that governed relationships between men and women in the family were broached for public discussion and women were encouraged to question the "spiritual shackles" of supposedly virtuous and proper deference to male authority.

Under the general rubric of criticizing Confucius's "feudal-patriarchal ideology" of "respecting men and despising women," local Party, women's and youth groups were reported to be holding meetings and carrying out education to change old customs and reform the practices which continued to reflect such attitudes. A number of specific issues were tied to the campaign. Discrimination against women in pay and the failure of men to take responsibility for household chores were put forward as examples of the old Confucian ideas that men were superior to women and that women should be "household slaves" of men.[8] Free-choice marriages were also promoted and bride prices and traditional ceremonial customs criticized. For example, in Heilungchiang, the efforts of thirty-eight young women in Mingcheng Commune, Chiangkiang County, who organized to promote free marriage, late marriage, the abolition of bride prices and expensive "ostentatious" traditional marriage ceremonies were publicized and praised for their rebellious spirit in "going against the tide."[9]

None of this even approached the dimensions of a new marriage reform campaign. Indeed, the issue of young women actually rejecting the marriage choice of their parents (as opposed to rejecting the parents' early timing and extravagant wedding plans) was treated quite gingerly in the media. Total defiance of parental influence, especially over whom one would marry, was not encouraged. More strikingly, women's divorce rights (which, as will be discussed later, are routinely violated in the countryside) were not even mentioned. Nonetheless, the campaign did provide greater attention to continuing problems of marriage and the family for young women than any previous effort since the early 1950s.

Perhaps the most significant issue raised in the context of the Anti-Confucian campaign, though not the most emphasized, was the promotion of matrilocal marriage. It seems clear that patrilocality came to be perceived as a problem at this time primarily because of family planning efforts, and not the problems of gender equality per se. Although some of the problematic implications of patrilocality had been glimpsed in earlier efforts to train women cadres and provide equal education to daughters in the countryside, these problems had mainly been seen as creating "ideological problems" to be overcome by educating against narrow localism in favor of a larger collective viewpoint. Now for the first time, the customs of patrilocality themselves were criticized and placed in the context of unacceptable "feudal-patriarchal" ideas of male supremacy.

Almost all rural families desired sons, and the preference for sons over daughters was one of the most frequently cited obstacles encountered by family planning cadres in trying to convince peasants to limit their families to two children, which had become the goal of national policy by the mid-1970s. This preference for sons had been previously understood to be caused by females' lesser productivity and therefore was expected to disappear as women became an important part of the labor force. Mao Tse-tung, in the vein of the Cultural Revolution approach to such issues, had commented in an interview with American journalist Edgar Snow in 1965 that the preference persisted mainly because of the backward, outmoded influences of "feudal ideology," especially in the minds of women, who insisted on bearing children until they had a son, regardless of how many daughters they had.[10] It was not until the mid-1970s, in the context of increased pressures to reduce rural birthrates, that it was finally realized that a major part of the problem was embedded in the patrilineal family and kinship structure itself, a structure which had previously seemed neutral in its impact on gender equality.

The fact was that regardless of whether or not females became as productive economically as males, the unquestioned patrilocal, and especially village exogamous patrilocal, traditional marriage practices made women only temporary members of their parents' family. Embedded in the meaning of "marriage" for women was the transfer of the value of women's labor to another family and women's adoption of primary obligations to their husbands' families. Bride prices, which were rarely made the subject of concerted official criticism after the early 1950s, both symbolized and reinforced these patterns and the transfer of women's labor and obligations from one patrilineal group to another.[11] These patrilineal assumptions were accepted not only by the "feudal minded" peasant women referred to by Mao, but also by the national media and commune leadership. In the 1960s, articles stressing the legal and moral obligations of adult children to care for aged parents explicitly stated that this meant "sons and daughters-in-law."[12] Furthermore, in determining whether or not a family should qualify for collective welfare relief, rural leadership generally took into account the ability of adult sons to provide support, but not married daughters.[13]

The promotion of matrilocal marriage and the questioning of patrilocality potentially strikes at the heart of a long-neglected source of gender inequality embedded in marriage practices and family structures. What is at stake is no less than the alteration of a process of family and community formation that to a large extent still is built around the exchange of women. Although the issue was raised in a much more narrow context than this during the Anti-Confucian campaign, the emergence of patrilocal marriage patterns as an issue represented a significant and long overdue contribution to the categories of reform thinking.

For the most part matrilocal marriage was presented as a means to ensure security in old age for parents who had no sons. It was hoped that this would also encourage reduced fertility among younger couples by convincing people that, in the absence of sons, daughters could fulfill these needs. Publicity was given to specific cases of successful matrilocal marriages where parents had feared being left alone in their old age after their daughters married.[14] Hsiaochinchuang, Chiang Ch'ing's model village in Hopeh, had reportedly carried out special ceremonies for matrilocal marriages and was frequently cited as an example to follow. It was clear from the publicity that popular disdain for matrilocal marriage needed to be confronted in most cases. Since matrilocal marriages had not been encouraged as a legitimate alternative since 1949 and since their incidence had probably declined in most areas, many people continued to view them as inferior arrangements violating a man's duty to his ancestors. According to one report some villagers "still influenced by feudal ideas" criticized a young man who was about to enter a matrilocal marriage:

> Some people said, "A fine young man like him has no difficulty finding a wife. Why then does he have to join the family of his wife? What a shame!" When [the young man's] father heard about these erroneous views, he also thought that as it had been a practice for women to marry into their husband's family since ancient times, his son would be looked down upon and meet "bad luck" if he did as planned.[15]

Such views were criticized as a manifestation of traditional, Confucian concepts, and it was pointed out that "if women could go settle in their husband's family, then men could also go settle in their wife's family."[16] Thus while matrilocal marriages tended to be promoted fairly narrowly as a solution to the problem of having no sons, rather than as an encouraged form of marriage under any circumstances, they were broadly linked to general attitudes which held women to be inferior to men and indirectly provided a critique of patrilocality.

One of the most successful areas in promoting matrilocal marriage practices was reportedly Ting Hsien, a relatively large county south of Peking in Hopeh Province. Here the need to promote matrilocal marriage had reportedly been realized as early as 1971 in response to problems encountered in family planning efforts. In 1975 it was reported that there had been over 6,800 matrilocal marriages in the county. As a result, it was claimed that family planning had become much more effective and that the number of "Five Guarantee Families" (families on collective welfare) had dropped. It was also claimed that the recruitment of female cadres had improved by drawing on the women who remained in their native villages, and that forty percent of these women were "politically active" in their units.[17] *People's Daily* lauded these developments as important concrete accomplishments in fighting the influence of "feudal" ideas of "respecting men and despising women."

Although the Anti-Confucian campaign was important in calling attention to the serious obstacles which traditional ideas and practices continued to create for women in the pursuit of equality, the campaign did not bring about effective and lasting changes throughout the countryside. The murky, behind-the-scenes political purposes of the campaign as well as the diffuse, shifting and often abstract ideological targets encompassed by it, certainly hindered its effectiveness in promoting women's status. By the mid-1970s, many people had become cynical and suspicious of the upper-level power struggles that lay behind, and were increasingly waged through, incessant calls for political and ideological mobilization. Out in the provinces, the various issues which ostensibly gave rise to these calls from Peking must have begun to appear as the masks of distant, struggling powerholders whose precise identities could only be surmised.[18] Under such circumstances, cadres at various levels were likely to be hesitant to identify themselves too closely with any one position. The mid-1970s was a period of great political uncertainty, and the political apparatus, even more than in the past, often attempted to protect itself by deflecting or delaying difficult policy decisions.

Furthermore, partly as a result of its mixed and uncertain purposes, the Anti-Lin Piao, Anti-Confucian campaign does not appear to have been backed by concerted, centrally directed organizational efforts to promote specific changes at local levels. It probably reached most local areas as merely one more propaganda campaign in the media without any clear, compelling injunctions for concrete actions, aside from the need to call some public meetings to denounce Lin Piao and Confucius, both of whom were dead. In some areas political groups, including groups of women and youth, did utilize the campaign to push for specific changes. But as the experience of the early years of the marriage reform campaigns demonstrated, ideological campaigns which involve contentious issues concerning the reform of women's status and rights are not likely to be effective when waged mainly through the media and without a concerted investment of organizational energies in local areas. Faced with a campaign of uncertain political origins and purposes, and one which might raise troublesome grievances among women, many local cadres probably found it a relatively easy campaign to deflect, avoiding yet another disruption of daily routine imposed from outside.

This neglect by local cadres was of course made all the more likely by the absence in most areas of strong village-level women's groups. While the slightly increased numbers of women in local governing groups might in some cases help, they were unlikely to have much influence or even inclination to try if they had no constituency outside the male leaders who wielded local power.

The scant evidence available suggests that the impact of the campaign was at best extremely uneven, although nationwide generalizations are impossible. For example, fairly extensive interviews with people who were living in various villages in rural Kwangtung in the mid-1970s, as well as coverage in the provincial Kwangtung paper, suggest that the campaign there was superficial and did not bring about concrete changes concerning women.[19] Visits to a number of communes near Canton in 1977 and 1978 also indicated that the period had not brought significant changes or even raised much discussion of the issues that had appeared in the national media. On the other hand, it appears in at least a few areas the campaign provided an occasion for more serious discussion and agitation on behalf of women.

The Provincial Women's Federation of Hopeh utilized the campaign to promote a number of efforts aimed at what its members had determined in 1973 to be major problems for women in the province.[20] In 1973–74, they obtained backing from the provincial Party committee to carry out work in three areas: (1) the promotion of free-choice marriage, late marriage, the abolition of bride prices and traditional marriage rituals symbolizing the "sale" of women; (2) the promotion of equal pay for equal work for women, including a major effort to redefine "equal work" as "work of comparable value" rather than the "same work," since much work in rural China is sex-typed; and (3) a provincewide effort to encourage the establishment of year-round nurseries and kindergartens, along with agitation for the idea that men should share in household chores. This work was carried out in 1974 through a series of provincial and county conferences and through the dispatching of trained Women's Federation work teams from the prefecture and county level down to the commune and brigade level.

As a result of these efforts, backed by the provincial Party committee and supported by the national media's campaign against male chauvinism in the Anti-Confucian campaign, the Hopeh federation claimed a number of concrete gains. Its detailed statistics showed a significant increase in the work-point rankings of women, an increase in the percentage of brigades supporting year-round nurseries and kindergartens, and an increase in the percentage of able-bodied women working full time in agriculture as a result of their higher pay and the increased availability of nurseries.[21] Although changes in men's willingness to help in household chores and a reduction of the obstacles to free-choice marriage and the abolition of bride prices were difficult to quantify, federation cadres felt from their follow-up investigations that their propaganda had also brought modest improvements in these areas.

My own investigations of four local areas in central Hopeh in the summer of 1978 support these claims. Cadres in each area marked 1974 as a period in which local women were successfully encouraged to agitate for more equitable work-point ratings, leading more women to join the work force full time and bringing a simultaneous expansion in childcare facilities and sewing groups supported by the collective. In at least one village, Wukung, a model village in Jaoyang County, the campaign had also brought meetings and organizational efforts to promote free-choice marriages, return bride prices and cajole men into at least publicly committing themselves to the principle of helping with childcare and household chores. A number of male cadres were shamed (or threatened by their wives) into "setting an example," at least temporarily. It was clear from observation of the village during meal times that women continued to do more than their share of household chores. Yet it was difficult to find a man in the village who would admit that he should not in principle share responsibility for such work. There seems to have been some change at least in publicly espoused opinions.

During this period, village Party committee and women cadres also raised the issue of matrilocal marriage publicly for the first time, although family planning cadres had begun to consider the issue a few years earlier. At least a few young women activists expressed the desire to have their future husbands move into their families' courtyard even though there were brothers present. Although by 1978 there were only a small handful of matrilocal marriages in the village (most but not all of them dating from the 1970s), there had been a dramatic and quite rapid increase in the percentage of intravillage marriages relative to village exogamous marriages for women.[22] While intravillage marriages had traditionally occurred in this large, multilineage village, they were a small minority up until the 1960s. Since the early seventies, the majority of women marrying began to remain within the village, with the percentage increasing throughout the decade. It is of course impossible to say precisely why the pattern shifted so rapidly for women who reached marriageable age in the 1970s.[23] But it seems likely that an important factor was the increased ability among young people to truly choose their own marriage partners from among the peers they knew from school, work, the militia and youth groups in the village, unimpeded by norms of village exogamy. The increased acceptability of women marrying within their native village, reinforced by the new argument that it was a male chauvinist "feudal" hangover to insist on women's "marrying away," certainly aided this development. The young activist women in the village themselves recalled that the activities around the time of the Anti-Confucian campaign helped to foster these trends.

That Hopeh was the cite of fairly vigorous agitation in combatting manifestations of "feudal" male chauvinism in family and public life, is also indicated from the models of women's work put forward in the media and other cases observed by visitors.[24] Both Hsiaochinchuang and Ting Hsien, mentioned above as models selected by the media for their work on various "women's issues" in the period, are in Hopeh.[25] An American woman living in another Hopeh village near Peking reported vigorous local activities to raise women's work-point ratings, foster matrilocal marriages and encourage men to share housework which resulted in some concrete changes (at least in the first two respects).[26]

It is conceivable that Hopeh, located near the center of competing leadership groups in Peking, was aided by a desire of one or more of these groups to make Hopeh a model in this work.[27] It is also probable that specific economic priorities of the state in the 1970s aided the Hopeh Women's Federation in gaining Party support in promoting its work for women, particularly the issue of equal pay and measures to reduce women's responsibility for housework. Hopeh produces cotton, an important cash crop which the state sought to increase beginning in the early 1970s.[28] Cotton-growing is done almost entirely by women and "equal pay for comparable work" was indeed sought to encourage more productivity from women. Since 1978, the price of cotton has increased significantly, and judging from my return visit to Wukung in 1980, women's cotton work (now remunerated on a quota-plus-bonus system previously dubbed "capitalist" by the Maoist left) has become one of the most highly remunerated types of agricultural work in the province.

Whatever the combination of specific factors which contributed to the success of these particular activities in Hopeh (and to the efforts that seem to have continued there), an important general point emerges from this example about the possibilities of using campaigns to promote reforms that aid women in the family and society.

Recent scholarship on rural China has tended to stress the ineffectiveness of mobilization campaigns and direct politically induced efforts in changing local social arrangements and peasant attitudes, except in superficial ways. This view has been reinforced by the current Chinese leadership's own negative assessment of the Cultural Revolution's political mobilizations and disruptions. The most recent and thorough study covering rural family practices and the role of women, that of Parish and Whyte, concludes that the normative and political influence of government policies and campaigns have had little effect in inducing change toward policy goals of family reform and women's roles in the family.[29] Using a structuralist view of change, Parish and Whyte attribute both changes and continuities in behavior and attitudes entirely to changes and continuities in broadly defined structural features of village life, including the patrilineal kinship patterns that have been stressed here. Thus, they argue that changes in the direction of government reform goals have occurred indirectly (and incidentally) as a result of changes in some of these structural features, while there has been no progress toward other goals precisely because other structural arrangements have failed to change sufficiently to induce behavioral and attitudinal adaptations.

I do not dispute that most of the changes that have occurred in the villages studied by Parish and Whyte can be explained as arising indirectly from structural changes rather than from direct government efforts to effect these changes. Nor do I dispute that more pervasive continuities in attitudes and practices persist because crucial structural bases for these have remained unchanged by the revolution in the countryside. However, Parish and Whyte, like most students of women, marriage and the family in China, have accepted an exaggerated view of the extent to which politically directed efforts have in fact accompanied the espoused family reform and gender equality goals of the government.[30] I have argued that the government has continually shied away from any serious mobilization efforts, aside from a brief period in 1953, and has been hesitant about applying even mild normative pressures apart from occasional national publicity. Even during the high tide of the marriage reform campaigns, the government paid mainly lip service to its national goals for women and the family, knowing that little effective organizational activity was being undertaken to support women and youth who sought to exercise new rights in the villages. Thus arguing that direct government efforts and normative pressures failed to influence change in the villages misses the point and incorrectly draws the conclusion that political and ideological forces can play little role in influencing either the speed or direction of family change.

Less obviously, such structuralist views come close to suggesting that the process of change in family and gender relations is largely an unconscious one which proceeds more or less in a conflict-free consensual manner. Yet, surely in addition to "rational adaptations" which arise from common corporate family interests in the face of structural changes, parents and children, men and women, old and young have different stakes in changes that potentially involve a redistribution of power and authority among family members. Historically, family change has produced characteristic conflicts and tensions between the generations and sexes, as weaker members gain access to new resources which could allow them to assert greater influence or freedom.[31] At the same time, stronger family members are likely to attempt to retain their traditional control in the face of challenges as some of the structural bases of this control begin to erode. It is in the context of these potential conflicts that a number of family historians have argued that ideological forces may play an important role in encouraging or legitimizing new claims made by traditionally subordinate family members.[32]

It is also arguable that larger political forces can affect the dynamics of change, by acting to either check or help legitimize new behavior and the assertions of weaker family members when these begin to emerge. Here the nature of local political power in rural China has appeared not only unlikely to encourage new rights for women and youth, but also likely to check the development of new behavior which threatens traditional patrilineal corporate family rights and interests. Top leadership political choices have in turn left these local political forces unchecked in most periods, and as will be discussed later, government legal reforms since the 1950s have weakened the role of local courts that operate outside of village power structures.

In this context, campaigns, if vigorously pursued with organizational commitment, can be crucial in providing external support for politically weak groups, such as women, and can help stimulate these groups to act on pre-existing grievances. Campaigns can also introduce ideas that shape and suggest new meaning and new solutions to vaguely perceived tensions. New ideas and political support can accelerate relevant embryonic structural changes (such as same-village marriages where these are desired by young people but opposed by parents) and they can help foster behavioral "adaptations" to the economic structural changes that have already occurred but which have not "naturally" led to the expected changes in attitudes and behavior (such as remuneration practices that fairly reflect the real value of women's labor and men sharing housework).

The Hopeh Women's Federation appears to have succeeded in the mid-1970s in tapping and supporting the grievances of at least a minority of local women on issues of remuneration and overwork in their families. They also appear to have provided new support to young people to arrange their own marriages, and they began to foster the apparently welcomed idea among young women that village exogamous patrilocal marriage need not be considered the preferred pattern of marriage. The vigorous promotion of free-choice marriage in itself, along with the strengthening of village youth peer group organizations, would tend to weaken certain structural impediments to women's community and family status inherent in traditional village exogamous marriage patterns. Young people, if freed from traditional taboos and norms of propriety, would tend to choose partners from among their known peers. And finally, such vigorous campaigns may also encourage intangible changes in the self-images of young women who begin to see themselves as stronger, more "modern" and more equal to their male peers in family and public roles.

In the absence of the external support and official legitimacy which a mobilization campaign, or other sustained organizational efforts, can provide, women are far less likely to pursue even widely held grievances through the local political structures. Given the political weakness of women as a group in the local power structures, externally generated campaigns and organizational activities seem all the more important; at the same time, the weakness of women's groups makes the success of campaigns more difficult. The young Women's Federation cadre working in a commune in rural Kwangtung in the 1970s, mentioned earlier, reported that able-bodied peasant women in her area *universally* complained of being underpaid and overworked.[33] Yet she was unable to get the women to act together on their shared complaints. She said the women did not dare raise such issues at public meetings for fear of being criticized as "selfish" and "petty" and for fear that cadres and other men might retaliate by insisting that women do the most physically strenuous work performed by men. She felt that organizing some of the braver women to raise the issue would do little good without outside support because local cadres were not sympathetic. The Anti-Confucian campaign might have provided such support had the Kwangtung Party Committee and Women's Federation pushed it, but the county and commune leadership in her area, including the county Women's Federation leadership, did little around campaign issues of male chauvinism.

There is no doubt that the ingredients of a successful campaign and of successfully regularizing lower-level efforts to promote gender equality and gradually alter family practices and traditional attitudes are complex and cannot be simply commanded at will from the top.

Politically directed change of this sort requires not only top-level commitment to publicize and promote issues through the media, but also the power to motivate relevant activities from the provincial level on down. Ultimately, such efforts require a willingness by the government to foster much greater autonomy and power within the nation's women's organizations. But given the current structures of power, given the weakness of the Women's Federation and its inability to act except with explicit Party support, the active support of provincial and lower-level Party committees must be obtained. Most important, politically directed campaigns and regular activities encouraging change must be able to find and encourage local groups of women who have been socially and politically disadvantaged to formulate and publicly articulate their grievances.

It is, of course, unlikely that local women would be enthusiastically unified in supporting changes toward all reform goals, especially those surrounding the family. As in the past, the current structure of the family and community is still likely to create recurring, patterned conflicts among older and younger women over issues such as unimpeded free-choice marriage (and the freer social interaction among youth which must necessarily accompany this), the loosening up of customary residence patterns at marriage and even the propriety of bride price exchanges. But it is also likely that these reforms could be made to appeal to, and build upon the support of, at least a segment of youth and women in many villages. Moreover, as will be discussed in the concluding chapter, the uterine family may already by eroding as a reliable source of influence even though the patrilocal, patrilineal structures which give rise to women's need to rely on it have not significantly changed. The state's current policies toward family planning—the one area in which the government has chosen to intervene forcefully and directly in the family despite considerble political liabilities—may make it impossible for many younger women to rely on the strategies that shaped their mothers' behavior. The greatest danger for women is that they will find their traditional sources of influence and control cut out from under them, while they still find themselves embedded in male-dominated family and community structures that do not (cannot) yet offer them commensurate alternatives.

14 Current Rural Practice

Before concluding and suggesting the current and future implications of the political dynamics that have surrounded reform, it is necessary to bring our account of rural family and marriage practices up to date. The most current evidence confirms that while there has been change in women's economic roles, there is still only limited progress toward the original family reform and women's rights goals enunciated over thirty years ago. In some respects very little progress at all seems to have been made.

Studies based on interviews, observations in China, and Chinese press accounts indicate that rural couples today do have somewhat greater say in their own marriages. There is no evidence that concubinage and the practice of taking a "foster daughter-in-law" still exist, and the truly blind arranged marriages of the past have sharply declined, though not disappeared everywhere.[1] Yet, true free-choice marriages in which the couple take the initiative in choosing each other (whether directly or, far more likely, through a third party) also appear to be rare. Most marriages are "semi-arranged." A substantial percentage of these may include cases where the real choosing is done by parents or relatives and the proposed spouses are not well known to each other, if known at all; the couple then consents to the marriage, perhaps on the basis of a brief meeting and marries without getting to know each other very well.[2] In most cases parents have maintained a considerable amount of influence and control (even if no longer absolute arbitrary power) over their children's marriages with the aid of taboos against same-lineage and same-village marriages and the traditional norms of propriety that continue to greatly restrict interactions between young people of the opposite sex, even when village young people often see each other in group meetings, work groups and schools.[3] Where same-village marriages are prohibited or frowned upon, only a small minority of young people may be more than vaguely familiar with someone they could marry because most young people have few opportunities to meet peers outside their village.[4]

Chinese parents, like parents everywhere, are likely to be loath to abandon the traditional taboos and moral standards that give them influence over their children's behavior, and they are likely to try to resist or at least blunt the development of new norms concerning free heterosexual interaction that tend to arise when peer groups become institutionalized among youth. This must be particularly true where parents still are in a situation in which their childrens' marriages will affect their own daily lives and future security, as is certainly true for the marriage of sons today in rural China. Since liberation, an organizational framework for the development of youth peer groups has been created in most villages through the establishment of coed rural schools, the militia, Youth League and nonfamilial work groups. But official "socialist morality" propagated through the media, official Youth League organs and schools has more often than not reinforced traditional moral standards in most respects. And the government has only recently and indirectly even questioned local traditional injunctions to village exogamous marriage for females. It was not until 1980, when a slightly revised version of the Marriage Law was issued, that the 1950 clause supporting existing local customs of exogamy was dropped—significantly, without comment.[5]

Evidence suggests that bride prices remain widespread and are in some places quite high, although there is probably considerable regional variation in the practice today as there was in the past. The Parish and Whyte study, which provides the most extensive data available on contemporary bride price practices, found that the payment of bride prices was nearly universal in the Kwangtung villages for which they had information, with the average amount quite high, perhaps equivalent to a family's annual income.[6] They cautiously conclude that this is actually higher than in the 1930s. Furthermore, they found that the ratio of bride price to dowry expenses had increased considerably as the dowry has become an insignificant part of marriage exchanges. They attribute both this absolute and relative increase in bride prices to the increased value of women's labor in agriculture, with the bride price signifying the transfer of rights to the woman's labor from one family to another. My own interviews with several peasants and cadres in villages near Canton in 1978 and 1979 also elicited information that bride prices were the norm in their areas and that the amounts given were at least of the magnitude indicated by Parish and Whyte's informants.[7] Bride prices have also been reported to be prevalent and high in some villages in neighboring Fukien.[8]

It seems quite likely that bride prices are more widespread and higher in Kwangtung and surrounding areas than in some other parts of the country. The Buck study in the 1930s indicated that in the double-cropping rice area, including Kwangtung and parts of Fukien, the ratio of bride prices to dowries was one of the highest in the country and that the absolute amount of the groom's family's expense was the highest in the country.[9] In Wukung, the village in the Hopeh plain discussed earlier, there did not seem to be any real bride price exchange at all any longer. Several young women claimed that there had been some paid as late as the early 1970s (when the custom was repeatedly criticized in public meetings), but the estimated size of these, as recounted to me, was quite small compared to the figures given in Kwangtung. Surrounding villages were said still to have cases of bride prices, but again the estimated value was relatively small, fifty to seventy yuan being the highest anyone had heard of.

As mentioned earlier, Hopeh was the site of particularly vigorous activities in the mid-1970s by the Women's Federation promoting a number of women's issues, including the abolition of bride prices, although this was not a major issue. In Wukung, bride prices appear to have finally disappeared in this period, along with village exogamous marriage patterns (which should make the abolition of bride prices easier). Yet traditional cultural factors may be most important in aiding this entire area in attaining relatively low bride prices. Buck's study from the 1930s indicated that in the winter wheat-kaoliang region, which includes the Hopeh plain, marriage exchanges and expenses were on the average roughly equal between the families of the bride and the groom, indicating that traditionally there was no outright bride price system in this area, the full value of the bride price probably being returned in the form of a dowry.[10] Another more detailed study conducted in the 1930s in Ting Hsien, a county in the Hopeh plain not far from Wukung and the other villages I visited in 1978, showed that dowries were in fact larger than bride prices there for all classes.[11] It seems that, even though many in the area I visited could not afford to do so in the 1930s, a large or at least equivalent dowry was considered necessary for a proper marriage. Significantly, this preferred pattern continues to be reflected in the practices that seem to prevail in and around Wukung today. While bride prices are understood to be officially stigmatized as a "feudal practice" signifying the sale of women and have diminished in value and incidence, dowries are still openly and proudly brought by a bride at marriage. These dowries provide much of the furniture, bedding and small personal items that the couple need to furnish their rooms in the house or courtyard of the groom's parents. The women formally considered these to be "gifts" of their parents, but, it was explained, gifts which now came from the labor earnings which the women themselves had contributed to their natal families before marriage.

Thus, in this one area, the pattern which emerges is opposite to the one found by Parish and Whyte in Kwangtung. Bride prices seem to have diminished to a level of relative insignificance, while dowries continue to be significant and perhaps fairly high in cost (though, seemingly, far from the ruinously expensive bride prices that have been reported in Kwangtung). While political factors related to the agitation against bride prices do not seem to be the most significant factor in producing this pattern (and indeed such agitation has not been sustained in most periods), the major structural factor Parish and Whyte argue to explain the continuation and intensification of bride prices in Kwangtung—the increased value of female labor—has not produced similar results in this part of Hopeh. Women are now a significant portion of the labor force in the Hopeh plain and they are largely responsible for the production of cotton, a crop particularly encouraged in recent years by the state. Hopeh has also done better than most areas in pressing for equal pay for women, and in 1978, I found the work-point ratings for women there were higher relative to men's than in any other area I have visited in China. It seems that the traditional dowry-dominant pattern of this area does more to predict and explain the pattern found today than current structural features related to women's expanded economic role. Similarly, political forces agitating against the sale of women through bride prices were enormously aided in this area by local customs.

None of this is to assert that new structural features are unimportant in shaping people's attitudes and behavior. But these contrasting patterns further support the notion that people tend to adapt to structural changes through the prisms of old values and behavior. Increasing bride prices in Kwangtung may reflect the increasing labor value of women in an area where bride prices were traditionally dominant, while in a part of Hopeh the same structural change (the increased value of female labor) is used to interpret and rationalize the continuation, and perhaps relative intensification, of dowries along with the dimunition of bride prices.

Obviously, bride price practices vary widely within China and generalizations based on our scanty evidence are necessarily speculative. But there seems to be little doubt that bride prices continue to be a problem in many, and perhaps most, rural areas as they were in the past. Even within Hopeh, the Women's Federation considers bride prices to be a serious problem in many areas, especially in the mountainous areas near the border of Shansi Province, an area within the winter wheat-millet region where Buck's 1930s study indicated that the bride price-dowry ratio was the highest in the country despite the fact that women's labor value in agriculture (and even handicrafts) was the lowest in China.[12] Leaders of the Hopeh Women's Federation also believed that bride prices continued to be a serious and pervasive problem in rural Shansi and Shensi and national federation leaders believed it was a problem in most other areas throughout the countryside as well.[13] In 1978, coinciding with the long-postponed convening of the national Women's Federation conference, a spate of newspaper articles and letters to the editor appeared complaining about the persistence of bride price practices in a variety of rural areas.[14]

The continuation of bride price practices in many rural areas represents far more than the persistence of ceremonial rituals drawn from a dying past. They are living customs which both reflect and, in many ways, positively reinforce women's continuing subordinate position in family and society. They symbolize the "exchange of women" between patrilineally defined families which continues to occur at marriage in very real and meaningful ways. They financially buttress a transfer of rights in the woman through the exchange, rights which the woman cannot therefore have in herself. In areas where bride prices involve a significant expenditure by the husband's family, bride prices are a real investment in the woman, paid to her natal group in return for the benefits of her future labor and offspring. They therefore are likely to reinforce expectations that the woman meet traditional role obligations in the family as a dutiful wife and daughter-in-law and they more firmly transfer the woman's future obligations of support from her own parents to her in-laws.[15] Indeed, the benefits of women's new economic roles have been largely absorbed, or channelled, by traditional obligations that treat women's labor as patrilineally defined family labor.

The payment of bride prices may also more directly infringe on women's rights. Heavy bride prices make it more likely that a husband and in-laws will resist a woman's efforts to seek a divorce, which makes it very difficult for her to obtain one through the courts. Parish and Whyte argue that bride prices result in the loss of certain divorce rights for women even when they obtain a divorce. If a divorce occurs early in a marriage, before the woman has contributed enough labor and children to "compensate" for the bride price, granting the divorce may be made contingent on the repayment of the bride price. If a woman divorces later in her marriage after producing children and contributing for years to the family's property through her labor earnings, she is usually expected to give up her claims to her earnings and, in most cases, her children when she leaves.[16] Thus in one way or another the woman is expected to "pay back" the investment paid to her parents and to buy her way out of a marriage contract that was solidified with a bride price. Even preliminary betrothal gifts and money spent on the meetings and "dates" through which a couple are to get to know, or at least meet, each other before marriage may be viewed as an investment by the man's side which a woman must pay back if she choses not to go through with the marriage.[17] Such practices clearly create pressures from both parents and in-laws against a woman exercising her rights to leave a marriage or to decide against entering one after preliminary arrangements have begun.

The decentralized and informal way in which divorces tend to be handled contributes to this sort of infringement on women's legal rights and power. Evidence suggests that most of the major decisions in rural divorce cases tend to be negotiated at local levels by cadres who are predominantly male and who are themselves likely to be tied by kinship and long-standing social networks to the husband's community, where the woman is still often an outsider. While county courts might be more impartial and more likely to uphold women's legal rights (especially against claims made on the basis of officially illegal bride prices and betrothal gifts), these courts often merely rubber-stamp the preliminary decisions sent up from the local levels.[18] Since the mid-1950s, government policy, especially in periods of antibureaucratic, Maoist "mass-line" legal reforms, has encouraged this community-based process.[19] While such a process might commend itself as a means to promote local community control over the legal process in noncriminal cases, it clearly has negative consequences for the development and protection of women's legal rights.

Women's divorce rights have in fact been an intentionally forgotten aspect of family reform since the mid-1950s. As the Party turned its attention to economic construction and cooperativization in the countryside, leaders became increasingly concerned with stablizing the bases of family and community solidarity upon which they hoped to build new cooperative village structures. Implicitly incorporating traditionalist objections to the "abuse" of Marriage Law freedoms, central policies began to encourage a more restrictive interpretation of the Marriage Law's divorce clause to reduce the peak divorce levels reached in the wake of the 1953 marriage reform campaign. The government's policy since the mid-1950s has been to discourage divorce. Only after a long process of informal and formal mediation aimed at reconciling the parties are local cadres or the courts supposed to entertain the demand for divorce. If both parties in fact want the divorce, this process may not be too long. But if one party contests it, the process may be extremely lengthy, requiring enormous perseverence on the part of the person seeking the divorce.[20] Although this policy of discouraging divorce is not viewed by the government as one which necessarily discriminates against women or hampers the development of a more egalitarian family, women still are probably far more likely to seek divorce than men, as they were in the early 1950s.[21] Thus, prolonged mediation is likely to operate disproportionately against women who seek to leave a marriage. After all, the right of divorce was initially considered an "antifeudal" reform which particularly benefited women's self-determination and alleviated patriarchal power over women.

Clearly, the government's policy on divorce has the effect of stabilizing and maintaining structures which are still highly patrilineal and patriarchal. The state, in effect, operates to help protect the patrilineal family's bride price investment. Male families can rest assured that once a marriage is formed, a woman will have an extremely difficult time getting out of it, even if she is willing to defy family and social pressures and seek a divorce. To be sure, the guarantees are not as absolute as they once were. But the government's tight policy on divorce coupled with policies that emphasize local cadre control over the legal negotiations in marital disputes provide a significant amount of support for the assertion of many traditional patrilineal family rights over women. Conversely, a free, less restrictive government policy on divorce and the encouragement of a legal process less easily permeated by local male power structures and interests (by, for example, making county courts more accessible to women), might help reduce bride price practices and lessen the strength of traditional patrilineal obligations that bind women to traditional roles. As it is, government policy has in a number of ways subverted family reform goals and indirectly supported the perpetuation of "feudal" practices.

Patrilocal exogamous marriage patterns give structural substance and support to continuing bride price practices which expropriate rights from women, to male supremacist attitudes which favor sons over daughters, to community power structures which perpetuate evaluations of economic worth that discriminate against women and exclude women from equal public authority, and to family practices which continue to assign subordinate traditional roles and obligations to women. Traditional attitudes, in turn, have helped to perpetuate discriminatory family and community structures, masked as "neutral" or "natural" even to the eyes of reformers. The interaction of these factors is a living dynamic which government policies and substantial economic and political changes in rural Chinese society have failed to break.

Government reform efforts might have broken into this dynamic more forcefully had they been pursued more consistently as a high-level priority over the years. The failure to identify and act to gradually alter some of the most crucial structural underpinnings of traditional attitudes and practices has further hampered the political efforts that have been made. This failure has led the government to miss opportunities to encourage and reinforce relevant behavioral changes that have begun to emerge on their own in some areas as a result of other structural changes. For example, in some areas, taboos preventing same-village and same-lineage marriages have weakened as a result of the development of youth peer groups and the greater role of youth in marriage choice.[1] Yet aside from the indirect and intermittent support for free-choice marriage initiated by the Marriage Law campaigns, these youth have received little support from the government in challenging taboos. The government has never directly and forcefully raised the issue of these proscriptions and the obstacles they pose for the full development of free-choice marriage and for gender equality.

The pervasiveness of old attitudes and practices is not merely related to government neglect and indifference. In many ways government policies have directly and indirectly supported the living dynamic of traditional values, behavior and family structure. We have already noted the conservative implications of the government's divorce policy and of an officially encouraged legal process in which major substantive decisions in the settlement of marital disputes are made by cadres in the local community outside of the lower levels of the court system. It was also suggested earlier that in a general way the rural development strategy pursued since the late 1950s has maintained the traditional family and community structures. This strategy has in effect undercut those processes often accompanying "modernization" and the development of new labor markets which encourage greater geographic mobility and neolocal living patterns and tend to weaken up

traditional kinship and marriage patterns. These conservative consequences probably have been especially accentuated during left Maoist
periods, when the closing down of traditional rural markets, stringent
interpretations of local "self-reliance" and particularly strict controls
on population movement have resulted in villages even more "closed"
than they were traditionally (the presence of small groups of politically
intimidated and socially isolated "sent-down youth" notwithstanding).

Since the late 1950s, the government, seeking to stem the growth of
urban areas and maintain the urban/rural ratio at about 20 percent to 80
percent, has more or less frozen the population in place and sought to
pursue the modernization and development of the countryside in ways
that do not create geographic mobility.[2] Rural modernization and
employment continue to rely on the development of decentralized,
small-scale rural industry, the development of sidelines, and labor
intensive agriculture and capital construction. As agricultural mechanization gradually proceeds, labor is to be absorbed mainly by expanding
local industry and sidelines and usually remains resident within the
original collective unit in the village. The basic collective units today
remain based on the traditional "natural" village or neighborhoods
within the village around which the early cooperatives were formed.
Indeed, it was the solidarity of these traditional communities that made
collectivization as successful as it was in the mid-1950s. In the Great
Leap commune movement, leadership found it difficult to exceed these
social boundaries and soon consolidated the smaller units based on
traditional communities as the main locus of socialist ownership and
organization. The larger commune remained but mainly as a loose
administrative structure. Post-1976 modernization policies may help
loosen these closed and frozen patterns (even as they further de-
emphasize the administrative power of higher collective units) by
reopening rural markets, emphasizing the development of more profitable nonagricultural sidelines and industries in the countryside, creating more nonagricultural jobs in towns and cities and somewhat
relaxing restrictions on population movement. As rural modernization
proceeds, nonagricultural jobs in small industries outside the villages
will become increasingly important sources of employment and may
encourage more neolocal living patterns. To date, however, current
policies have not radically altered the patterns discussed here. Even in
more developed rural areas (such as suburban communes) people who
do work outside their villages in nonagricultural jobs (usually males)
still generally maintain their household registration and their families in
their natal villages.

Thus much of the social fabric of traditional communities, the old
lineages and patrilineally shaped community networks, has been
reinstitutionalized within the collective structures developed since

1949. The only significant population movement since the 1950s has consisted of women marrying in or out of these communities. Males are almost always patrilineal descendents of residents at liberation, and in most villages (except in those areas most seriously disrupted in the twentieth century) there are many men who can trace their lineages back generations, if not centuries, before liberation. The organization of the collectives and the government's economic strategies have both preserved and built upon these rooted male-centered communities of preliberation rural China. In the context of the brutal social, economic and military disruptions earlier in the century, millions of destitute peasants had painfully faced the loss of their rooted communities and ancestral ties. In concrete ways, their "restorationist" aspirations have been realized, albeit at the expense of viable economic opportunities outside the villages, opportunities which many peasants today no doubt would welcome as an escape from their modern-day "enserfment" on the land.

Other features of collectivization and the government's development strategies have further reinforced traditional family orientations in rural areas. The government's emphasis on self-reliance in rural development has meant that lower-level collective units are expected to deal with the welfare and social security needs of their own members without access to outside funds. These communities, in turn, have tended to rely very heavily on the continuing strength of traditional forms of corporate family security and welfare whenever possible—that is, the traditional obligations of adult sons and their families to support elderly parents or other disabled members of the family. Only a tiny minority of areas has moved in recent years to establish social security and retirement systems which go beyond providing minimal case-by-case subsistence subsidies as charity to those who have no family who can support them, meaning those without adult sons and daughters-in-law.[3] Radical, "Maoist" periods, such as the Cultural Revolution, have created some political pressures on local areas to strengthen collective welfare responsibilities (including the distribution and sale of collectively subsidized grain on a per capita, rather than work point basis). Yet at the same time these periods have created even stronger central pressures to attain high collective reinvestment rates which have reinforced the local tendency to rely on families and keep collective welfare expenditures as low as possible. And, of course, collectivization eliminated the possibility of the elderly or widows supporting themselves by renting out private land when they can no longer work. The labor power of sons has been made the first and most important guarantee of a decent old age.

Thus in a variety of ways, the "Chinese Road to Socialism"—in both its radical and moderate incarnations—has restored, preserved

and utilized traditional rural communities and traditional family orientations and obligations. Indeed, it could be argued that the reluctance
of the government to vigorously pursue family reform goals after the
early 1950s and the failure of the government to perceive and act on the
patrilocal, exogamous patterns which maintain traditional male-centered community and family structures (until these conflicted with the
urgent priority of lowering population growth) are at least partly
attributable to the leaderships' recognition of the utility of strong
families and rooted communities for its other economic and political
goals. Tinkering too much with the basic traditional structures of these
institutions might risk weakening them in ways that would contribute
to the state's problems of control and might increase its responsibilities
for providing social welfare.[4]

The resulting patterns are a sort of hybrid fusion of new collective
structures and attitudes with old traditional structures and attitudes,
existing in tension in many respects but mutually supportive in others.
In orthodox Marxist terms, the pattern might be viewed as illustrative
of the problems of building socialism on a "feudal" social base. Marx
assumed that capitalism and its highest stage, imperialism, would
thoroughly atomize traditional structures and sweep away traditional
values before the capitalist order would itself be overthrown, leaving in
effect a society without a living precapitalist past upon which to build a
new socialist society.[5] It was not expected that socialists would have to
confront the problems of the "old society." Even less was it expected
that a revolution which brought socialists to power would partially
restore or save threatened features of the old society. It is not
surprising that Chinese revolutionaries who led that revolution, most
notably Mao, developed a view of change that stood many Marxists'
assumptions on their heads. Mao implicitly stressed the "advantages
of backwardness" in building a socialist society and we have in fact
pointed to a number of those "advantages."[6]

Yet it should not be forgotten that many of the traditional features of
rural communities also have posed problems for a number of important
government policies, as well as for goals of gender equality. When top
leadership priorities have been at stake, the government often has
moved to alter rather than accommodate traditional orientations,
sometimes with success.

Traditional clan loyalties, for example, often cut across and blocked
the development of class struggle against landlords during land reform.
In some places, large and powerful corporate lineages, whose power
was based not only on land ownership but on the organization and
control of village religious life, threatened the new government's
political control of villages. During collectivization, traditional peasant
aspirations for family land ownership coupled with traditional clan

hostilities and familistic loyalties sometimes factionalized villages along very narrow lines and hindered the development of new cooperative structures. In these cases the government broadly utilized its considerable political power and invested significant organizational energies to fight these threatening "feudal tendencies." The use of successive mass campaigns to mobilize and give strength to mass supporters (often beginning with only a "progressive minority"), as well as the use of outside work teams, economic rewards and sanctions and political and legal coercion, has succeeded in bringing about significant transformations in those aspects of traditional structures and orientations which the government has found most threatening to its top priorities.[7]

In other words, the Chinese revolution did not bring to power a Marxist leadership deterministically trapped by its inheritance of a disrupted but largely untransformed "feudal social base" in the countryside. Having built up a reservoir of rural mass political support and a strong organizational base in the countryside through the revolution, the Party and government have in many ways succeeded, through conscious politically directed social and economic change, in transforming many aspects of rural society by selectively destroying, repressing and reforming, as well as building on, the structure and values of the "feudal base" it inherited. However, the government has tended to accommodate or even utilize traditional orientations when these have not been seen as conflicting with its major priorities.

The relative neglect of family reform and gender equality, despite the government's continually reiterated commitment to them, is in many ways a political result of sharply conflicting values and expectations of the revolutionary coalition of intellectuals and male peasants and their different experiences and understanding of nineteenth and twentieth century disruptions of traditional family institutions. In mediating these two political forces over these issues, Party leaders, many of whom came from and shared the intellectual's experience, have maintained the visions and aspirations of the former as ideological goals, but have made choices in actual political priorities and policies that have directly and indirectly undercut the political force of this vision in the countryside.

In this political context, orthodox Marxist theory has offered theoretical means to bridge the conflicting aspirations within the revolutionary coalition. It has helped provide a general theoretical rubric for guiding, rationalizing, and maintaining a relatively depoliticized, low priority approach to reform issues concerning women and the family—an approach which has permitted accommodation with male peasant supporters—while sustaining the ideological commitment to goals of gender equality. Engels, who has been made the highest theoretical authority on such matters, has served these needs particularly well. His major theses on women's subordination effectively depoliticize many of the culturally embedded issues of women's status and the family, leaving family structures, practices, and attitudes to evolve "naturally" on their own in response to economic changes outside the family. It is only in the economy, where Party development strategies have relied heavily on increasing the utilization of female labor, that the Engelsian theory insists on the necessity of directing change in women's roles. Thus, the dominant Chinese theoretical view of women and the family, in sharp contrast to many other issues, has remained firmly rooted in the mechanistic, materialistic, economistic mainstream of the inherited orthodoxy.

The main exception to this pattern was during the Marriage Law campaigns of the early 1950s when, for a brief period, leadership groups actively agitated to mobilize government and mass support to promote new antipatriarchal ideas and practices concerning women's rights and status in the family. In many ways, the views put forward by the early 1950s marriage reform activists concerning the independent importance of dominant cultural norms and values and the need to promote reform through politically directed efforts as well as through indirect structural changes were more realistic in understanding the problems of family reform than the orthodox Engelsian position. To be sure, the analysis presented in the preceding chapters suggests that the marriage reform advocates of the early 1950s shared a crucial blindness with the Engelsian approach. They failed to identify (or perhaps were prohibited from identifying) as targets of change important noneconomic structural features of rural society and family arising from the larger patrilineal, kinship patterns that shaped marriage patterns and the composition of families and communities. They therefore failed to raise the custom of patrilocality as well as village exogamous taboos for women as targets for criticism and change. As we have seen, these customs pose severe limitations and obstacles to change for women in a variety of ways. By focusing narrowly on the attitudes and hierarchy within individual families and the treatment of women within their husband's families, the reformers never raised issues and practices that touched on the basic patrilineal definition of "family" and the meaning of marriage as an "exchange of women" within this context. Thus they tended to disengage the reform of values and behavior from larger patterns of rural society and structure which encouraged them and missed an opportunity to try directly to loosen these patterns through encouraging new marriage patterns.

Nonetheless, those behind the marriage reform campaigns implicitly understood that the relationship between values and structure is not unidirectional, that, in the absence of new ideological forces, people tend to adapt to structural changes through the lenses of old values.[8] They realized that new ideological and political forces may play an important role in shaping and accelerating reform in conjunction with structural changes, as had happened among educated May Fourth youth, many of whom became marriage reform leaders.[9] Similarly, in contrast to those who advocated a narrow Engelsian approach, marriage reformers understood correctly that the family institution, and women's position within it, were important factors shaping and limiting women's roles outside the family, and were not merely a reflection of those other roles.[10] Thus, marriage reform advocates explicitly refuted the notion that the general revolutionary process in the countryside, aimed primarily at altering class political power and economic organization, would automatically liberate women from male domination and eliminate women's subordination in the family. Rather, their policy prescriptions emphasized the need to introduce new ideological forces into the countryside and to undertake political action aimed specifically at reforming the family, its practices, values and norms. Perhaps most importantly, their approach took account of the fact that local political forces, enmeshed as they were in culturally conservative male networks of kin and community were not likely without upper-level pressure and supervision to act to ensure, let alone promote, the new legal rights of those women and youth who were pioneers in trying to act on the new ideas.

While the Party appeared prepared to put some effort behind this approach, and actually did so for a brief period in late 1952–53, it quickly retreated in the face of the inevitable conflict and traditionalist resistance that arose. Not even the moderate proposals of the National Committee for the Thorough Implementation of the Marriage Law to periodically check up on local cadres and strengthen the role and discipline of lower courts were ever undertaken on a systematic basis. Rather, more conservative forces, well represented in village political structures, were allowed to reassert themselves in an atmosphere which effectively decentralized and depoliticized family reform and related women's rights issues. The Party's abandonment of a politically directed approach again left the responsibility of overseeing and checking up on the reforms to local male cadres. A single propaganda campaign of a month's duration could not be expected to transform these cadres' basic political, cultural and social orientations which were so heavily shaped by patrilineal kinship ties in their native villages. Even if individual cadres had become more personally sympathetic to the reforms, they could hardly be expected to jeopardize their most important working relationships in the villages in order to push reforms which the government itself was unwilling to support. While the marriage reformers' approach certainly provided no panacea, the total abandonment of their approach undercut ideological, political and legal sources of support which might have allowed women and youth to translate the weakening of direct patriarchal economic control which developed with collectivization and the gradual expansion of women's economic roles into greater self-determination and influence in marriage and the family.

Politically, then, the leadership has mediated the revolutionary coalition's conflicting aspirations by incorporating the egalitarian May Fourth visions as official goals, while allowing the implementation process to accommodate, and indeed make more decisive, the aspirations and political force of a peasant base dominated by male cadres and patrilineally shaped networks of solidarity within village communities. Collectivization, which the Party claimed to be the key to fully realizing family reform and women's emancipation, has actually reinforced these networks.

The political strength of forces advocating reform for women has not been sufficient to sustain significant leadership efforts on behalf of what are considered secondary priorities in the face of inevitable conflict and difficulties. The failure of the government to maintain strong central support, in turn, has further weakened reform forces by depriving local groups and individuals desiring change of a major external source of power and legitimacy, without which they have been far less able to act in the midst of local power structures. The most hopeful political links for promoting reform in the countryside have been those between urban-based women activists (and other progressive urban forces) and rural young women and youth. These links have always been tenuous and dependent on larger political forces and they have emerged only rarely.

The groups most likely to politically articulate and spontaneously support reform issues probably have continued to be relatively well-educated groups in the major urban areas, the old social base of radical intellectuals and the women's movement in the early part of the century. As we have seen the early activists who first tried to venture into the countryside behind the Northern Expedition's revolutionary armies to bring marriage reform and women's rights to village women were predominantly urban female students. In Kiangsi, it was claimed that the most ardent (indeed too ardent) activists promoting these issues were "petty bourgeois" (intellectual) young women, although they almost certainly included young women of peasant background as well. The Yenan feminists, whose best-known spokesperson was Ting Ling, were predominantly urban intellectual women, though they, like the earlier activists, seem to have successfully appealed to and influenced young village women, something for which they were criticized. The top leaders most prominently associated with the active promotion of the Marriage Law in the early 1950s were, similarly, individuals who were closely associated with or politically shaped by the early progressive urban movements or the urban wing of the Party (such as Teng Ying-ch'ao, Shih Liang, Ho Hsiang-ning, Ch'en Shao-yu and Liu Ching-fan).

Although the major urban areas were politically relatively dormant when they were liberated in 1949, there is no doubt that the progressive, modern ideals of the earlier May Fourth era, including those of family reform and women's rights, had taken hold among urban students, intellectuals, and probably many young women workers. Although these were not politically powerful groups, they were an important source of needed skills, and the government sought to win their support in the early years. The Marriage Law and the government's espoused policy on gender equality probably helped in this respect.[11] For such groups, the symbolic value of the enunciated policy was likely to be politically important whether or not there was an effective government commitment to implement it in distant and largely invisible rural areas. Not only was implementation of the Marriage Law more effective in the urban areas, but the lives of these relatively elite groups, were already likely to be relatively nontraditional, "liberated" and socially distant from the majority of the population, especially the rural women who were to be the main beneficiaries of such reforms. Many urban reform supporters were probably persuaded by the passage of the Marriage Law, along with the highly sanguine national press reports which were typical before 1952 and after 1953, that the government was effectively moving to support a new social status for women throughout the country. General policy pronouncements indicated that the government now considered women politically, socially and economically equal to men, symbolically fulfilling the demands of the early women's rights movement. While the enunciation of such policies did little to transform women's lives in the countryside, they probably helped legitimize and benefit the lives of urban women leaders who lived in a subculture already substantially transformed.[12]

Urban intellectuals and students in China have remained very isolated and socially distant from rural society in most periods. The enormous cultural gap that probably widened in the first part of the twentieth century has been further accentuated since the early 1950s by policies restricting population movement and by the paucity of realistic, nondidactic information in the public media concerning rural conditions, including rural women's family and social status. Although the Cultural Revolution introduced millions of educated urban youth for the first time to the realities of rural life through their relocation in the countryside, the conditions of this contact did far more to overwhelm these youth as a political force (as indeed, it was intended to in some respects) and to create widespread cynicism than to motivate them to alleviate the cultural "backwardness" of rural areas.

We have seen how the most relevant and potentially receptive groups in the villages—young women and youth—are not only isolated from outside sources of support and politically disadvantaged locally, but live in a context which is culturally and structurally unconducive to the development of strong interest groups around reform issues. Even under the best of circumstances, the development in the countryside of women's groups capable of pressing their rights and interests would be difficult. Party attitudes, policies and structures have operated to maintain this weakness even while sometimes seeking to strengthen the organization of women in order to implement the leadership's other priority policies. Always insisting that the embryonic "women's movement," as developed in the wake of the revolutionary armies in the countryside, not be allowed to become "separate from the revolutionary movement as a whole under the leadership of the Party," the Party has at times been particularly sensitive to "deviations" of the "women's movement." Women have not been allowed the leeway in defining and acting on their grievances that has sometimes been allowed male peasant supporters. During the years of revolutionary upheaval and land revolution, many revolutionary leaders insisted that it was necessary for peasants themselves to act to liberate themselves from landlord domination in order to raise their consciousness.[13] For this reason, Mao and others at times sought to protect male peasants from too much Party control in spontaneously acting out their pent-up hostility and grievances, even when their actions were extreme, unruly, particularistic, and aimed against targets that were not Party priorities.[14] Yet the Party leadership has often demonstrated that even in the minority of areas where women acted more or less spontaneously on gender issues after they were organized, it has not been willing to allow women to build and act independently on a consciousness defined in their own way from their own particularistic experiences. Similarly, in the revolutionary base areas, leaders bluntly stated that the Party should avoid publicizing women's legal family rights because they feared that poor women might respond all too spontaneously and uncontrollably to the invitation, disrupting the army's political base among poor male peasants.[15] Since 1949, warnings against the women's movement "separating itself" or "causing divisiveness" have accompanied virtually every general mobilization undertaken, including at the height of the marriage reform campaigns.

Given the Party's long-time insistence that village women's groups only be organized under the control of village political structures monopolized by local male peasants, given the local cultural and

structural obstacles to women's political involvement and to raising
women's issues, and given the fact that women themselves have built-
in conflicting interests on many reform issues, it is perhaps surprising
that there have been "deviations" at all worthy of leadership concern.
The fact that there have been is perhaps a good indication that a real
women's movement has been a possibility in some rural areas. Yet
when one adds to the formidable local social and political obstacles the
leadership's concern to control potential "deviations," it is hardly
surprising that effective women's interests groups have failed to
develop in most villages.

Yet despite the weakness of the political and ideological forces
historically and potentially favorable to reform over the years, there
are reasons to believe that the coming decades will see greater efforts
by the government to alter the rural family. The impetus for such
efforts arises not from the ideals of gender equality or egalitarian family
reform, nor from any impending political empowerment of youth or
women, but from the government's policies on population control.
Population control has emerged as an increasingly urgent government
priority since the early and mid-1970s. Today, many government
leaders see it as the linchpin of all other priorities and crucial goals.
Hua Kuo-feng, then Party chair, in an address to the Fifth National
People's Congress in September 1980, expressed the sense of urgency
and importance that leaders currently attach to population control:

> If population growth is not controlled, there will be a dizzy peak,
> making it virtually impossible for the economy and all our social
> institutions to cope. Upon careful study, the State Council deems
> it necessary to launch a crash program over the coming 20 or 30
> years calling on each couple . . . to have a single child, so that the
> rate of population growth may be brought under control as soon as
> possible. Our aim is to strive to limit the population to a maximum
> of 1.2 billion by the end of this century.[16]

It is now understood that while agricultural production has grown
considerably over the last thirty years, per capita output has increased
very little since the early 1950s. Indeed, per capita labor productivity in
agriculture is said to be almost identical to what it was in the Han
dynasty, two-thousand years ago.[17] Improving upon this record is
believed to be dependent on rapidly reducing birth rates in the
countryside.

Although the government has backed off in the past from direct
efforts to alter the family, the felt urgency of population control is
leading to radical and forceful interventions in the family despite the
risk of considerable political conflict and costs among peasant supporters. As long as the present views remain dominant in the leadership,

the government is not likely to back off from these efforts, although it may adjust its policies in order to minimize popular resentment and increase the effectiveness of its measures.

It is clear that lack of progress in the low priority areas of women's rights and the family directly and adversely affect population control. Problems which were all too easily slighted when they were seen as related merely to "women's issues" and problems of gender equality have now come back to haunt the leadership in other guises. With population control an increasingly urgent priority since the early and mid-1970s, greater attention has been paid to some of the ways in which family structures and attitudes discriminate against females and continue to lead peasants to prefer sons to daughters. Some of the changes that emerge from the government's vigorous family planning efforts are likely to weaken traditional family orientations and patrilineal definitions that have made women unequal members of families and communities. However, as the government moves hard and fast against behavior that arises from unreformed traditional attitudes and structures, women are likely to be caught in the cross-fire and again bear a disproportionate burden as the cost of change.

There is considerable evidence that by the mid-1970s changes in economic organization, improved health care and the birth planning infrastructure established in family planning efforts during the preceding decade already reduced fertility motivation and birth rates in the countryside.[18] Collectivization has eliminated one traditional economic motivation for having numerous sons, that is, the use of sons' accumulated earnings to increase family landholdings. While family wealth today is based on the number of full-bodied laborers and adult sons continue to mean greater wealth, the value of many sons cannot be invested to increase wealth exponentially as in the past. Since a family's economic well-being at any particular time is based almost entirely on the ratio of able-bodied adult labor to dependents—so that too many young children pose an economic burden, at least temporarily—economic calculations have probably been tipped in favor of fewer children. In light of still inadequate childcare and household services, women are expected to carry a heavy double burden and some female labor earnings are inevitably lost while they care for preschool-age children, adding to the cost of having many young children. Moreover, improved health care means that children are more likely to survive and, with some time lag, families begin to feel more secure that they need not bear extra children in order to be assured of surviving sons.

Yet it is now clear that, even if reduced, birth rates have remained relatively high in the countryside and peasants still desire three or four children, including at least one son and preferably two.[19] Prior to the 1970s, family planning campaigns were relatively low-key and were rationalized mainly in terms of the health of women and children and the need to help women contribute to socialist construction through public roles. These campaigns were not as successful as demographers once thought, and the government has clearly decided a new approach is necessary.

If the government's current "crash program," which has been building up since the mid-1970s, is to be successful, it must directly or indirectly affect some of the unreformed structures and attitudes of family and community that have maintained the unacceptably high fertility levels in the countryside. We have seen how patrilocal marriage patterns, especially village exogamous patrilocal patterns, reproduce traditional preferences for sons. While studies in other traditionally patriarchal societies indicate that parents tend to increasingly rely on the strength of their emotional ties with daughters for support in old age once they lose economic control over their sons' employment opportunities, the perpetuation of patrilocal marriage patterns and government policies which tie sons to the land of their fathers have operated against the emergence of these trends in the Chinese countryside.[20] The traditional reliance on sons has remained virtually unchanged.[21] These patterns coupled with the rural collective's and the state's reliance on the family for rural social security needs provide powerful reasons for families to want sons—indeed, they virtually require that families do. Under such circumstances, even if parents could be persuaded that two sons were unnecessary and could accept the desirability of smaller families, the need for at least one son makes the two-child ideal, much less a one-child ideal, extremely difficult to attain.

In some ways, young women could be the government's strongest ally in moving toward smaller families. Women, far more than men, experience the strain of increased domestic responsibilities which many young children create, and there is a limit to the double burden which women are able to bear. Indeed, there is evidence that young women are far more likely to desire fewer children than their husbands and in-laws.[22] Yet the impact of women's desires on actual fertility rates is lessened because they do not enjoy equal power in the family and because family attitudes and structures continue to restrict rights of self-determination for young women. Certainly the fact that young women work outside the home for income and the fact that they now have the external support of a vigorous family planning program if they desire fewer children have increased their ability to override family pressures for more children. Nevertheless, family practices such as bride prices and the very meaning of "marriage" for a woman reinforce the presumption that her fertility belongs to her husband and his family more than to herself.

Furthermore, women themselves are likely to continue to have powerful motivations for having families with sons. Not only do older women share older men's need for sons to provide social security in old age, but the impact of traditional marriage patterns and unreformed structures on women's position in their husband's family and community continue to make women's traditional uterine family very important to them. As long as women remain outsiders in their husband's communities and families and lack significant new sources of power and prestige, they will rely on male children as an important, perhaps primary, source of status, influence, and membership in family and community.

The government's concern over population control has begun to lead it to deal with some of these traditional patterns, patterns which not only motivate people to want large families, but also sustain male-centered families and communities. To the extent that the government truly tries to reform these patterns, increased gender equality in both the family and community should result. As we have already seen, the issue of matrilocality was finally raised in the mid-1970s and along with it some indirect encouragement to abandon village exogamy for women. To the extent such developments take hold, new old age strategies of relying on daughters become more likely. Daughters and women are more likely to become valued family and community members. There also seems to be some tendency within at least wealthier communes to move toward a social security system independent of the family. As such developments progress, less familial community identities become more possible. Parents will have less need to differentiate between sons and daughters, to exert control over their children's marriages and behavior, and to restrict the rights of women.

Yet these government efforts come late, considering the complexity of the problem and the need for gradual change over time before such patterns can be fundamentally altered. Reform efforts remain surprisingly weak even now. In the short run, the government's "crash program" is relying more on overriding than on reforming the traditional structures and attitudes by providing direct economic incentives (for one child) and punishments (for three and in some places two children).[23] These rewards and punishments are being coupled with enormous political and normative pressures that all too easily become direct coercion. The hope is that with these tough measures, the number of children will drop and that this in turn will eventually alter the traditional patterns that stand in the way.

In the meantime, women are, in effect, being placed at the vortex of strongly conflicting pressures and they are likely to bear the brunt of a policy that has moved so fast and so far ahead of what current structures, values and practices can easily allow.[24] In the cross-fire, women's rights and control over their own bodies are made as irrelevant as they ever were in traditional China. Additionally, government policies are demanding that women abandon an important traditional source of influence before new sources have truly emerged for them. At the extreme, the consequences of the current policy for females could be dangerous and life-threatening, depending on the amount of coercion that develops in its implementation. The clash between unreformed structures and attitudes and coercively implemented government demands for one-, or at most two-, child families could all too easily lead to a revival of female infanticide in some areas, repeating the fate of unknown numbers of unwanted females during the worst circumstances of poverty and disruption in the past. There is already some suggestion that this is occurring, although concrete evidence is lacking and the nature of such a crime would, in any event, make it very hard to detect since it may require no more than inconspicuous neglect.[25] Such instances may be blamed on overzealous cadres' coercive implementation, but the larger forces making such developments possible are clear; they have been set in motion by central policy and have been exacerbated by earlier failures to make not only population control but gender equality a consistent priority since 1949. To avoid the possibility of these crimes, the government needs to be extraordinarily vigilant, more so than it seems to have been to date.

Whether the extreme measures now being taken by the government to control population growth are warranted by the severity of the problem is perhaps debatable. But, it is clear that the government now finds itself trapped between a rock and a hard place. It is faced with extremely difficult choices, all of which require sacrifices. In the short run, one may accept the government's judgment that urgent measures such as direct rewards and penalties are necessary; changing the underlying causes of fertility motivation cannot be accomplished rapidly. But in the long run, such fundamental changes must be made. The current policies are not only politically costly, but economically unviable except as a stopgap measure.[26] A return to serious implementation of family reform goals would be both helpful and more humane, especially in relieving women of the pressures they now experience from being trapped between new policies and old structures.

While greater gender equality and more egalitarian family structures, attitudes and practices would not necessarily or automatically produce the low fertility rates the government desires, these developments could create greater receptivity to lower fertility rates. Many demographers have noted that women's fertility becomes lower with higher status and more freedom from traditional family roles and pressures.[27] Many of the original family reform ideals would indirectly contribute to this result. For example, the more vigorous development of free-choice marriage norms would help keep women in or very near their natal communities, making it possible for stronger parent-daughter ties to develop and creating a better community base for women to develop public roles and influence not dependent on their children or their husbands' families. Free-choice marriages are also likely to create stronger conjugal bonds, which would relieve the loneliness traditionally felt by women at marriage. Margery Wolf has found this loneliness to be a major factor leading young brides to desire children (and particularly sons) as soon as possible after marriage. Similarly, the reduction of bride price practices—which becomes more likely with the loosening of exclusive patrilocal residence and village exogamous marriage and with the implementation of divorce rights for women— would help reduce traditional family claims to control women's fertility, allow women to reduce fertility in response to their expanded economic and community roles and permit closer ties and mutual obligations to continue between daughters and parents after marriage. Indeed, any loosening of patrilineal patterns is likely to lead to closer relations between daughters and parents and to the greater relative value of women in their communities, making sons less of a necessity.

Yet even today, with the greater awareness of the structural and attitudinal underpinnings of female subordination arising from family planning efforts, the government seems more intent on overriding those structures than in investing in efforts to reform them. Of course, the desire for fast results requires such an approach. But alongside the stopgap measures, more serious long-term reform, including the full range of gender equality issues, is certainly necessary. While some promotion of matrilocal or village endogamous marriage has accompanied family planning efforts, they remain relatively low priority, their value for fertility reduction, as well as gender equality, still not fully appreciated.

On issues of women and the family, Marxist theory in general, and Engel's theoretical exposition in particular, have proved extremely inadequate for understanding, and trying to alter, the dynamics of women's subordination. Engels' failure to take any account of the importance of larger kinship structures in shaping the family, community, and women's position in both, and his tendency to see "the family" throughout "civilization" as a reflection of the relatively isolated, bourgeois nuclear family of his own Protestant and capitalist society, make him a particularly inappropriate starting point for

understanding China. Certainly an understanding of issues of women
and the family in China requires that central consideration be given to
the role of kinship and of the familial-religious underpinnings of
community in peasant society. For an understanding of how these
dimensions of family and community relate to female subordination
one would do far better to begin with theoretical frameworks such as
those suggested by Lévi-Strauss and Rubin.[28] Lévi-Strauss not only
sees the creation of kinship (rather than the development of private
property) as the origin of "civilization," but as Rubin shows, his work
suggests the ways in which kinship shapes both social organization and
the position of women within that organization. Marxist theory, on the
other hand, merely reinforces blinders to these crucial features so
strongly embedded in Chinese society and culture.

The impetus for promoting women's rights and family reform within
the revolutionary coalition which the May Fourth heritage once
provided, while not completely exhausted, has been overwhelmed
repeatedly by other political forces and priorities. It was first sub-
merged within the political exigencies and inhospitable social environment of peasant-based revolution; later it was pushed aside by the
economic and political priorities of a modernizing bureaucratic state
attempting to consolidate its power and control in a desperately poor
agrarian society; still later it was pushed into obscurity by the political
struggles of an embattled, leftist minority within the leadership.

What appeared to be forgotten over the years was that the "antifeudal" cultural revolution of May Fourth, which gave rise to a generation
of revolutionary leaders and which was a crucial force in bringing
about the conditions of revolution, remained sorely incomplete. Some
say it has failed.[29] It is not necessarily dead. In the mid-1970s, the anti-
Confucian, iconoclastic cultural critique appeared to re-emerge in
some ways—perhaps as the result of a strange political dynamic
generated between an ultra-leftist woman leader (Chiang Ch'ing), who
had struggled all her life within a male-dominated political culture that
despised her for her ambitious pretensions as much as for her politics,
and a veteran moderate (Chou En-lai), who remained more committed
than most leaders to the promise of intellectual enlightenment of his
May Fourth days and the meaning it held for women's emancipation.
Nonetheless, the most crucial fact is that the organization and political
empowerment of social forces capable of continuing the May Fourth
spirit and completing the cultural revolution have not yet clearly
emerged.

Family reform remains a major uncompleted task of that original
cultural revolution, and it remains as crucial today as before for the
emancipation of Chinese women. It also remains as urgent. Marriage

reformers in the early 1950s echoed a number of impassioned May Fourth writers, including Mao Tse-tung, in arguing that family reform was a life and death matter for tens of thousands of Chinese women. Today unreformed family structures and attitudes coupled with a seemingly desperate government program for population control again may threaten an unknown number of female lives in China.

Appendix
The 1950 Marriage Law

General Principles

Article 1. The feudal marriage system based on arbitrary and compulsory arrangements and the supremacy of man over woman, and in disregard of the interests of the children, is abolished.

The new democratic marriage system, which is based on the free choice of partners, on monogamy, on equal rights for both sexes, and on the protection of the lawful interests of women and children, is put into effect.

Article 2. Bigamy, concubinage, child betrothal, interference in the remarriage of widows, and the exaction of money or gifts in connection with marriages, are prohibited.

The Marriage Contract

Article 3. Marriage is based upon the complete willingness of the two parties. Neither party shall use compulsion and no third party is allowed to interfere.

Article 4. A marriage can be contracted only after the man has reached twenty years of age and the woman eighteen years of age.

Article 5. No man or woman is allowed to marry in any of the following instances:

(a) Where the man and woman are lineal relatives by blood or where the man and woman are brother and sister born of the same parents or where the man and woman are half brother and half sister. The question of prohibiting marriage between collateral relatives by blood (up to the fifth degree of relationship) is determined by custom.

Text taken from a government pamphlet, Peking 1950.

(b) Where one party, because of certain physical defects, is sexually impotent.

(c) Where one party is suffering from venereal disease, mental disorder, leprosy, or any other disease which is regarded by medical science as rendering a person unfit for marriage.

Article 6. In order to contract a marriage, both the man and the woman should register in person with the people's government of the district or township in which they reside. If the proposed marriage is found to be in conformity with the provisions of the law, the local people's government should, without delay, issue marriage certificates.

If the proposed marriage is not found to be in conformity with the provisions of this law, registration should not be granted.

Rights and Duties of Husband and Wife

Article 7. Husband and wife are companions living together and enjoy equal status in the home.

Article 8. Husband and wife are in duty bound to love, respect, assist and look after each other, to live in harmony, to engage in productive work, to care for their children, and to strive jointly for the welfare of the family and for the building up of the new society.

Article 9. Both husband and wife have the right to free choice of occupation and free participation in work or in social activities.

Article 10. Husband and wife have equal rights in the possession and management of family property.

Article 11. Husband and wife have the right to use his or her own family name.

Article 12. Husband and wife have the right to inherit each other's property.

Relations between Parents and Children

Article 13. Parents have the duty to rear and to educate their children; the children have the duty to support and to assist their parents. Neither the parents nor the children shall maltreat or desert one another.

The foregoing provision also applies to foster parents and foster children.

Infanticide by drowning and similar criminal acts are strictly prohibited.

Article 14. Parents and children have the right to inherit one another's property.

Article 15. Children born out of wedlock enjoy the same rights as children born in lawful wedlock. No person is allowed to harm them or discriminate against them.

Where the paternity of a child born out of wedlock is legally established by the mother of the child or by other witnesses or material evidence, the identified father must bear the whole or part of the cost of maintenance and education of the child until the age of eighteen.

With the consent of the mother, the natural father may have custody of the child.

With regard to the maintenance of a child born out of wedlock, if its mother marries, the provisions of Article 22 apply.

Article 16. Neither husband nor wife may maltreat or discriminate against children born of a previous marriage by either party and in that party's custody.

Divorce

Article 17. Divorce is granted when husband and wife both desire it. In the event the husband or the wife alone insisting upon divorce, it may be granted only when mediation by the district people's government and the judicial organ has failed to bring about a reconciliation.

In cases where divorce is desired by both husband and wife, both parties should register with the district people's government in order to obtain divorce certificates. The district people's government, after establishing that divorce is desired by both parties and that appropriate measures have been taken for the care of children and property, should issue the divorce certificates without delay.

When one party insists on divorce, the district people's government may try to effect a reconciliation. If such mediation fails, it should, without delay, refer the case to the county or municipal people's court for decision. The district people's government should not attempt to prevent or to obstruct either party from appealing to the county or municipal people's court. In dealing with a divorce case, the county or municipal people's court should, in the first instance, try to bring about a reconciliation between the parties. In case such mediation fails, the court should render a decision without delay.

After divorce, if both husband and wife desire the resumption of marriage relations, they should apply to the district people's government for a registration of remarriage. The district people's government should accept such a registration and issue certificates of remarriage.

Article 18. The husband is not allowed to apply for a divorce when his wife is pregnant, and may apply for divorce only one year after the birth of the child. In the case of a woman applying for divorce, this restriction does not apply.

Article 19. In the case of a member of the revolutionary army on active service who maintains correspondence with his or her family, that army member's consent must be obtained before his or her spouse can apply for divorce.

Divorce may be granted to the spouse of a member of the revolutionary army who does not correspond with his or her family for a period of two years subsequent to the date of the promulgation of this law. Divorce may also be granted to the spouse of a member of the revolutionary army, who had not maintained correspondence with his or her family for over two years prior to the promulgation of this law, and who fails to correspond with his or her family for a further period of one year subsequent to the promulgation of the present law.

Maintenance and Education of
Children after Divorce

Article 20. The blood ties between parents and children are not ended by the divorce of the parents. No matter whether the father or the mother has the custody of the children, they remain the children of both parties.

After divorce, both parents continue to have the duty to support and educate their children.

After divorce, the guiding principle is to allow the mother to have the custody of a breast-fed infant. After the weaning of the child, if a dispute arises between the two parties over the guardianship and an agreement cannot be reached, the people's court should render a decision in accordance with the interests of the child.

Article 21. If, after divorce, the mother is given custody of a child, the father is responsible for the whole or part of the necessary cost of the maintenance and education of the child. Both parties should reach an agreement regarding the amount and the duration of such maintenance and education. Lacking such an agreement, the people's court should render a decision.

Payment may be made in cash, in kind, or by tilling land allocated to the child.

An agreement reached between parents or a decision rendered by the people's court in connect with the maintenance and education of a child does not obstruct the child from requesting either parent to increase the amount decided upon by agreement or by judicial decision.

Article 22. In the case where a divorced woman remarries and her husband is willing to pay the whole or part of the cost of maintaining and educating the child or children by her former husband, the father of the child or children is entitled to have such cost of maintenance and education reduced or to be exempted from bearing such cost in accordance with the circumstances.

Property and Maintenance after Divorce

Article 23. In case of divorce, the wife retains such property as belonged to her prior to her marriage. The disposal of other family property is subject to agreement between the two parties. In cases where agreement cannot be reached, the people's court should render a decision after taking into consideration the actual state of the family property, the interests of the wife and the child or children, and the principle of benefiting the development of production.

In cases where the property allocated to the wife and her child or children is sufficient for the maintenance and education of the child or children, the husband may be exempted from bearing further maintenance and education costs.

Article 24. In case of divorce, debts incurred jointly by husband and wife during the period of their married life should be paid out of the property jointly acquired by them during this period. In cases where no such property has been acquired or in cases where such property is insufficient to pay off such debts, the husband is held responsible for paying them. Debts incurred separately by the husband or wife should be paid off by the party responsible.

Article 25. After divorce, if one party has not remarried and has maintenance difficulties, the other party should render assistance. Both parties should work out an agreement with regard to the method and duration of such assistance; in case an agreement cannot be reached, the people's court should render a decision.

By-Laws

Article 26. Persons violating this law will be punished in accordance with law. In cases where interference with the freedom of marriage has caused death or injury to one or both parties, persons guilty of such interference will bear responsibility for the crime before the law.

Article 27. This law comes into force from the date of its promulgation.

In regions inhabited by minority nationalities in compact communities, the people's government (or the military and administrative committee) of the greater administrative area or the Provincial People's Government may enact certain modifications or supplementary articles in conformity with the actual conditions prevailing among minority nationalities in regard to marriage. But such measures must be submitted to the government administration council for ratification before enforcement.

Notes

CB Current Background
CKCN Chung-kuo ch'ing-nien (China Youth)
CKCNP Chung-kuo ch'ing-nien pao (China Youth Paper)
CKFN Chung-kuo fu-nu (Women of China)
ECMM Extracts of China Mainland Magazines
FBIS Foreign Broadcast Information Service
HCKFN Hsin chung-kuo fu-nu, (Women of New China), later changed to
  Chung-kuo fu-nu (Women of China)
JMJP Jen-min jih-pao (People's Daily)
JPRS Joint Publications Research Service
NCNA New China News Agency
SCMP Survey of China Mainland Press

Introduction

1. See for example Richard Wilhelm's introduction to *The Secret of the Golden Flower* (London: Routledge and Kegan Paul, 1962), p. 12. Also see Andrea Dworkin, *Woman Hating* (New York: E. P. Dutton, 1974), pp. 155–73.

2. See Lin Yu-tang, "Feminist Thought in Ancient China," *Tien Hsia Monthly*, 1, no. 2 (Sept. 1935, Nanking), and Wolfram Eberhard, *Guilt and Sin in Traditional China* (Berkeley: University of California Press, 1967).

3. See, for example, Margery Wolf, "Women and Suicide in China," in Margery Wolf and Roxane Witke, eds., *Women in Chinese Society* (Stanford: Stanford University Press, 1975); Arthur Smith, *Village Life in China* (New York: Fleming Revell, 1899), p. 326; Arthur Wolf, "The Women of Hai-shan: A Demographic Portrait," in M. Wolf and Witke, *Women in Chinese Society*.

4. See Hou Chi-ming, "Man-power, Employment and Unemployment," in Alexander Eckstein, et. al., eds., *Economic Trends in Communist China*, (Chicago: Aldine, 1968), pp. 336–38. Undernumeration of females in population registration is also thought to contribute to the high male/female sex ratios reported.

5. Olga Lang, *Chinese Family and Society* (New Haven: Yale University Press, 1946), chap. 1.

6. Chow Tse-tsung, *The May Fourth Movement: Intellectual Revolution in Modern China* (Cambridge: Harvard University Press, 1960), especially pp.

241

300–13. For reform attitudes during the Ch'ing dynasty see Mary Backus Rankin, "The Emergence of Women at the End of the Ch'ing: The Case of Ch'iu Chin," in M. Wolf and Witke, *Women in Chinese Society*.

Chapter 1

1. For the purposes of this chapter the designation "traditional" is being used in an admittedly imprecise and static manner. Our knowledge of the practices of the traditional Chinese family is heavily weighted by evidence from the nineteenth and early twentieth centuries as are most of the general works used as references in this chapter. There are a number of general sociological and anthropological accounts of the traditional Chinese family system. Two of the most comprehensive are Olga Lang, *Chinese Family and Society* (New Haven: Yale University Press, 1946), and Marion J. Levy, *The Family Revolution in Modern China* (Cambridge: Harvard University Press, 1949), chaps. 3–7. Also see Maurice Freedman, ed., *Family and Kinship in Chinese Society* (Stanford: Stanford University Press, 1970). The most recent and in some ways the best, general account is Hugh Baker, *Chinese Family and Kinship* (New York: Columbia University Press, 1979).

2. Arthur Wolf, "Women of Hai-shan," in Margery Wolf and Roxane Witke, eds., *Women in Chinese Society* (Stanford: Stanford University Press, 1975); Irene Tauber, "The Families of Chinese Farmers," in Freedman, *Family and Kinship in Chinese Society*.

3. James Scott, "Hegemony and the Peasantry," *Politics and Society*, 7, no. 3 (1977).

4. Much of the following discussion of kinship draws on C. K. Yang, *The Chinese Family in the Communist Revolution* (Cambridge: MIT Press, 1958), pp. 7–10, 191–96. Also see Maurice Freedman, *Lineage Organization in Southeastern China* (London: Athlone, 1958).

5. See, for example, Margery Wolf, *Women and the Family in Rural Taiwan* (Stanford: Stanford University Press, 1972), pp. 134–36; Burton Pasternak, *Kinship and Community in Two Chinese Villages* (Stanford: Stanford University Press, 1972), pp. 63–66; Jean A. Pratt, "Emigration and Unilineal Descent Groups: A Study of Marriage in Hakka Villages in the New Territories," *Eastern Anthropologist*, no. 13, pp. 147–58.

6. Yang, *Chinese Family*, p. 191.

7. For estimates of average family size and composition see ibid., p. 7, and William Parish and Martin Whyte, *Village and Family in Contemporary China* (Chicago: University of Chicago Press, 1978), pp. 132–34.

8. See William G. Goode, *World Revolution and Family Patterns* (New York: Free Press, 1963), pp. 27–80. Also see Parish and Whyte, *Village and Family*, p. 157.

9. See Jane Fishburne Collier, "Women in Politics," and Louise Lamphere, "Strategies of Cooperation and Conflict among Women in Domestic Groups," both in Michelle Zimbalist Rosaldo and Louise Lamphere, eds., *Women, Culture and Society* (Stanford: Stanford University Press, 1974). Also see Ernestine Friedl, "The Position of Women: Appearance and Reality," *Anthropological Quarterly*, no. 40 (1967), pp. 97–108.

10. M. Wolf, *Women and the Family in Rural Taiwan*.

11. Lang, *Chinese Family and Society*, p. 37.

12. Levy, *Family Revolution*, p. 96; Lang, *Chinese Family and Society*, p. 37.

13. Parish and Whyte, *Village and Family*, pp. 180–82; Lang, *Chinese Family and Society*, p. 44.

14. Levy, *Family Revolution*, p. 96; Lang, *Chinese Family and Society*, p. 37.

15. John Lossing Buck, *Land Utilization in China* (Nanking: University of Nanking Press, 1937), pp. 468–69.

16. See Ester Boserup, *Women's Role in Economic Development* (London: Allen and Unwin, 1970), p. 48, and Jack Goody and S. J. Tambiah, *Bridewealth and Dowry* (Cambridge: Cambridge University Press, 1973).

17. Parish and Whyte appear to have misread the data presented in Buck, pp. 468–69, when they say that the ratio of male family expenses to female family expenses was highest in the double-cropping rice region of the South (being 305 yuan to 169 yuan). While the *absolute amount* of the male's expense was highest in the relatively wealthy double-cropping rice region, the *ratio* of male to female expenses was highest in the poor winter wheat-millet region of the Northwest, being 2½ to 1. Thus the variations within China do not fit the expected pattern quite as neatly as Parish and Whyte's account suggests (*Village and Family*, p. 181, 188).

18. Many, if not most, sociological works on the status of women consider women's economic participation to be among the most important variables in determining their social status. See, for example, Rae Blumberg, "Structural Factors Affecting Women's Status: A Cross-Cultural Paradigm" (Paper presented at the International Sociological Association Meetings, Toronto, August 1974). Also see Boserup, *Woman's Role in Economic Development*. Later we shall discuss the classic and highly influential theoretical statement for this economic approach, Friedrich Engels, *Origin of the Family, Private Property and the State* (New York: International, 1942).

19. A. Wolf, "The Women of Hai-shan."

20. For example, see Fei Hsiao-tung and Chang Chih-I, *Earthbound China* (Chicago: University of Chicago Press, 1945), pp. 113–14. They comment that matrilocal marriages were possible in the Yunnan villages they studied in the 1930s because of the presence of numerous rootless and landless poor, young male immigrants to the area.

21. A. Wolf, "The Women of Hai-shan."

22. See, for example, Sidney D. Gamble, *Ting Hsien: A North China Rural Community* (Stanford: Stanford University Press, 1968), pp. 28, 384.

23. A. Wolf, "The Women of Hai-shan."

24. M. Wolf, *Women and the Family in Rural Taiwan*, pp. 171–77.

25. Statistics cited by A. Wolf, "The Women of Hai-shan," p. 95.

26. Marilyn Strathern, *Women Between* (New York: Seminar Press, 1972), similarly argues that bridewealth systems make divorce difficult or impossible for women.

27. See, for example, Jan Myrdal, *Report from a Chinese Village* (New York: Signet, 1966), p. 241, and Gamble, *Ting Hsien*, p. 37.

28. Ida Pruitt, *A Daughter of Han: The Autobiography of a Chinese Working Woman* (Stanford: Stanford University Press, 1967), p. 29.

29. Arthur Smith, *Village Life in China* (New York: Fleming Revell, 1899), p. 262.

30. See, for example, Elizabeth Johnson, "Women and Childbearing in Kwan Mun Hau Village: A Study of Social Change," in M. Wolf and Witke, *Women in Chinese Society*, especially pp. 218–19.

31. Fei and Chang, *Earthbound China*, pp. 23, 36.

32. See Craig Dietrich, "Cotton Culture and Manufacture in Early Ch'ing China," and Mark Elvin, "The High-level Equilibrium Trap: The Causes of the Decline of Invention in the Traditional Chinese Textile Industries," both in W. E. Wilmott, ed., *Economic Organization in Early Chinese Society*, (Stanford: Stanford University Press, 1972). Also see Battya Weinbaum, "Women in the Transition to Socialism: The Chinese Case," *Review of Radical Political Economics*, 8, no. 1 (Spring 1976), especially pp. 34–50.

33. See the Introduction to M. Wolf and Witke, *Women in Chinese Society*, p. 8. In the same volume see Delia Davin, "Women in the Countryside of China," p. 249.

34. A number of cross-cultural analyses have shown that participation rates are not related to women's status in a direct and simple way. See, for example, Peggy R. Sanday, "Female Status in the Public Domain," in Rosaldo and Lamphere, *Woman, Culture and Society*.

35. Buck, *Land Utilization*, pp. 292–93.

36. Boserup, *Women's Role in Economic Development*, p. 35. For a general theoretical explanation of these patterns see Blumberg, "Structural Factors Affecting Women's Status."

37. This is not to deny that unusual circumstances might create local or personal exceptions to this generalization. For an example of how an unusual, complex combination of local cultural, economic and demographic factors combined with high rates of female economic participation could and did give rise to significantly greater female independence and control see Marjorie Topley, "Marriage Resistance in Rural Kwangtung," in M. Wolf and Witke, *Women in Chinese Society*. For an example of what I would argue is a more typical case, where very high rates of female agricultural participation (equal to or slightly higher than men's) did not translate into a significantly different female status position in the family or society, see Fei and Chang, *Earthbound China*.

38. Practices which could be termed female "hobbling," such as footbinding, have existed in many cultures. Examples range from bustling, to weighting wive's legs with heavy metal bracelets, to corsetting, to chastity belts, to genital mutilation. Such practices are variously understood as a means to display family wealth, enhance women's erotic appeal, or protect female property. They all, however, at least partially restrict women physically and symbolically underscore women's position in family and kinship as "goods for exchange" or display.

39. For a description and history of footbinding, see Howard S. Levy, *Chinese Footbinding: The History of a Curious Erotic Custom* (New York: W. Rawls, 1966).

40. For a feminist discussion of the sexual functions of footbinding see Andrea Dworkin, *Woman-Hating* (New York: E. P. Dutton, 1974), pp. 95–117.

41. For example see Gamble, *Ting Hsien*, p. 46–48.

42. Fei and Chang, *Earthbound China*, p. 111, indicate that footbinding was practiced in the Yunnanese villages they studied even though women did as much or more field work as men. Also see Davin, "Women in the Countryside," p. 248.

43. Quoted in Lang, *Chinese Family and Society*, p. 46.

44. Wolfram Eberhard, *Guilt and Sin in Traditional China* (Berkeley: University of California Press, 1967), pp. 76–80.

45. Cordia Ming-yeuk Chu, "Menstrual Beliefs and Practices of Chinese Women," (Paper presented to the California Regional Seminar in Chinese

Studies, Center for Chinese Studies, Berkeley, February 1977); Emily Ahern, "The Power and Pollution of Chinese Woman," in M. Wolf and Witke, *Women in Chinese Society*, p. 209. Also see Robert H. Van Gulik, *Sexual Life in Ancient China* (Leiden: E. J. Brill, 1961).

46. Yi-tse Feuerwerker, "Women as Writers in the 1920s and 1930s," in M. Wolf and Witke, *Women in Chinese Society*, p. 148. For a discussion of misogynous perceptions of women's dangerous power in traditional literature see the chapter on the novel *Shui-Hu Chuan* (Water Margin), in C. T. Hsia, *The Classic Chinese Novel: A Critical Introduction* (New York: Columbia University Press, 1968). The Chinese language also reflects these cultural stereotypes. The character for *yin* (in the *yin-yang* dichotomy mentioned in the Introduction) stands for gloomy, dark, vicious (*yin-hsien*), conspiracy (*yin-mou*), as well as feminine character (*yin-hsing*).

47. Collier, "Women in Politics," p. 92.

48. Such dichotomous imagery abounds in Hindu mythology. Some Muslim societies also present extreme examples of this phenomena. See, for example, Fatima Mernissi, *Beyond the Veil: Male-Female Dynamics in a Modern Muslim Society* (New York: John Wiley and Sons, 1975).

49. Collier, "Women in Politics."

50. M. Wolf, *Women and the Family in Rural Taiwan*.

51. Evalyn Jacobson Michaelson and Walter Goldschmidt, "Female Roles and Male Dominance among Peasants," *Southwestern Journal of Anthropology*, 27 (1971), pp. 330–52.

52. M. Wolf, *Women and the Family in Rural Taiwan*, pp. 172–73, 189–90. Also see A. Wolf, "Women of Hai-shan," p. 100.

53. See Arthur Wolf, "Childhood Association, Sexual Attraction and the Incest Taboo," *American Anthropologist*, 68 (1968), pp. 883–98, "Women of Hai-shan," pp. 104–6.

54. See, for example, E. Friedl, "The Position of Women: Appearance and Reality."

55. M. Wolf, *Women and the Family in Rural Taiwan*, pp. 32–52. Also see Margery Wolf, "Chinese Women: Old Skills in a New Context," in Rosaldo and Lamphere, *Woman, Culture and Society*.

56. Collier, "Women in Politics," p. 92.

57. Collier, "Women in Politics," and Lamphere, "Strategies, Cooperation and Conflict among Women in Domestic Groups."

58. This discussion of the patterns and dynamics of women's behavior in the traditional Chinese family system suggests some interesting parallels with other oppressed groups. Indeed my own thinking about the double-edged nature of women's strategies and their simultaneous resistance and complicitly in the larger system of domination has been informed by Eugene Genovese's analysis of the North American slave system and "the world the slaves made," particularly his analysis of the dynamics of "accommodation within resistance" (Eugene Genovese, *Roll Jordan Roll: The World the Slaves Made* [New York: Vintage, 1967]). I am also indebted to my colleague, Margaret Cerullo, for insightful discussions on the historiography of slavery which suggested to me some of these parallels with my work on Chinese women.

59. See, for example, Pruitt, *Daughter of Han*, pp. 32–33.

60. See Sherry Ortner, "Is Female to Male as Nature Is to Culture?" in Rosaldo and Lamphere, *Woman, Culture and Society*, p. 85. Also see Nancy Chodorow, "Family Structure and Feminine Personality" in the same volume.

61. For example, Mao, like many others, has characterized older women as among the most superstitious and "culturally backward" elements within the peasantry. See Mao Tse-tung, "Report on an Investigation into the Peasant Movement in Hunan," *Selected Works of Mao Tse-tung*, vol. 1 (Peking: Foreign Languages Press, 1975).

62. Similar explanations, often drawing on the sociological concept of the "total institution" as developed by Irving Goffman, *Asylums* (Garden City, N.Y.: Anchor Books, 1961), have been put forward to explain the "slavish personalities" of other oppressed groups, particularly slaves and colonized peoples. See, for example, Stanley Elkins, *Slavery* (Chicago: University of Chicago Press, 1959), and Albert Memmi, *The Colonized and the Colonizer* (New York: Orion Press, 1965). Perhaps the classic work in the psychology of the oppressed is Frantz Fanon, *Black Skin, White Masks* (New York: Grove Press, 1967).

63. See, especially, Claude Lévi-Strauss, *The Elementary Structures of Kinship* (Boston: Beacon Press, 1969), and "The Family," in H. Shapiro, ed., *Man, Culture and Society* (London: Oxford University Press, 1971). Gayle Rubin, "The Traffic in Women: Notes on the 'Political Economy' of Sex," in Rayna Reiter, ed., *Toward an Anthropology of Women* (New York: Monthly Review Press, 1975).

64. Lévi-Strauss, *Elementary Structures*, p. 115.

65. Two works which, I believe, point in particularly fruitful directions for such an undertaking are Heidi Hartmann, "Capitalism, Patriarchy and Job Segregation by Sex," *Signs*, 1, no. 3, part 2, (Spring 1976), and Nancy Chodorow, *The Reproduction of Mothering* (Berkeley: University of California Press, 1978).

66. For example, the traditional family heritage of Europe and England is far more mixed in regard to rules of residence, female property ownership and inheritance, the importance of affinal ties and matrilineal descent. See, for example, Jean-Louis Flandrin, *Families in Former Times* (London: Cambridge University Press, 1979), especially pp. 74–78, 125–26 and Lawrence Stone, *The Family, Sex and Marriage In England, 1500–1800* (New York: Harper and Row, 1977).

67. J. L. Dull, "Marriage and Divorce in Han China: A Glimpse at 'Pre-Confucian' Society," in David C. Buxbaum, ed., *Chinese Family Law and Social Change in Historical and Comparative Perspective* (Seattle: University of Washington Press, 1978), pp. 23–24.

68. See, for example, Nancy Swann, *Pan Chao: Foremost Woman Scholar of China* (New York: Century Co., 1932). Pan Chao's "Lessons for Women" written around 100 A.D., became accepted as part of the classic Confucian tradition and was reprinted and quoted approvingly up until the Ch'ing dynasty.

69. This is one of the major implications of Dull, "Marriage and Divorce in Han China." The feudal period in Europe prior to the rise of the centralized monarchical state is also seen by many scholars as less rigid and deleterious to women in a variety of ways. For example greater flexibility in female property rights, matrilocal residence and matrilineal naming practices seem to have characterized parts of feudal Europe. See Marc Bloch, *Feudal Society*, vol. 1 (Chicago: University of Chicago Press, 1961), p. 137. For the negative impact on women of the central state and the erosion of medieval common law in England in the sixteenth century, see Stone, *Family, Sex and Marriage*, p. 137 ff.

Chapter 2

1. Mary Backus Rankin, "The Emergence of Women at the End of the Ch'ing: The Case of Ch'iu Chin," in Margery Wolf and Roxane Witke, eds., *Women in Chinese Society* (Stanford: Stanford University Press, 1975).

2. The most comprehensive study of the May Fourth movement is Chow Tse-tsung, *The May Fourth Movement: Intellectual Revolution in Modern China* (Cambridge: Harvard University Press, 1960). Also see Lucien Bianco, *Origins of the Chinese Revolution, 1915–1949* (Stanford: Stanford University Press, 1971), chap. 2.

3. A well-known illustration of this personal struggle is contained in an interview Mao Tse-tung gave to the American journalist Edgar Snow in which Mao discusses his youthful struggle against the patriarchal authority of his father. This struggle, which Mao described in highly political terms, included Mao's refusal to accept a marriage arranged for him by his father and Mao's tacit alliance with his oppressed mother against his father's authority. See Edgar Snow, *Red Star over China* (New York: Grove Press, 1961).

4. Pa Chin, *Family* (New York: Anchor Doubleday, 1972).

5. See Stuart Schram, *The Political Thought of Mao Tse-tung*, rev. ed. (New York: Praegar, 1969), pp. 334–37, and Roxane Witke, "Mao Tse-tung, Women and Suicide," *China Quarterly*, no. 31 (July–September 1967).

6. Lu Hsun, "New Year's Sacrifice," *The Selected Works of Lu Hsun*, Yang Hsien-yi and Gladys Yang, trans. (Peking: Foreign Languages Press, 1972).

7. Jou Shih, "Slave's Mother," in W. J. F. Jenner, trans., *Modern Chinese Short Stories* (London: Oxford University Press, 1970).

8. For a much celebrated May Fourth era article on the role of individualism and on the liberation of women from Confucianism see Ch'en Tu-hsiu, "The Confucian Way and Modern Living," translated in Theodore DeBary, Wing-tsit Chan, and Chester Tan, eds., *Sources of Chinese Tradition*, vol. 2 (New York: Columbia University Press, 1964), p. 153. A detailed discussion of the attitudes of three famous May Fourth writers toward women is provided in Christine Chan, "May Fourth Discussions of the Woman Question: Hu Shih, Ch'en Tu-hsiu and Lu Hsun" (Master's thesis, University of Wisconsin, Madison, 1980).

9. Edward Friedman, *Backward toward Revolution* (Berkeley: University of California Press, 1974).

10. Numerous studies of early twentieth-century rural China argue that a variety of forces were leading to increasing maldistribution of wealth and a steady decline in average peasant income throughout the first three or four decades. See R. H. Tawney, *Land and Labor in China* (London: Allen and Unwin, 1932); Ch'en Han-seng, *Landlord and Peasant in China: A Study of the Agrarian Crisis in South China* (New York: International, 1936); Fei Hsiao-tung, *Peasant Life in China* (London: Routledge and Kegan Paul, 1939). For an account that disputes many of the arguments made by the "distribution theories" of the above authors see Ramon Myers, *The Chinese Peasant Economy: Agricultural Development in Hopei and Shantung, 1890–1940* (Cambridge: Harvard University Press, 1970). Also see Bianco, *Origins of the Chinese Revolution*, pp. 104–7.

11. For detailed discussions of these factors see Ho Ping-ti, *Studies on the Population of China, 1368–1953* (Cambridge: Harvard University Press, 1959); Victor Lippit, "The Development of Underdevelopment in China," *Modern China*, 4, no. 3 (July 1978).

12. See Bianco, *Origins of the Chinese Revolution*, pp. 104–7.

13. The painful and poignant stories told by peasants in Liu Ling Village, Shensi Province, are typical. See Jan Myrdal, *Report from a Chinese Village* (New York: Signet, 1965). Also see Bianco, *Origins of the Chinese Revolution*, pp. 87–90.

14. See, for example, Fei Hsiao-tung and Chang Chih-I, *Earthbound China* (Chicago: University of Chicago Press, 1945), pp. 58–60, 114; Fei Hsiao-tung, *Peasant Life*, p. 52; Sidney Gamble, *Ting Hsien: A North China Rural Community* (Stanford: Stanford University Press, 1954), p. 28; Hugh Baker, *Chinese Family and Kinship* (New York: Columbia University Press, 1979), pp. 4–9.

15. Bianco, *Origins of the Chinese Revolution*, p. 105.

16. See, for example, Gamble, *Ting Hsien*, p. 405; Fei Hsiao-tung, *China's Gentry* (Chicago: University of Chicago Press, 1953), especially chaps. 4, 6, 7.

17. For an example of the weight of such concerns on the mind of one poor woman, see Ida Pruitt, *A Daughter of Han: The Autobiography of a Chinese Working Woman* (Stanford: Stanford University Press, 1967), pp. 44–45, 50–53, 57–62. These passages tell of the poor woman's struggles to approximate the proper burial rituals, scraping together her last pennies to do so. Significantly, in China's first poor peasant union, organized by P'eng P'ai in Hailufeng, Kwantung, in 1923, the first collective welfare measure was to establish a fund to guarantee its members a proper funeral. See P'eng P'ai, *Seeds of Peasant Revolution: Report on the Haifeng Peasant Movement*, translated by Donald Holoch (Ithaca: Cornell University Press, 1973), p. 32. Also see Fei, *China's Gentry*, pp. 129–30.

18. For a discussion of the early urban-based women's movement see Roxane Witke, "Woman as Politician in China in the 1920s," in Marilyn Young, ed., *Women in China* (Ann Arbor: Center for Chinese Studies, University of Michigan, 1973). Also see Elizabeth Croll, *Feminism and Socialism in China* (London: Routledge and Kegan Paul, 1979), chaps. 3 and 4.

19. See Friedrich Engels, *The Peasant War in Germany* (New York: International, 1966); E. J. Hobsbaum, *Primitive Rebels* (New York: Norton, 1959); Eric Wolf, *Peasant Wars of the Twentieth Century* (New York: Harper and Row, 1969); James Scott, *The Moral Economy of the Peasant: Rebellion and Subsistence in Southeast Asia* (New Haven: Yale University Press, 1976), and "Hegemony and the Peasantry," *Politics and Society*, 7, no. 3 (1977). Edward Friedman discusses this body of theory and its usefulness for understanding twentieth-century Chinese peasants in "Primitive Rebel vs. Modern Revolutionary: A Case of Mistaken Identity?" (Paper presented at the Annual Meeting of the Association for Asian Studies, Boston, 1974). Also see Friedman's rejoinder in *Modern China*, 2 (April 1976), pp. 198–204.

20. Friedman, *Backward toward Revolution*, especially part 3 and the Conclusion; Ralph Thaxton, "Tenants in Revolution: The Tenacity of Traditional Morality," *Modern China*, 1, no. 3, (July 1975).

21. Many scholars have noted that popular consciousness was informed by conceptions of a romanticized, heroic past and the brotherhood of the social bandit. Edgar Snow reported that *Water Margin*, a thirteenth-century epic novel filled with legendary bandit-heroes, was one of Mao Tse-tung's favorite childhood novels and that Mao, like many other village boys, had been inspired by the outlaw heroism of the novel's characters. See Friedman, *Backward toward Revolution*, p. 158; Vincent Y. C. Shih, *The Taiping Ideology* (Seattle: University of Washington Press, 1972); Schram, *The Political Thought of Mao Tse-tung*, pp. 22–23, 238.

22. Scott, "Hegemony and the Peasantry."

23. Friedman, *Backward toward Revolution*, p. 120. As Friedman comments, when trying to understand the meaning of the revolutionary commitment for peasant participants "one should not stress the radical intellectual's looking forward to a strong nation and exclude consideration of the ancestor-worshipping, family-oriented, backward-looking rural dweller" (p. 147).

24. Scott, "Hegemony and the Peasantry."

25. Even in those parts of Kwangtung where such notions helped inspire a "marriage resistance movement" among some women in the late nineteenth and early twentieth centuries, the movement did not advocate family reform, but sexual segregation and celibacy, in other words, opting out of the Confucian family system while coexisting with it. Indeed, the movement was apparently uninterested in finding converts, perhaps partly because it was believed that the Fates decided whether or not a woman should marry. Marjorie Topley, "Marriage Resistance in Rural Kwangtung," in M. Wolf and Witke, *Women in Chinese Society.*

26. See Yi-tse Feuerwerker, "Women as Writers in the 1920s and 1930s," in M. Wolf and Witke, *Women in Chinese Society*, pp. 147–48; C. T. Hsia, *The Classic Chinese Novel: A Critical Introduction* (New York: Columbia University Press, 1972), pp. 105–6.

27. This analysis also has been suggested by Phil Billingsley in unpublished notes. See his Ph.D. thesis, "Banditry in China 1911–1928, with particular reference to Henan Province" (Center for Research on China, University of Leeds, U.K.); and Friedman, *Backward toward Revolution*, part 3 and Conclusion. For a complementary analysis of the role of fraternal societies in Europe, see Mary Ann Clawson, "Early Modern Fraternalism and the Patriarchal Family," *Feminist Studies*, 6, no. 2 (Summer 1980).

28. Battya Weinbaum, "Women in the Transition to Socialism: Perspectives on the Chinese Case," *Review of Radical Political Economics*, 8, no. 1, (Spring 1976).

29. See Olga Lang, *Chinese Family and Society* (New Haven: Yale University Press, 1946), interviews with women factory workers.

30. See, for example, Pruitt, *Daughter of Han*, p. 25.

31. Baker, *Chinese Family*, pp. 4–9, *Peasant Life*, p. 52.

32. Myrdal, *Report from a Chinese Village*, pp. 234–36. Also see Pruitt, *Daughter of Han*, especially pp. 55–56, 62–73.

33. See Clara Zetkin, "My Recollections of Lenin: An Interview on the Woman Question," in the Appendix to V. I. Lenin, *The Emancipation of Women* (New York: International, 1972), pp. 97–123.

34. Heidi Hartmann and Amy Bridges, "The Unhappy Marriage of Marxism and Feminism" (unpublished paper); Joan Landes, "Our Praxis of Pain: The Feminist Challenge to Socialist Thought and Practice" (Paper presented at the Midwestern Meetings of the American Political Science Association, Chicago, April, 1979).

Chapter 3

1. To classify a woman villager as "middle peasant," "rich peasant" or "landlord," as the Communist Party later did during land reform, was merely to assign her the class label of the men in the family to which she "belonged" and into which she had, in most cases, been sold. Objectively, this was tantamount to ascribing to the slave the class status of her slaveowner. The

only meaning that such a class category could have for women was that it presumably reflected her material standard of living. Yet even here the classification would not automatically take into account her subordination within the family which might very well, and so often did, lower her personal material standard of living relative to the men in her family.

2. See, for example, "Sixth CCP Congress Resolution on the Women's Movement," *Chinese Studies in History*, 4, no. 4 (Summer 1971), especially pp. 229–32. Also see Janet Salaff and Judith Merkel, "Women and Revolution: The Lessons of the Soviet Union and China," in Marilyn Young, ed., *Women in China* (Ann Arbor: Center for Chinese Studies, University of Michigan, 1973).

3. Conrad Brandt, Benjamin Schwartz, and John K. Fairbank, eds., *A Documentary History of Chinese Communism* (New York: Atheneum, 1966), pp. 64–65.

4. Ch'en Kung-po, *The Communist Movement in China* (New York: Octagon Books, 1966), p. 129.

5. Roxane Witke, "Woman as Politician in China of the 1920's," in Young, *Women in China*, pp. 38–39.

6. Hsiang Ching-yu, *Lieh Shih Hsiang Ching-yu* (Martyr Hsiang Ching-yu) (Peking, 1948), pp. 50–62. Also, see Suzette Leith, "Chinese Women in the Early Communist Movement," in Young, *Women in China*, pp. 50–51.

7. Witke, "Woman as Politician," pp. 40–41. Also see the remarks of Ts'ai Ch'ang in Helen Foster Snow, *Women in Modern China* (The Hague: Mouton and Co., 1967), p. 247.

8. Witke, "Woman as Politician," p. 40.

9. Helen Snow, *Women in Modern China*, pp. 70–88.

10. Chiang Ch'ing's association with YWCA work has not been well known and she, herself, seemed somewhat embarrassed by it many years later. But her contact with progressive Christian activities was not atypical of radical young women in the 1920s and 1930s. See Roxane Witke, *Comrade Chiang Ch'ing* (Boston: Little Brown, 1976), p. 182.

11. Helen Snow, *Women in Modern China*, pp. 254–58.

12. See Nym Wales [Helen Foster Snow], *The Chinese Labor Movement* (New York: John Day, 1945), p. 16; Jean Chesneaux, *The Chinese Labor Movement, 1919–1927* (Stanford: Stanford University Press, 1968), pp. 74–75; Fang Fu-an, *Chinese Labor* (London: P. S. King and Son, 1931), p. 31.

13. Hsiang Ching-yu, "The Recent Chinese Women's Movement," in *Lieh Shih Hsiang Ching-yu*, pp. 53–55.

14. Wales, *Chinese Labor Movement*, pp. 31–34.

15. Helen Snow, *Women in Modern China*, p. 247.

16. Interview with Ts'ai Ch'ang, Yenan, 1937, in ibid., p. 247.

17. Anna Louise Strong, *China's Millions* (New York: Coward-McGann, 1928), pp. 113–14. From an interview with Ho Hsiang-ning.

18. Ibid., p. 114.

19. Ibid., p. 113.

20. Strong, *China's Millions*, p. 125.

21. Helen Foster Snow [Nym Wales], *The Chinese Communists: Sketches and Autobiographies of the Old Guard* (Westport, Conn.: Greenwood Publishing Co., 1972), pp. 119–202. Interview with Ts'ai Ting-li.

22. See P'eng P'ai, *Seeds of Peasant Revolution: Report on the Hailufeng Peasant Movement*, translated by Donald Holoch (Ithaca, N.Y.: Cornell University Press, 1973), pp. 8–17.

23. Strong, *China's Millions*, p. 125.

24. Ibid., pp. 130–31.

25. C. Martin Wilbur and Julie Lien-ying How, eds., *Documents on Communism, Nationalism, and Soviet Advisers in China, 1918–1927* (New York: Columbia University Press, 1956), pp. 308–10.

26. Strong, *China's Millions*, pp. 115–16.

27. "Sixth CCP Congress Resolution on the Women's Movement," p. 237.

28. Ibid., pp. 145–46.

29. Ibid., pp. 116.

30. Ibid., pp. 138–54.

31. Mao Tse-tung, *Selected Works of Mao Tse-tung*, vol. 1 (Peking: Foreign Languages Press, 1965), pp. 23–59.

32. Ibid., p. 46.

33. Strong, *China's Millions*, pp. 116, 163–64.

34. "Sixth CCP Congress Resolution on the Women's Movement," p. 238.

Chapter 4

1. For information about a model township's efforts to organize women, see Mao Tse-tung, "Investigation of Ch'ang-kang Township," in *Mao Tse-tung chi* (Collected Works of Mao Tse-tung), vol. 4 (Tokyo: Hokobu Sha, 1970–73), pp. 163–65.

2. "Plan for Work among Women," translated in M. J. Meijer, *Marriage Law and Policy in the Chinese People's Republic* (Hong Kong: Hong Kong University Press, 1971), p. 38.

3. Han Nien, "Summary of the Mobilization Plan of the Workers Division of the Young Communist International and the Mobilization Plan for the Next Four Months," in *Kung-fei huo kuo shih-liao lei-pien* (Collection of Historical Materials on the Communist Bandits) (hereafter *Kung-fei*), vol. 2 (Taipei: Chung-hua min-kuo kuo-chi kuan-hsi yen-chiu suo, 1961), p. 404.

4. Ibid., p. 397.

5. Kiangsi Provincial Women's Federation, *Chiang-hsi fu-nu ke-ming tou-cheng ku-shih* (Stories of the Revolutionary Struggles of Kiangsi Women) (Peking: Chung-kuo fu-nu tza-chih she, 1963), p. 3.

6. John Lossing Buck, *Land Utilization in China* (Nanking: University of Nanking Press, 1937), p. 293.

7. Chung Kung-hsun, "An Investigative Report on Kiangsi Villages," in *Kung-fei*, vol. 5, pp. 417, 419. Also see Lu Ch'eng, "Rehabilitation Work and the Situation in the Bandit Areas of Hsing-kuo," in *Kung-fei*, vol. 5, p. 455.

8. Mao Tse-tung, "Be Concerned with the Well-being of the Masses, Pay Attention to Methods of Work," in *Selected Works of Mao Tse-tung*, vol. 1, p. 148; Ilpyong J. Kim, *The Politics of Chinese Communism: Kiangsi under the Soviets* (Berkeley: University of California Press, 1973), p. 147.

9. Interview with Liu Chien-hsien in Helen Foster Snow, *The Chinese Communists: Sketches and Autobiographies of the Old Guard* (Westport, Conn.: Greenwood Publishing Co., 1972) pp. 244–45.

10. Interview with K'ang K'e-ch'ing in ibid., pp. 213–14.

11. Ibid, p. 218. Dick Wilson, *The Long March 1935: The Epic of Chinese Communism's Survival* (London: Hamish Hamilton, 1971), p. 69.

12. For example, see Chu Teh's remarks in Helen Foster Snow [Nym Wales], *My Yenan Notebooks* (Madison, Conn.: Mimeographed, 1961), pp. 61–63.

13. Mao Tse-tung, "Investigation of Ts'ai-hsi Township," in *Mao Tse-tung chi*, vol. 4, 178–79. For army recruitment figures for Ts'ai-hsi see *Selected Works of Mao Tse-tung*, vol. 1, p. 148.

14. "Report of the President of the Central Executive Committee of the Chinese Soviet Republic, Mao Tse-tung—Before the Second National Soviet Congress," translated in Victor Yakhontoff, *The Chinese Soviets* (Westport, Conn.: Greenwood Publishing Co., 1972), p. 254.

15. Liu Ch'un-hsien in Helen Snow, *The Chinese Communists*, p. 244.

16. Mao Tse-tung, "Investigation of Ch'ang-Kang Township."

17. Conrad Brandt, Benjamin Schwartz, and John K. Fairbank, eds., *A Documentary History of Chinese Communism* (New York: Atheneum, 1966), p. 223.

18. Ibid., pp. 224–25.

19. For these demands, see Anna Louise Strong, *China's Millions* (New York: Coward-McGann, 1928), pp. 108–9.

20. Text of 1931 Labor Code in Yakhontoff, *Chinese Soviets*, pp. 228–29.

21. Text of 1931 Marriage Regulations in Meijer, *Marriage Law and Policy*, pp. 281–82.

22. Interview with K'ung Hsiang-p'an in Wang Chien-min, ed., *Chung-kuo kung-ch'an-dang shih-kao: Chiang-hsi shih-ch'i* (A Draft History of the Chinese Communist Party: The Kiangsi Period), vol. 2 (Taipei: Wang Chien-min, 1965), pp. 446–47. K'ung Hsiang-p'an was a woman Communist Party cadre who worked in the Kiangsi Soviet for several years. At the time of the collapse of the Soviet, she was captured and interrogated by the KMT. The interview reprinted above occurred sometime after her capture. The excerpts I have referred to seem very credible and do not bear the ideologically stilted earmarks of a "confession." Indeed, many of her remarks contradict the propaganda image of the CCP which the KMT sought to project at that time.

23. See, for example, "Plan for Work among Women," translated in Meijer, *Marriage Law and Policy*, p. 38.

24. Mao Tse-tung, "Hsing-kuo Investigation," in *Kung-fei*, vol. 5., pp. 219–22.

25. Ibid.

26. See interview with K'ung Hsiang-p'an in Wang, *Chung-kuo kung-ch'an dang*, vol. 2, pp. 446–47.

27. Translated in Meijer, *Marriage Law and Policy*, pp. 40–41.

28. Interview with K'ung Hsiang-p'an in Wang, *Chung-kuo kung-ch'an dang*, vol. 2, pp. 446–47.

29. Strong, *China's Millions*, pp. 138–54.

30. The two Kiangsi reports were originally printed in *Kuo-wen chou-pao*, 10, no. 32 (August 14, 1933), reprinted in Wang, *Chung-kuo kung-ch'an dang*, vol. 2, pp. 445. Counties in the Soviets varied in size from 80,000 to 270,000. There were 4,200 divorces reported for Yi-yang and Heng-feng counties (the two counties cited above) from March through June 1931. See Hu Chi-hsi, "The Sexual Revolution in Kiangsi," in *China Quarterly*, no. 59 (July–Sept. 1974), p. 486n. Also see Lu Ch'eng, "Rehabilitation Work," in *Kung-fei*, vol. 5, p. 455.

31. Mao, "Investigation of Ch'ang-kang Township."

32. K'ung Hsiang-p'an's interview in Wang, *Chung-kuo kung-ch'an dang*, vol. 2, pp. 445–46.

33. This observation appears in the original, unexpurgated versions of Mao's, "An Investigation into the Peasant Movement in Hunan." However,

later versions published in China after 1949 have these lines deleted. See Stuart Schram, *The Political Thought of Mao Tse-tung* (New York: Praeger, 1969).

34. K'ung Hsiang-p'an in Wang, *Chung-kuo kung-ch'an dang*, vol. 2, pp. 445–46. See note 22 above.

35. Hu, "Sexual Revolution," pp. 480, 483. Also see Wang, *Chung-kuo kung-ch'an dang*, vol. 2, p. 447.

36. Hu, "Sexual Revolution," p. 484.

37. Mao Tse-tung, *Selected Works of Mao Tse-tung*, vol. 1, p. 135.

38. Translated in Meijer, *Marriage Law and Policy*, p. 42.

39. Hu, "Sexual Revolution," p. 484.

40. Ibid.

41. Text in Meijer, *Marriage Law and Policy*, pp. 283–84.

42. Mao Tse-tung, "Conclusions Concerning the Central Executive Committee's Report," in *Kung-fei*, vol. 2, p. 80.

43. See Meijer, *Marriage Law and Policy*, pp. 112–13 for a chart on the recorded number of divorces for various provinces and cities in the early 1950s. If one assumes an estimated population of 12 to 13 million for the province in the early 1950s, Kiangsi's divorce rate from mid-1950 to mid-1951 was about 10 per 1,000 population. Even by international standards, this is a very high rate. The estimated national divorce rate for China in 1953—the year with the highest number of recorded divorces—is 2.2 per 1,000 for an estimated population of 550 million. The divorce rate for the United States in 1974 was less than 4.5 per 1,000.

44. Interview with Liu Chien-hsien in Helen Snow, *The Chinese Communists*, p. 245.

Chapter 5

1. John L. Buck, *Land Utilization in China* (Nanking: University of Nanking Press, 1937), p. 293.

2. Helen Foster Snow [Nym Wales], *Inside Red China* (New York: Doubleday, Doran and Co., 1939), p. 192.

3. Helen Foster Snow, *Women in Modern China* (The Hague: Mouton and Co., 1967), pp. 223–24.

4. Mark Selden, *The Yenan Way in Revolutionary China* (Cambridge: Harvard University Press, 1971), pp. 115–16.

5. Ts'ai Hsiao-Ch'ien, *Kiang-hsi su-ch'u hung-ch'un hsi ts'uan huei-yi* (Remembrances of the Kiangsi Soviet and the Westward Flight of the Red Army) (Hong Kong: Ta chung-hua ch'u-pan she, 1970), p. 185.

6. Ibid.

7. Selden, *Yenan Way*, pp. 115–16.

8. Helen Snow, *Inside Red China*, p. 192.

9. Selden, *Yenan Way*, p. 142.

10. Ibid.

11. For example, see Isabel and David Crook, *Revolution in a Chinese Village: Ten Mile Inn* (London: Routledge and Kegan Paul, 1959), pp. 42–46.

12. Ibid., p. 43; Delia Davin, "Women in the Liberated Areas," in Marilyn Young, ed., *Women in China* (Ann Arbor: Center for Chinese Studies, University of Michigan, 1973), p. 79.

13. Selden, *Yenan Way*, p. 257.

14. Helen Snow, *Inside Red China*, p. 195.

15. Edgar Snow, *Red Star over China* (New York: Grove Press, 1961), p. 237. While travellers to Yenan report that footbinding was still being practiced there when the Red Army arrived, in the area around Ting Hsien, located in the northern plains area where the Central Hopeh Base Area was established, footbinding is known to have ceased quite rapidly between 1910 and 1915. See Sidney Gamble, *Ting Hsien* (Stanford: Stanford University Press, 1968), pp. 47–48. In such areas, most of the women under thirty years of age probably had natural feet by the time of the Anti-Japanese War and were therefore more likely to be able to participate in agriculture.

16. Selden, *Yenan Way*, p. 165. Also see Harrison Forman, *Report from Red China* (New York: Book Find Club, 1945), p. 60, for the 1941 election platform on women.

17. Selden, *Yenan Way*, p. 165.

18. Helen Snow, *My Yenan Notebooks* (Madison, Conn.: Mimeographed, 1960), p. 85.

19. Calculated from Roy Hofheinz, "The Ecology of Chinese Communist Success: Rural Influence Patterns, 1923–45," in A. Doak Barnett, ed., *Chinese Communist Politics in Action* (Seattle: University of Washington Press, 1972), p. 24.

20. Helen Snow, *Inside Red China*, p. 194; Edgar Snow, *Red Star*, p. 230.

21. Texts of four of these and notes on later revisions in M .J. Meijer, *Marriage Law and Policy in the Chinese People's Republic* (Hong Kong: Hong Kong University Press, 1971), pp. 285–99.

22. P'eng Teh-huai, "Report Concerning Work in the North China Base Areas," in *Kung-fei huo kuo shih-liao lei-pien* (Collection of Historical Materials on the Communist Bandits), vol. 3, especially pp. 380–82.

23. See Selden, *Yenan Way*, pp. 208–12, for summary of these policies.

24. Ibid., pp. 258–60.

25. "Decision of the CCP, CC Concerning the Policy on Current Women's Work in the Anti-Japanese Base Areas, February 26, 1943," in *Chung-kuo fu-nu yun-tung ti chung-yao wen-chien* (Important Documents on the Chinese Women's Movement) (Peking: Jen-min ch'u-pan she, 1953), p. 103.

26. Crook and Crook, *Revolution in a Chinese Village*, pp. 69–71.

27. Davin, "Women in the Liberated Areas," p. 78.

28. Crook and Crook, *Revolution in a Chinese Village*; p. 71, Davin, "Women in the Liberated Areas," p. 79.

29. Selden, *Yenan Way*, p. 256.

30. Jack Belden, *China Shakes the World* (New York: Monthly Review Press, 1970), p. 316.

31. Davin, "Women in the Liberated Areas," pp. 79–80.

32. Belden, *China Shakes the World*, pp. 314–15.

33. For example, see Gunther Stein, *The Challenge of Red China* (New York: McGraw-Hill Book Co., 1945), p. 249.

34. Ting Ling related her autobiography to Helen Snow in *Women in Modern China*, pp. 194–221.

35. Helen Snow, *Women in Modern China*, p. 30; *My Yenan Notebooks*, p. 156; *The Chinese Communists: Sketches and Autobiographies of the Old Guard* (Westport, Conn.: Greenwood Publishing Co., 1972), p. 262.

36. Ting Ling, *When I Was in Sha Chuan and Other Stories* (Bombay: Kutub Publishers, 1945), pp. 5–35.

37. Also see Ting Ling's portrayal of women in "Night," ibid., pp. 108–18.

38. For a reprint of the complete text see *JMJP*, August 23, 1957, p. 8. Also see Merle Goldman, *Literary Dissent in Communist China* (Cambridge: Harvard University Press, 1967), pp. 23–24.

39. For example, see Liu Shao-ch'i, "Several Basic Understandings from the Summary of Women's Work," in *Fu-nu yun-tung wen-hsien* (Documents of the Women's Movement) (Hong Kong: Hsin min-chu ch'u-pan she, 1949), pp. 24–33.

40. Stein, *Challenge of Red China*, p. 257.

41. Ts'ai Ch'ang, "Welcome the New Direction in Women's Work" (March 1943), in *Chung-kuo chieh-fang ch'u fu-nu yun-tung wen-hsien* (Documents on the Chinese Women's Movement in the Liberated Areas) (Shanghai: Hsin-hua shu-tien, 1949), pp. 4–11.

42. Helen Snow, *Inside Red China*, pp. 179, 193.

43. *Chung-kuo fu-nu ta fan-shen* (Chinese Women Stand Up) (Hong Kong: Hsin min-chu ch'u-pan she, 1949), p. 2.

44. Isabel and David Crook, *The First Years of Yangyi Commune* (London: Routledge and Kegan Paul, 1966), p. 241.

45. "The Stages of Development of Laboring Women in Kao-chuang-tse," NCNA, February 1948, in *Chung-kuo fu-nu ta fan-shen*, pp. 9–11.

46. Ibid. Also see "Women during the Land Reform Struggle in Pin County," in *Chung-kuo fu-nu ta fan-shen*, pp. 14–15; Davin, "Women in the Liberated Areas," p. 81.

47. Helen Snow, *Women in Modern China*.

48. Crook and Crook, *Revolution in a Chinese Village*, pp. 100–108.

49. Ibid., p. 107.

50. Suzanne Pepper, *Civil War in China: The Political Struggle, 1945–1949* (Berkeley: University of California Press, 1978), pp. 263–64.

51. "Women during the Land Reform Struggle in Pin County," pp. 14–15.

52. Janet Salaff's interviews show that even in the late 1960s villagers might still suspect the moral standards of women who served as cadres because they sometimes associated with men in their work. Janet Salaff, "Institutionalized Fertility Limitation in China," in Young, *Women in China*, p. 119.

53. Edward Friedman, *Backward toward Revolution*, part 3.

54. Pepper, *Civil War in China*, p. 267.

55. Davin, "Women in the Liberated Areas," p. 81. Also see, for example, "Examples of Accomplishments of the Women's Movement during Land Reform," in *Chung-kuo fu-nu ta fan-shen*, pp. 16–17; Liu Chih, "Women of Ting Hsien Stand Up," in *Chung-kuo chieh-fang ch'u nung-ts'un fu-nu fan-shen yun-tung su-miao*, (The Movement in which Village Women of China's Liberated Areas Stand Up) (1949), pp. 17–21.

56. William Hinton, *Fanshen: Documentary of Revolution in a Chinese Village* (New York: Vintage, 1968), p. 158.

57. Ibid., pp. 454–58.

58. Belden, *China Shakes the World*, pp. 275–317; Crook and Crook, *The First Years of Yangyi Commune*, pp. 241–42.

59. Several articles advertising marriage reform were published in the liberated areas, but no campaign to implement reform was advocated. See "Hun-yin t'iao-lieh ti chueh-ting yu t'ui-hsing" (Decision and Implementation of Marriage Regulations), in *Chung-kuo fu-nu ta fan-shen*, pp. 21–30.

60. "Decision of the CCP, CC Concerning Current Women's Work in the Liberated Zones, December 20, 1948," in *Chung-kuo fu-nu yun-tung ti chung-yao wen-chien*, pp. 4–11.

61. Crook and Crook, *The First Years of Yangyi Commune*, pp. 241–42.

62. Selden, *Yenan Way*, p. 115.

63. Mao Tse-tung, "Report on an Investigation into the Peasant Movement in Hunan," *Selected Works of Mao Tse-tung*, vol. 1, p. 29.

64. Ibid.

Chapter 6

1. Maurice Meisner, *Mao's China* (New York: Free Press, 1977), pp. 10–19.

2. See Olga Lang, *Chinese Family and Society* (New Haven: Yale University Press, 1946). For an excellent study of women workers in this period see Emily Honig, "Women Cotton Mill Workers, 1919–1949" (Ph.D. thesis, Stanford University, 1982).

3. See Mark Selden, *The Yenan Way in Revolutionary China* (Cambridge: Harvard University Press, 1971).

4. Tachai is the most famous example. Shaoshihyu, Wang Kuo-fan's "Pauper's Coop," and Li Shun-ta's Hsi-kou brigade also have been among the few most important Maoist models and they also fit this type.

5. Author's interviews with Hopeh Women's Federation cadres, summer 1978.

6. As we shall see in part 3, the old Shen-Kan-Ning Base Area seems to have had one of the worst records on marriage reform in the 1950s. Some evidence indicates that such issues as women's political participation and women's marriage rights were pursued more vigorously and successfully at the local level in some of the plains counties that had been part of the other base areas, such as Ting Hsien and Jaoyang in Hopeh. See Liu Chih, "Women of Ting Hsien Stand Up," in *Chung-kuo chieh-fang ch'u nung-ts'un fu-nu fan-shen yun tung su-miao* (The Movement in which Village Women of China's Liberated Area's Stand Up) (1949). My own interviews with women residents of Jaoyang County, Summer 1978 also suggest this. Significantly, models in promoting new family customs for women around the time of the Anti-Confucian campaign in the mid-1970s came from these plains areas.

7. Friedrich Engels, *The Origin of the Family, Private Property and the State* (New York: International, 1942).

8. Juliet Mitchell, *Women's Estate* (New York: Vintage, 1973), especially pp. 73–84. Also see Joan Landes, "'Our Praxis Of Pain': The Feminist Challenge to Socialist Thought and Practice" (Paper presented at the Midwestern Political Science Association Meetings, Chicago, Spring 1979).

9. These sorts of assumptions characterize much of the postwar study of modernization. See, for example, Cyril E. Black, *The Dynamic of Modernization* (New York: Harper and Row, 1966); Walt Rostow, *Stages of Economic Growth* (Cambridge: Harvard University Press, 1960); Daniel Lerner, *The Passing of Traditional Society* (Glencoe, Ill.: Free Press, 1958); Karl Deutsch, "Social Mobilization and Political Development," *American Political Science Review*, 55 (September 1961); Gabriel Almond and James Coleman, eds., *Politics of Developing Areas* (Princeton: Princeton University Press, 1960). For a discussion of modernization theories and sex roles, see Gail Lapidus, "Sex Roles and Modernization in Critical Perspective," in Jane Jaquette, ed., *Women in Politics* (New York: John Wiley and Sons, 1974).

Chapter 7

1. William J. Goode, *World Revolution and Family Patterns* (New York: Free Press, 1970), pp. 18–19, 56, 372–73. Eli Zaretsky, *Capitalism, the Family*

and Personal Life (New York: Harper and Row, 1976), also argues for the important role ideological forces may play in shaping change for women and the family, but he identifies somewhat different forces.

2. Joan Scott and Louise Tilly, "Women's Work and the Family in Nineteenth-Century Europe," in Charles Rosenberg, ed., *The Family in History* (Philadelphia: University of Pennsylvania Press, 1977).

3. The classic literary statement of the leading role of ideology in the repudiation of the traditional family system by intellectual youth is Pa Chin's *Family* (New York: Anchor Doubleday, 1972).

4. Maurice Meisner, *Mao's China* (New York: Free Press, 1976), chap. 2.

5. Editorial, *JMJP*, April 16, 1950.

6. An Tzu-wen, "Carry Out the Marriage Law and Wipe Out the Remnants of Feudal Thought," in *Hun-yin fa chi-ch'i yu-kuan wen-chien* (The Marriage Law and Related Documents) (Shanghai, 1950).

7. Maurice Meisner, *Li Ta-chao and the Origins of Chinese Marxism* (Cambridge: Harvard University Press, 1967); Stuart Schram, ed., *The Political Thought of Mao Tse-tung* (New York: Praeger, 1969).

8. See Goode, *World Revolution*, pp. 10–26; Wilbert E. Moore, *Industrialization and Labor* (Ithaca: Cornell University Press, 1951), chaps. 9, 10, 11; Robert Heilbronner, *The Great Ascent* (New York: Harper and Row, 1963). Such views also prevail among Marxist sociologists and social historians, though they question the "liberating" outcome of the process. See Zaretsky, *Capitalism*.

9. Editorial, *JMJP*, April 16, 1960.

10. Shih Liang, "Answers to Some Questions Concerning the Marriage Law," *HCKFN*, 11 (May 1950).

11. On the importance of redefining the political by "politicizing the personal," and on the relationship of this process to the process of consciousness-raising in the contemporary feminist movement in the United States, see Nancy McWilliams, "Contemporary Feminism, Consciousness-Raising, and Changing Views of the Political," in Jane S. Jaquette, ed., *Women and Politics* (New York: John Wiley and Sons, 1974).

12. For example, M. J. Meijer, *Marriage Law and Policy in the Chinese Peoples Republic* (Hong Kong: Hong Kong University Press, 1971). Gregory Massel comes to this conclusion about political assaults on the traditional family in Soviet Central Asia in *The Surrogate Proletariat: Moslem Women and Revolutionary Strategies in Soviet Central Asia, 1919–1929* (Princeton: Princeton University Press, 1974).

13. Goode, *World Revolution*, p. 57.

14. Teng Ying-ch'ao, "Report on the Marriage Law of the People's Republic of China," *JMJP*, May 24, 1950. (Reprinted in *Hun-yin fa chi-ch'i yu-kuan wen-chien*.)

15. Samuel Huntington discusses, in a general way, this sort of dilemma for the reformer in *Political Order in Changing Societies* (New Haven: Yale University Press, 1968), chap. 6.

Chapter 8

1. See, for example, M. J. Meijer, *Marriage Law and Policy in the People's Republic* (Hong Kong: Hong Kong University Press, 1971). Sui-ning Prudence Chou, "The Chinese Communist Policies toward Rural Women from 1949–

1955" (M.A. thesis, University of California, Berkeley, 1968). Also see Note 2 below.

2. C. K. Yang, *The Chinese Family in the Communist Revolution* (Cambridge: MIT Press, 1959), chap. 11, Janet Salaff and Judith Merkle, "Women and Revolution: The Lessons of the Soviet Union and China," in Marilyn Young, ed., *Women in China* (Ann Arbor: Center for Chinese Studies, University of Michigan, 1973), p. 163.

3. Toward the end of the marriage reform period, some directives did explicitly exempt land reform areas from marriage reform work, although such areas were few by this time. See, "Government Administrative Council Directive on the Thorough Implementation of the Marriage Law," *JMJP*, February 1, 1953.

4. William Hinton, *Fanshen: A Documentary of Revolution in a Chinese Village* (New York: Vintage, 1966), p. 457.

5. See, for example, "Resolutely Carry Out the Principle of Mobilizing Peasant Men and Women Together," editorial, *HCKFN*, 14 (September 1950); Liu Mien-chih, "The Need to Thoroughly Carry Out the Principle of Mobilizing Both Men and Women Simultaneously in Land Reform and of Defending the Legal Rights of Women," *JMJP*, December 4, 1951.

6. "Experience of Mobilizing Women during the Land Reform Movement in Pei-yueh District," in *Chung-kuo chieh-fang ch'u nung-tsun fu-nu fan-shen yun-tung su-miao* (The Movement in which Village Women of China's Liberated Areas Stand Up) (1949). Quoted excerpt translated in Chou, "Chinese Communist Policies," p. 51.

7. *JMJP*, June 30, 1950.

8. "Directive Concerning the Strengthening of Women's Work during Preparations for Land Reform," *HCKFN*, 14 (September 1950).

9. Ch'u Meng-chiao, "The Relationship between Village Women's Work and the Peasant Movement," *HCKFN*, 14 (September 1950).

10. Li Cheng, "Strengthen the Study of the Marriage Law among Sub-District (*ch'u*) and Village (*hsiang*) Cadres," *JMJP*, October 9, 1951.

11. Ibid.

12. "Women's Liberation through Struggle," *China Reconstructs* (March 1973).

13. See "The Stages of Development of Laboring Women in Kao-chuang-tse," and "Women during the Land Reform Movement in Pin County," in *Chung-kuo fu-nu ta fan-shen* (Chinese Women Stand Up) (Hong Kong: Hsin min-chu ch'u-pan she, 1949).

14. "Experience of Mobilizing Women during the Land Reform Movement in Pei-yueh District."

15. Liu Mien-chih, "The Need to Carry Out the Principle of Mobilizing both Men and Women." Also see *Chung-kuo fu-nu ta fan-shen*, pp. 16–20.

16. Ts'ai Ch'ang, "Actively Train More and Better Women Cadres," *Hsin-hua pan-yueh-k'an* (New China Semi-Monthly), November 6, 1956, cited in Janet Salaff, "Institutionalized Motivation for Fertility Limitation," in Young, *Women in China*, p. 126.

17. Margery Wolf, "Chinese Women: Old Skills in a New Context," in Michelle Rosaldo and Louise Lamphere, *Woman, Culture and Society*.

18. See, for example, Ida Pruitt, *A Daughter of Han: Autobiography of a Chinese Working Woman*. Also see the discussion in chapter 2 above.

19. For examples of such women see, William Hinton, *Fanshen* (Old Lady Wang); David and Isabel Crook, *Revolution in a Chinese Village: Ten Mile Inn*

(London: Routledge and Kegan Paul, 1959) ("Blackie"), see note 24 below; Chen Yuan-tsung, *The Dragon's Village* (New York: Pantheon, 1980) (the "Broken Shoe"). Also see chapter 5 above.

20. See chapter 5, above. Also see Chen, *The Dragon's Village*.

21. Hinton, *Fanshen*, p. 397.

22. From an interview with Teng Ying-ch'ao in Dymphna Cusack, *Chinese Women Speak* (Sydney: Angus and Robertson, 1958), p. 198.

23. See, for example, Teng Ying-ch'ao, "Land Reform and Women's New Tasks," in *Chung-kuo chieh-fang ch'u fu-nu yun-tung wen-hsien*.

24. The Crooks in their first village study describe such a woman, named Wang Hsiang, who was an exception in the village. She was a widow whose husband had been an indigent opium addict. Even while he was alive, Wang, with the help of her young son, did all of the field work on her husband's land. She was given the (less than complimentary) nickname of "Blackie" because she was suntanned "like a man" from working all day in the sun. Furthermore, her general personality traits and habits were considered inappropriately masculine and she was, therefore, morally suspect among other villagers. There were, of course, other poor women in the village whose husbands were indigent, absent, dead, or otherwise unable to support them. But they apparently had to find ways other than tilling the land to fend for themselves, such as prostitution or being rented out to other men. They too, of course, were morally suspect. Crook and Crook, *Revolution in a Chinese Village*, pp. 104–6.

25. Rae Blumberg, "Structural Factors Affecting Women's Status: A Cross-Cultural Paradigm" (Paper presented at the International Sociological Association Meetings, Toronto, August 1974).

26. See, for example, Peggy Sanday, "Female Status in the Public Domain," in Michelle Zimbalist Rosaldo and Louise Lamphere, eds., *Woman, Culture and Society* (Stanford: Stanford University Press, 1974).

27. Joan Scott and Louise Tilly, "Women's Work and the Family in Nineteenth-Century Europe" in Charles Rosenberg, ed., *The Family in History* (Philadelphia: University of Pennsylvania Press, 1977), p. 42.

28. David and Isabel Crook, *The First Years of Yangyi Commune* (London: Routledge and Kegan Paul, 1966), pp. 241–42.

29. Liu Chih, "The Women of Ting Hsien Stand Up," in *Chung-kuo chieh-fang ch'u nung-ts'un fu-nu fan-shen yun-tung su-miao*, p. 19.

30. Crook and Crook, *The First Years of Yangyi Commune*, p. 241.

31. Ch'en Yu-t'ung, "Destroy the Old Legal View in Order to Thoroughly Implement the Marriage Law," *HCKFN*, 9 (September 1952).

32. See, for example, Natalie Zemon Davis, "Ghosts, Kin, and Progeny: Some Features of Family Life in Early Modern France," *Daedalus*, Spring 1977; Scott and Tilly, "Women's Work and the Family."

33. "Women during the Land Reform Movement in Pin County," in *Chung-kuo fu-nu ta fan-shen*.

34. *Women in New China* (Peking: Foreign Languages Press, 1950).

35. Even in societies with long-standing, traditional jural rules of near sexual equality in ownership or access to the means of production and in actual participation in production, patrilineal, patrilocal marriage customs create a "sexual asymmetry" which undermines the actual power and control of women as a group. Paradigms which overemphasize socioeconomic factors tend to overlook the independent, even contradictory impact of marriage patterns. See Bridget O'Laughlin, "Meditation of Contradiction: Why Mbum

Women Do Not Eat Chicken," in Rosaldo and Lamphere, *Woman, Culture and Society*.

36. Margery Wolf, "Chinese Women: Old Skills in a New Context," in Rosaldo and Lamphere, *Woman, Culture and Society*, pp. 168–70.

37. Shih Liang, "Report of the Central Inspection Group on the Situation Concerning the Implementation of the Marriage Law," *JMJP*, July 4, 1952.

Chapter 9

1. Olga Lang, *Chinese Family and Society* (New Haven: Yale University Press, 1946), especially chaps. 9 and 10.

2. William Goode, *World Revolution and Family Patterns* (New York: Free Press, 1970), pp. 371–72.

3. This was certainly one of the major effects of land reform. Furthermore, as I discuss in part 4, one of the generally overlooked consequences of Maoism for the liberation of rural women from traditional family control and norms has been the conservative effect on the family of the distinctively Maoist effort, emerging in the late 1950s, to organize socioeconomic development so as to de-emphasize geographic mobility and urbanization with its attendant "atomization" of rooted rural dwellers.

4. Later in the 1950s, when the government was becoming increasingly concerned with rural-urban migration, young village women were often criticized for seeking marriages that would get them away from the villages into the cities where they had the prospect of living neolocally with their husbands without in-laws. See, for example, Tzu Chi, "In Handling Divorce Cases, We Must Struggle against Bourgeois Ideology," in *ECMM*, no. 65, pp. 5–11.

5. Hou Chi-ming, "Manpower, Employment and Unemployment," in Alexander Eckstein et. al., eds., *Economic Trends in Communist China* (Chicago: University of Chcago Press, 1968), pp. 365–66.

6. See, for example, Ester Boserup, *Women's Role in Economic Development* (London: Allen and Unwin, 1970); Judith Van Allen, "Memsahib, Militante, Femme Libre: Political and Apolitical Styles of Modern African Women," in Jane Jaquette, ed., *Women in Politics* (New York: John Wiley and Sons, 1971). The trends which these authors emphasize are similar to the increasing "specialization" and "differentiation" of family sex roles and functions which Talcott Parsons identifies as characteristic of the modernization process, although Parsons views these changes positively (Talcott Parsons and Robert F. Bales, *Family, Socialization, and Interaction Process* [New York, 1955]). All of these views stand in contrast to views of William Goode and others who see processes associated with industrialization as broadening women's role opportunities, helping to break down specialized, ascriptively defined female roles, increasing women's freedom from family control, and potentially (but not necessarily or completely) weakening sexual role differentiation inside and outside the family. In fact the complex processes that fall under the rubric of modernization may have contradictory effects, creating pressures toward increased sex-role "specialization" and dependence while also opening new possibilities and sources of independence for some women. Whether these processes, overall, increase or decrease women's status depends on the nature of traditional roles and on a host of specific cultural, economic, political and historical factors.

7. Lang, *Chinese Family and Society*, pp. 210–12. Lang found that the new potential economic power of women factory workers in their families had not

necessarily created parallel changes in the values and beliefs about proper women's roles, although younger women were adopting some of the new progressive ideas. She concluded that, while many women had increased their family decision-making power, they felt defensive because their new roles violated "the old Chinese idea of propriety." Lang's findings fit well with the theoretical perspective of Scott and Tilly.

8. Shih Liang, "Seriously Attend to the Thorough Implementation of the Marriage Law," *JMJP*, October 13, 1951. Also see C. K. Yang, *The Chinese Family in the Communist Revolution* (Cambridge: MIT Press, 1959), pp. 70–72. Given the fragmentary nature of reported divorce statistics it is hard to estimate the overall divorce rate and how it changed in response to marriage reform work and publicity. It does seem clear that there was an increase in the early years following the passage of the law. According to divorce figures for the years 1953 to 1956 which were reported in *JMJP* (April 13, 1957), it appears that divorces reached a peak in 1953 (1.1 million, a rate of about 2 per 1,000 population) and then fell off sharply each year until 1956 (the last year for which figures are given, when there were only 15,000). As we shall see, the divorce rate rose and fell with the rise and fall of the marriage reform campaigns. There were no overall figures given for 1951–52, but M. J. Meijer has estimated that the average yearly divorce rate for the 1950–53 period was 1.3 per 1,000 per year (*Marriage Law and Policy in the Chinese People's Republic* [Hong Kong: Hong Kong University Press, 1971], p. 114). (This is lower than the relatively high U.S. rate in 1962 of 2.2, but higher than most of Western Europe and Canada which had rates around .4 in the early 1960s.) This estimate is most likely too low because it is based on figures which probably only include court cases. Furthermore, it obscures the yearly differences (with the rate growing from 1950 to 1953) and what were probably considerable regional differences. Based on statistics given for June 1950 to June 1952, the yearly divorce rate in Kiangsi Province was a very high 4.5 (based on an estimated population of 16 million). See "Implementation of the Marriage Law in Different Parts of the Country Is Very Uneven," NCNA, Peking, January 31, 1953, translated in *CB*, no. 236. This was a very high rate even by international standards. By past Chinese standards it was, of course, extremely high.

9. Shih Liang, "Seriously Attend to the Thorough Implementation of the Marriage Law."

10. *Shanghai News*, June 28, 1951, in *SCMP*, no. 132, pp. 20–21; Shih Liang, "Seriously Attend to the Thorough Implementation of the Marriage Law"; *Hun-yin fa chi-ch'i yu-kuan wen-hsien* (The Marriage Law and Related Documents) (Shanghai, 1950), p. 72.

11. *JMJP*, March 29, 1951, p. 2.

12. Sidney D. Gamble, *Ting Hsien: A North China Rural Community* (Stanford: Stanford University Press, 1968), pp. 379–80. Lang, *Chinese Family and Society*, pp. 122–23.

13. Teng Ying-ch'ao, "Report on the Marriage Law of the People's Republic of China," *JMJP*, May 24, 1950.

14. See, for example, Shih Liang, "Answers to Some Questions Concerning the Marriage Law," *HCKFN*, 11 (May 1950).

15. For examples and references see Yang, *Chinese Family*, pp. 33–34.

16. *Hun-yin fa hsin-hua* (New Talks on the Marriage Law) (Shanghai, 1950), pp. 9–10, cited by Yang, *Chinese Family*, p. 34.

17. For example, see *Shanghai News*, June 25, 1951, in *SCMP*, no. 132, p. 20.

18. For an interesting study of the changes in the image of women in literature, see Chin Ai-li, "Family Relations in Modern Chinese Fiction," in Maurice Freedman, ed., *Family and Kinship in Chinese Society* (Stanford: Stanford University Press, 1970).

19. See, for example, Liu Ching-fan, "The Thorough Implementation of the Marriage Law" (broadcast speech), NCNA, Peking, March 19, 1953, translated in *CB*, no. 243, pp. 10–12.

20. See, for example, Min Kang-hou, "Judicial Cadres Must Correctly and Promptly Dispose of Cases of Marriage Disputes," *HCKFN*, 10 (October 1951); *JMJP*, October 9, 1951, p. 3. For an example where cadres prevented the local militia from taking action against the free courtship of a young couple, see Tzu Ping, "Wang Kuei-ying: Model Cadre in the Implementation of the Marriage Law," *HCKFN*, 1 (January 1953).

21. Teng, "Report of the Marriage Law of the People's Republic of China."

22. The directive appeared in *Ch'ang-chiang jih-pao*, July 5, 1950, paraphrased in Meijer, *Marriage Law*, pp. 120–21.

23. This potential dilemma was implicit in the way the cadres of Long Bow Village handled the village's first divorce case, although in this instance the cadres were successful in winning some popular support and avoided having to make the choice. William Hinton describes the divorce proceedings: At the outset of the case, "if the work team could have granted Hsien-e a divorce, they would have done so without any public spectacle. But the question was not so simple. The attitude of all the villagers had to be taken into account. Divorce had never before been sanctioned in Long Bow. . . . It could be taken for granted that the overwhelming majority of men would oppose such a step. . . . If a divorce was to be granted a much wider section of the female population had to be mobilized [to support Hsien-e]." Hsien-e therefore had to present her case before a mass meeting (a brave act which many women would hesitate to follow). A persuasive and sympathetic figure, the young woman was able, after some discussion and debate, to win over a large segment of the women and a small group of progressive men (seemingly in part because her husband was disliked by them). As it turned out, this was a most effective way of introducing women's rights of divorce to the village. It helped educate other women about their new rights and the divorce was legitimized by the public support of at least a significant minority of villagers as well as village leaders. But the fact remains that this process of change precariously tied the woman's rights, indeed her life, to her own and the cadres' ability to win over some segment of public opinion. William Hinton, *Fanshen* (New York: Vintage, 1966), pp. 454–60.

24. For a post-Cultural Revolution discussion of Chinese Marxism in general and, in particular, of Mao the Leninist verses Mao the populist that seeks to explain the balance between these contradictory strains see Introduction to Stuart Schram, ed., *Authority, Participation and Cultural Change in China* (Cambridge: Cambridge University Press, 1973), pp. 1–108.

25. Tzu Ping, "Wang Kuei-ying: Model Cadre."

26. Author's interview, June 1971. Cf. Edward Friedman, "Primitive Rebel versus Modern Revolutionary: A Case of Mistaken Identity?" (Paper presented at the Annual Meeting of the Association for Asian Studies, Boston, 1974.)

27. See Hinton, *Fanshen*, pp. 353–54 for an account of the reaction of one older woman who was soon to be a mother-in-law to the notion of according

higher status to daughters-in-law in the family and to the perceived threat of free-choice marriage.

28. David and Isabel Crook, *Revolution in a Chinese Village* (London: Routledge and Kegan Paul, 1959), pp. 102–3.

29. Obviously many male cadres found it easier to accept marriage and family reform as an attack on the mother-in-law than on the patriarch. This not only helped protect men but was congruent with traditional notions about women. Traditional myths about the terrible powers of women to lead men astray, to bring moral decline and even dynastic ruin, often blamed women for the cruel or foolish acts of men. These sorts of attitudes often informed the attitudes toward the mother-in-law in marriage reform cases. For example, a village leader after witnessing the trial and execution of a mother-in-law and her husband for the murder of their daughter-in-law commented on how he had become enlightened about the need for marriage reform at the trial and would carry the message back to his village. The message was, he said, "there are many cruel mothers-in-law in our village . . . I now know how to tell [oppressed women] to rebel against them." He did not mention learning about cruel fathers-in-law or the need to rebel against patriarchal authority (*JMJP*, October 22, 1951, p. 3).

30. "Outline of Propaganda on the Thorough Implementation of the Marriage Law," NCNA, Peking, February 25, 1953, translated in *CB*, no. 236, pp. 22–29.

31. See chapter 2, note 14, and the discussion in the text.

32. On proscribing the custom of a woman's family "adopting a son-in-law" (*chui-fu*) see, Meijer, *Marriage Law*, pp. 59, 72, 285.

33. See, for example, William Parish and Martin Whyte, *Village and Family in Contemporary China* (Chicago: University of Chicago Press, 1978), p. 136.

34. Li Cheng, "Strengthen the Study of the Marriage Law among Subdistrict and Village Cadres," *JMJP*, October 9, 1951.

35. See, for example, "Be Determined in the Thorough Implementation of the Marriage Law and the Protection of Women's Rights," editorial, *JMJP*, September 29, 1951; "Resolutely Protect Women's Lives and Security," editorial, *JMJP*, December 6, 1951.

36. All three reports appeared in *Ch'ang-chiang jih-pao*, August 30, 1951. Partial translations of the Government Council's and Party Bureau's reports appear in Meijer, *Marriage Law*, pp. 121–22. The Women's Federation report is translated in full in *CB*, no. 136, pp. 37–39.

37. *CB*, no. 136, pp. 37–39.

38. These kinds of attitudes and the vulnerability of women cadres to accusations against their moral character are still problems in rural areas. See Janet Salaff, "Institutionalized Motivation for Fertility Limitation in China," *Population Studies*, 26, no. 2 (July 1972).

39. Margery Wolf, "Women and Suicide in China," in Margery Wolf and Roxane Witke, eds., *Women in Chinese Society* (Stanford: Stanford University Press, 1975).

40. Ch'en Yu-t'ung, "Destroy the Old Legal View in Order to Thoroughly Implement the Marriage Law," *HCKFN*, 9 (September 1952).

41. See, for example, "Women Still Persecuted and Murdered as Marriage Law Fails to Be Thoroughly Implemented," NCNA, in *SCMP*, no. 499, pp. 22–24.

42. *JMJP*, May 30, 1953, p. 3; *JMJP*, February 25, 1953, p. 2.

43. "Government Administrative Council Directive on the Investigation of Conditions Relating to the Implementation of the Marriage Law," *JMJP*, September 29, 1951.

44. Shih Liang, "Report of the Central Inspection Group on the Situation Concerning the Implementation of the Marriage Law."

45. See chapter 1, note 17. On the significance for women of the bride price/dowry ratio also see chapter 1.

46. "Implementation of the Marriage Law in Different Parts of the Country Is Very Uneven," *Kuang-ming jih-pao* (Peking), January 31, 1953; translated in *CB*, no. 236.

47. Li Cheng, "Strengthen the Study of the Marriage Law."

48. Ma Chao-kao, "Basic Understanding of the Campaign for the Implementation of the Marriage Law," *Hsin chien-she* (New Reconstruction), February 1953, translated in *Chinese Communist Propaganda Review*, no. 36. Also see Shih Liang, "Seriously Attend to the Thorough Implementation of the Marriage Law."

49. "Implementation of the Marriage Law in Different Parts of the Country Is Very Uneven."

50. The account of the model woman cadre in Lu Shan County describes the kind of hard, continuous, time-consuming work which could lead to some success in encouraging women and young people, preventing violence, and easing the fears of traditional-minded peasants. See Tzu Ping, "Wang Kuei-ying: Model Cadre."

Chapter 10

1. Mao Chao-kao, "Basic Understanding of the Campaign for the Implementation of the Marriage Law," *Hsin chien-she* (New Reconstruction), no. 2 (February 1953), in *Chinese Communist Propaganda Review*, no. 36.

2. See, for example, Wang Tse-ying, "Why We Should Push the Campaign for the Thorough Implementation of the Marriage Law," *Nan-fang jih-pao* (Southern Daily), January 25, 1953, translated in *CB*, no. 37, pp. 24–25.

3. Edward Friedman, *Backward toward Revolution* (Berkeley: University of California Press, 1974), pp. 117–18. Also see C. S. Chen and C. P. Ridley, *Rural People's Communes in Lien-chang* (Stanford: Hoover Institution Press, 1969).

4. "Government Administrative Council Directive on the Thorough Implementation of the Marriage Law," NCNA, Peking, February 1, 1953, translated in *CB*, no. 236.

5. "Cadres Trained throughout the Country for Marriage Law Publicity Campaign," *JMJP*, March 19, 1953.

6. For a report on one keypoint experimental area, carried out in Yunnan Province in August 1952, see Liang Hung, "Experience in the Implementation of the Marriage Law in Cheng Kung County, Yunnan Province," *HCKFN*, no. 1 (January 1953).

7. "Government Administrative Council Directive on the Thorough Implementation of the Marriage Law."

8. It is difficult to determine whether Ho Hsiang-ning was very active in this capacity. Nonetheless, her membership is symbolically important, since, as head of the KMT Central Women's Department during the KMT-CCP alliance, she was in charge of the first efforts to carry out marriage reform and she was a major early spokesperson for the importance of such reforms. Also significant

was the conspicuous absence from committee membership of Ts'ai Ch'ang, still the only woman Communist Party Central Committee member at the time. In fact, throughout the early 1950s, Ts'ai was never closely associated with marriage reform and rarely even discussed it in her public speeches. It is likely that her absence from the marriage reform front reflected her disinclination to become involved as an advocate of the policies of the period, given her history as a major opponent of "narrow bourgeois feminism"—a charge she had, more than once, levelled at those who placed emphasis on family reform issues, most notably in Yenan. By contrast, Teng Ying-ch'ao emerged as a major marriage reform spokesperson in the early 1950s. She had never been closely associated with the antifeminist Yenan policies and was in fact absent from Yenan during much of that period. Furthermore, as we have seen, her earliest political activity was as an organizer of a women's rights group among teachers and students in Tientsin and she had been active in Ho's KMT-CCP Central Women's Department in 1925–27. Whatever the reason for Ts'ai's lack of active involvement in marriage reform in the 1950s, it is significant that China's most highly placed woman in the political hierarchy was not an active public advocate of the marriage reform policies of this period.

9. "Outline of Propaganda on the Thorough Implementation of the Marriage Law," NCNA, February 25, 1953, in *CB*, no. 236.

10. For example, when officials in Tientsin submitted that their preparations had been completed, the committee's work teams found that, owing to the "careless manner in which the original training scheme was carried out," the work had to be started again ("Cadres Trained throughout the Country for Marriage Law Publicity Campaign").

11. Victor Li, "Chinese Law and Society," in Michael Oksenberg, ed., *China's Developmental Experience*, New York Academy of Political Science, Proceedings, vol. 31, no. 1 (New York, 1973).

12. "All-China Democratic Women's Federation Decision on Changes in Structures and Tasks," NCNA, Peking, December 20, 1952, in *SCMP*, no. 477.

13. The December 26 directive is referred to in the second directive issued by the Central Committee on February 18, 1953.

14. See note 4 above.

15. "Supplementary Directive of the Central Committee, Chinese Communist Party, on the Movement for the Thorough Implementation of the Marriage Law," NCNA, Peking, February 19, 1953, translated in *CB*, no. 236.

16. "National Committee on Campaign for Thorough Implementation of Marriage Law Holds Second Session," NCNA, Peking, March 18, 1953, in *SCMP*, no. 535.

17. Liu Ching-fan, "The Thorough Implementation of the Marriage Law" (broadcast speech), *NCNA*, Peking, March 19, 1953, in *CB*, no. 243, pp. 10–12.

18. Ibid.

19. Tzu Ping, "Wang Kuei-ying: Model Cadre in the Implementation of the Marriage Law," *HCKFN*, no. 1 (January 1953).

20. Liang Hung, "Experience in the Implementation of the Marriage Law" in Cheng Kung County, Yunnan Province," *HCKFN*, no. 1 (January 1953).

21. Liu, "The Thorough Implementation of the Marriage Law."

22. See note 9 above.

23. This was presumably due in part to the death of Stalin and the official mourning period which occupied most newspaper space for several days around March 7 and which prompted the cancellation of March 8th Internation-

al Women's Day celebrations. It was also due in part to the failure of cadres in some areas to complete their campaign preparations on time.

24. Liu Ching-fan, "General Summary Report on the Movement for the Thorough Implementation of the Marriage Law," *JMJP*, November 19, 1953. Also see "Achievements throughout Country in Movement to Publicize Marriage Law," NCNA, Peking, May 6, 1953, in *CB*, no. 243.

25. "Achievements throughout the Country in Movement to Publicize Marriage Law."

26. Ibid.

27. See chapter 9, note 8.

28. "The Thorough Implementation of the Marriage Law Is a Very Important Regular Task," editorial, *JMJP*, May 6, 1953.

29. See note 24 above.

30. For a discussion of welfare policies and their implications for the family see William Parish and Martin Whyte, *Village and Family in Contemporary China* (Chicago: University of Chicago Press, 1978), pp. 74–75.

31. See, for example, Tzu Chi, "In the Handling of Divorce Cases, We Must Struggle against Bourgeois Ideology," in *ECMM*, no. 65, pp. 5–11.

32. See chapter 9, note 8.

33. See, for example, "Arranged Buying and Selling Marriages Are Serious in Shensi Villages," *CKCNP*, August 30, 1956; also see "Give Correct Guidance to the Marriage and Love Problems of Rural Youth," *CKCN*, no. 21 (November 1, 1956), translated in *ECMM*, no. 66, pp. 13–15.

Chapter 11

1. Friedrich Engels, *The Origins of the Family, Private Property and the State* (New York: International, 1942), quoted in Foreword to *New Women in New China* (Peking: Foreign Languages Press, 1972), p. 4.

2. Lu Yu-lan, "A Liberated Woman Speaks," in *New Women in New China*, pp. 7–8.

3. Editorial, "Mobilize Women to Join the Cooperativization Movement," *JMJP*, November 5, 1955.

4. Vivienne Shue, *Peasant China in Transition: The Dynamics of Development toward Socialism, 1949–1956* (Berkeley: University of California Press, 1980), p. 155.

5. Marina Thorborg, "Chinese Employment Policy in 1949–78, with Special Emphasis on Women in Rural Production," in United States Congress, Joint Economic Committee, *Chinese Economy Post-Mao* (Washington, D.C.: U.S. Government Printing Office, 1978), p. 576.

6. "Women of the Whole Country Realize the Draft Program for National Agricultural Development, 1956–67," *JMJP*, March 9, 1956.

7. See, for example, An Tzu-wen, "A Correct Approach to the Problem of the Retirement of Women Cadres," *CKFN*, no. 2 (February 1958). Also see, Delia Davin, "The Implications of Some Aspects of CCP Policy towards Urban Women in the 1950s," *Modern China*, 1, no. 4 (October 1975).

8. John Philip Emerson, "Employment in Mainland China: Problems and Prospects," in United States Congress, Joint Economic Committee, *An Economic Profile of Mainland China* (New York: Praeger, 1968), pp. 433–34. Also see Hou Chi-ming, "Manpower, Employment and Unemployment," in Alexander Eckstein et. al., eds., *Economic Trends in Communist China* (Chicago: Aldine, 1968), p. 380.

9. Thorborg, "Chinese Employment," pp. 570–71.

10. "The People's Commune Is an Excellent Form of Organization for the Complete Emancipation of Women," *Hung-ch'i* (Red Flag), no. 5 (March 1, 1960).

11. Thorborg, "Chinese Employment," p. 582.

12. See, for example, Ch'en Chien-wei, "The Breaking Down of the System of Feudal Patriarchy," *Hopeh Jih-pao* (Hopeh Daily), April 8, 1959, in *SCMP*, no. 2039; Feng Ting, "The Patriarchal System and the Family," *CKCN*, no. 23 (December 1, 1958), in *ECMM*, no. 157.

13. Maurice Meisner, *Mao's China: History of the People's Republic of China* (New York: Free Press, 1977), p. 204.

14. See, for example, Juliet Mitchell, *Woman's Estate* (London: Penguin, 1971); Sheila Rowbotham, *Women, Resistance and Revolution* (New York: Vintage, 1974); Gayle Rubin, "The Traffic in Women: Notes on 'The Political Economy of Sex,'" in Rayna Reiter, *Toward an Anthropology of Women* (New York: Monthly Review Press, 1975).

15. Meisner, *Mao's China*, p. 234.

16. For a discussion of these policies in the Great Leap and the Cultural Revolution, see Stephen Andors, "Revolution and Modernization: Man and Machine in Industrializing Societies, the Chinese Case," in Edward Friedman and Mark Selden, eds., *America's Asia: Dissenting Essays on Asian-American Relations* (New York: Vintage, 1969).

17. Shue, *Peasant China* pp. 153–63.

18. G. William Skinner, "Marketing and Social Structure in Rural China," *Journal of Asian Studies*, 24, nos. 1, 2 and 3 (1964–65).

19. Meisner, *Mao's China*, pp. 242–43; Mark Selden, *The People's Republic of China: A Documentary History of Revolutionary China* (New York: Monthly Review Press, 1979), pp. 98–99.

20. Thorborg, "Chinese Employment," p. 584.

21. See, for example, Yang Liu, "Reform of Marriage and Family Systems in China," *Peking Review*, 7, no. 11, (March 13, 1964), p. 19.

22. Thorborg, "Chinese Employment," p. 596.

23. Statistics on rural women's labor participation for Hopeh Province in the 1970s, obtained in my interviews with leaders of the Hopeh Women's Federation, July 1978, indicate that women's participation rates increased from around 75 percent in the early 1970s to nearly 90 percent by 1978. Women were said to average 188 work days per year, compared to an average of 255 for the male labor force.

24. See, for example, William Parish and Martin Whyte, *Village and Family in Contemporary China* (Chicago: University of Chicago Press, 1978), p. 205.

25. Jean Adams, "The Utilization of 'Surplus' Labor in the People's Republic of China," *Bulletin of Concerned Asian Scholars*, 11, no. 4, (1979); Maria Mies, "Capitalist Development and Subsistence Reproduction: Rural Women in India," *Bulletin of Concerned Asian Scholars*, 12, no. 1 (1980); Irene Tinker, "The Adverse Impact of Development on Women," in Irene Tinker and Michele Bo Bramson, eds., *Women and World Development* (Washington, D.C.: Overseas Development Council, 1976).

26. See Xue Mu-qiao, *China's Socialist Economy* (Peking: Foreign Languages Press, 1981), pp. 41–43.

27. Thorborg, "Chinese Employment," p. 599.

28. See, for example, "Criticize Lack of Concern for Women," *JMJP*, May 16, 1956; "Labor Protection for Women Peasants," NCNA, December 11,

1956, in *SCMP*, no. 1432; "Teng Ying-ch'ao on Women Work at September 22nd Meeting of the Party Congress," NCNA, September 22, 1956, in *SCMP*, no. 1377.

29. See, for example, "She Holds Thirteen Jobs!" October 1, 1956, *ECMM*, no. 55, p. 16; *Shih-ssu-ke nu hsien-chin sheng-ch'an-che* (Fourteen Advanced Women Producers) (Peking: Women of China Magazine Publishing House, 1956).

30. See "National Women's Draft Program for Realizing the 'National Program for Agriculture'—Proposed by All China Democratic Women's Federation," NCNA, March 8, 1956, in *SCMP*, no. 1258; "Teng Ying-ch'ao on Women's Work at September 22nd Meeting of the Party Congress." Also see "How to Correctly Handle 'Equal Pay for Equal Work' among Men and Women," *JMJP*, September 9, 1956; Thorborg, Chinese Employment," pp. 544–47.

31. Thorborg, "Chinese Employment," p. 566.

32. Li Teh-ch'uan, "Maintain Firm Support for Women's Health," *CKFN*, no. 3 (1959), p. 1. Also see Phyllis Andors, "Social Revolution and Woman's Emancipation: China during the Great Leap Forward," *Bulletin of Concerned Asian Scholars*, 7, no. 1 (January-March 1975).

33. See Phyllis Andors, "Social Revolution," p. 37.

34. Parish and Whyte, *Village and Family*, p. 81.

35. Author's interviews, July 1978.

36. Barbara Wolfe Jancar, *Women under Communism* (Baltimore: Johns Hopkins University Press, 1978).

37. Parish and Whyte, *Village and Family*, pp. 204, 244.

38. See, for example, Fang Shu-min, "The Moon on a Frosty Morning," in W. J. F. Jenner, trans., *Modern Chinese Short Stories* (London: Oxford University Press, 1970). Also see, Chin-Ai-li, "Family Relations in Modern Chinese Fiction," in Maurice Freedman, *Family and Kinship in Chinese Society* (Stanford: Stanford University Press, 1970).

39. Eli Zaretsky, *Capitalism, the Family and Personal Life* (New York: Harper and Row, 1976), especially chap. 2. For the classical Marxist view, see Karl Marx, *The Communist Manifesto*.

40. Some critics add to this the value to capitalism of using social cleavages and prejudices as a basis for "labor segmentation" which helps capital control labor. See Richard Evans, David Gordon and Michael Reich, eds., *Labor Market Segmentation* (Lexington, Mass.: C. D. Heath, 1976).

41. For an excellent discussion of the way women's position in the labor force has aided state accumulation see Batya Weinbaum, "Women in Transition to Socialism: Perspectives on the Chinese Case," *Review of Radical Political Economics*, 8, no. 1 (Spring 1976).

42. Thorborg, "Chinese Employment," p. 604.

43. Women on average put in longer days of work than men. See Parish and Whyte, *Village and Family*, pp. 204–5.

44. Shulamith Firestone, *The Dialectics of Sex: The Case for Feminist Revolution* (London: Cape, 1971), p. 248.

Chapter 12

1. For a typical example of a Cultural Revolution article illustrating these themes, see "Working Women Resolutely Following Chairman Mao's Road," *JMJP*, March 17, 1968.

2. Wan Mu-ch'un, "How to Look at the Women Question," *Hung-ch'i* (Red Flag), no. 20 (October 16, 1964), reprinted in *JMJP*, October 28, 1964. A translation of the article appears in *JPRS*, November 23, 1964.

3. "What Do Women Live For?" *CKFN*, nos. 6–9 (June–September 1963). Also see, "The Relationship between Work, Children and Household Tasks Should Be Treated in a Revolutionary Way," *CKFN*, no. 11 (November 1963).

4. Wan Mu-ch'un, "How to Look at the Women Question."

5. For criticism of Tung Pien, see, *CKFN*, no. 8 (August 1966). Also see, "Chairman Mao Gives Inscription to *Women of China* Magazine," *JMJP*, August 25, 1966.

6. Author's interviews with Wang Fu-chen, then member of Shanghai's Revolutionary Committee, Wu Kuei-hsien, member of the Central Committee and other national women leaders, July 1971.

7. For example, the Cultural Revolution's adaptations of the Model Revolutionary Ballets *Red Detachment of Women* and *White-Haired Girl* eliminated references and incidents which dealt too directly with female sexuality, including intimations of how women in the "old society" were brutalized through rape. The movie *Li Shuang Shuang*, made in the 1950s, which portrayed a young peasant woman's struggle with her feudal-minded (but ultimately educable) husband over the unequal distribution of household chores and the unfair treatment of women in the village labor force, was criticized and banned during the Cultural Revolution for dwelling on "petty bourgeois" personal matters and thereby degrading women!

8. Janet Salaff, "Institutionalized Motivation for Fertility Limitation," in Marilyn Young, ed., *Women in China: Studies in Social Change and Feminism* (Ann Arbor: Center for Chinese Studies, University of Michigan, 1973).

9. For a detailed personal account of the experiences of a Red Guard, see, Gordon Bennett and Ronald Montaperto, *Red Guard: The Political Biography of Dai Hsiao-ai* (New York: Doubleday, 1971).

10. Author's interviews with former Red Guards/"sent-down youth," Hong Kong, 1978. In Hong Kong, in 1978–79, I interviewed a total of 22 people who had been "sent-down youth" in the late 1960s and early 1970s, mostly in Kwangtung. Also see, Parish and Whyte, *Village and Family*, p. 170.

11. Parish and Whyte, *Village and Family*, p. 170. Several similar incidents were reported to me in interviews with "sent-down youth," Hong Kong, 1978. Such incidents were not confined to rural areas. A young man interviewed in China in 1980 reported that in 1970 he was arrested in Nanking by local security forces when he was found alone with his "girlfriend" listening to old waltz records. The charges against him included listening to "pornographic music" and "engaging in chaotic relations with the opposite sex." In 1980, when the leadership was attempting to clear the records of those unjustly charged during the Cultural Revolution, he successfully appealed to have his record purged of the antisocialist label that had resulted from the arrest.

12. See, for example, Ke Ch'ang-yueh, "Do Not Start Making Love (sic) Too Early," *Chung-hsueh-sheng* (Middle School Student), no. 4 (April 1956), in *ECMM*, no. 41.

13. See, for example, Tzu Chi, "In the Handling of Divorce Cases, We Must Struggle against Bourgeois Ideology," *Hua-tung cheng-fa hsueh-pao* (East China Journal of Political Science and Law), no. 3 (December 15, 1956), in *ECMM*, no. 65.

14. See, for example, "Give Correct Guidance to the Marriage and Love Problems of Rural Youth," *CKCN*, no. 21 (November 1, 1956), in *ECMM*, no.

65; and "Will Young Women Working Together with Men Bring Disrepute to the Family?" *CKCNP*, October 27, 1964, in *SCMP*, no. 3339.

15. See, for example, "Youth of Luching Commune Take the Lead in Eliminating Outmoded Habits and Customs," *CKCNP*, May 16, 1964, in *SCMP*, no. 3237; Lo Tung-lin, "How I Broke from Outmoded Rules and Old Customs in Conducting My Wedding," *CKCNP*, November 19, 1964, in *SCMP*, no. 3352.

16. Hsuan-hua County, Hopeh, Revolutionary Committee Investigation Group, "How to Realize Equal Pay for Equal Work among Men and Women," *Hung-ch'i*, no. 3 (1972). The Hopeh Women's Federation cadres interviewed by the author in 1978 reported that charges of "bourgeois economism" and "putting work points in command" plagued their provincewide efforts to mobilize village women to demand equal pay in the mid-1970s.

17. Heilungchiang Revolutionary Committee and Lan-hsi County Revolutionary Committee Investigation Group, "Village Women are a Great Revolutionary Force," *Hung-ch'i*, no. 10 (1969), reprinted in *JMJP*, October 18, 1969.

18. Although I know of no published account of this directive, its existence was widely reported in interviews in China in 1971 and later by informants who were working in the countryside at the time.

19. For specific cases of women's increased political participation in the wake of the Cultural Revolution, see Committee of Concerned Asian Scholars, *China! Inside the People's Republic* (New York: Bantam, 1971); Jan Myrdal, *China: The Revolution Continued* (New York: Vintage, 1970); Kansu Provincial Service (Lanchow), "Kansu Women's Federation Lauds the Historic Role of Women," *FBIS*, February 12, 1974. For general estimates and statistics on women's participation after the Cultural Revolution see Salaff, "Institutionalized Motivation for Fertility Limitation"; Joan Maloney, "Chinese Women and Party Leadership: The Impact of the Cultural Revolution," *Current Scene*, 19, no. 4 (1972); Ying Kuei-fang, "The Current Women's Movement on the Chinese Mainland," *Issues and Studies*, no. 10 (July 1974).

20. Myrdal, *China: The Revolution Continued*, pp. 137–38.

21. Author's interviews, Hong Kong, 1978.

22. Salaff, "Institutionalized Motivation," pp. 119–20.

23. See chapter 5, note 19 for the basis of this earlier estimate.

24. Chang Yun, "Speech at Rally Held by Women of All Circles in Peking to Mark the International Women's Day on March 8," *JMJP*, March 9, 1956, in *SCMP*, no. 1258.

25. Peggy Sanday, "Female Status in the Public Domain," in Michelle Zimbalist Rosaldo and Louise Lamphere, eds., *Woman, Culture and Society* (Stanford: Stanford University Press, 1974).

26. Karen Sachs, "Engels Revisited: Women, Organization of Production and Private Property," in Rosaldo and Lamphere, *Woman, Culture and Society*; Rae Blumberg, "Structural Factors Affecting Women's Status: A Cross-cultural Paradigm" (Paper presented at the International Sociological Association Meetings, Toronto, August 1974).

27. Sanday, "Female Status," p. 200.

28. On a return visit to Hung-ch'iao commune near Shanghai in 1980, I found that the female representation on commune and brigade leadership bodies had declined since my first visit there in 1971. The findings of the 1971 visit are reported in Committee of Concerned Asian Scholars, *China!* Women's representation at the highest levels of the Party, the Presidium and Central Committee, declined somewhat between the Tenth and Eleventh Party Con-

gresses. For the Eleventh Party Congress figures, see, *Beijing Review*, no. 35 (August 26, 1977), p. 14.

29. "Will Young Women Working Together with Young Men Bring Disrepute to the Family?"

30. Salaff, "Institutionalized Motivation," pp. 118–19.

31. Parish and Whyte, *Village and Family*, pp. 169–72; Jack Chen, *A Year in Upper Felicity* (New York: Macmillan, 1973), pp. 72–74. In response to inquiries I have made on visits to thirteen communes and brigades, mostly since 1977, informants in all claimed that patrilocal residence was nearly universal and in all but one, that village exogamy continued to be the norm, although not exclusively so in some places. In the one exceptional case, Wukung brigade in central Hopeh, a household survey showed a significant breakdown in village exogamy in the last ten years. Wukung is a large, multilineage, model village and is the subject of an upcoming book by Edward Friedman, Paul Pickowicz, Mark Selden and myself.

32. Jan Myrdal, *Report from a Chinese Village* (New York: Signet, 1965), pp. 243, 245; Myrdal, *China: The Revolution Continued*, pp. 132–33.

33. Hugh Baker, *Chinese Family and Kinship* (New York: Columbia University Press, 1979).

34. See Salaff, "Institutionalize Motivation," pp. 119–20. Also see chapter 5 above.

35. Norma Diamond, "Collectivization, Kinship and the Status of Women in Rural China," *Bulletin of Concerned Asian Scholars*, 7, no. 1 (January–March 1975).

36. Parish and Whyte, *Village and Family*, p. 242.

37. Ta-ho Brigade Party Committee, Hsin-hsu Commune, Ching-hsi County, Kwangtung, "Pay Attention to Developing Women Party Members," *JMJP*, September 13, 1971.

38. See, for example, "Determining to Pass a New Spring Festival of Reforming Customs," *Kung-jen Jih-pao* (Workers Daily), Peking, February 7, 1964, in *SCMP*, no. 3194; Lo Tung-lin, "How I Broke from Outmoded Rules and Old Customs in Conducting My Wedding,"

39. Elizabeth Croll, *Feminism and Socialism in China* (London: Routledge and Kegan Paul, 1978); Judith Stacey, "When Patriarchy Kowtows: The Significance of the Chinese Family Revolution for Feminist Theory," *Feminist Studies*, 2, no. 43 (1975).

40. An example of this exceptional view is Hunan Provincial Party Committee Writing Group, "Bring the Role of Women in to Full Play in Revolution and Construction," *Hung-ch'i*, no. 10 (September 1, 1971).

Chapter 13

1. See, for example, Hunan Provincial Party Committee Writing Group, "Bring the Role of Women into Full Play in Revolution and Construction," *Hung-ch'i* (Red Flag), no. 10 (September 1, 1971); Ta-ho Brigade Party Committee, Hsin-hsu Commune, Ching-hsi County, Kwangtung, "Pay Attention to Developing Women Party Members," *JMJP*, September 13, 1971.

2. Soong Ching-ling, "Women's Liberation in China," *Peking Review*, no. 6 (February 11, 1972).

3. For example, in 1956 the federation was active in calling attention to the abuse of female labor and unfair remuneration practices in the cooperatives. See, "National Women's Draft Program for Realizing the National Program for

Agriculture—A Proposal by the All China Women's Federation," NCNA, Peking, March 8, 1956, in *SCMP*, no. 1258.

4. Author's interview with Women's Federation cadres, July 1978.

5. Merle Goldman, "China's Anti-Confucian Campaign, 1973–74," *China Quarterly*, no. 63 (September 1975).

6. Hsiaochinchuang was widely hailed in the media in the mid-1970s and, like other national models, cadres from around the country were sent there to study their experience. See, for example, Chou Ke-chou, "How Our Village Got Equal Pay for Equal Work," *China Reconstructs*, March 1975; "Tientsin Brigade: 'Ten New Things'," *FBIS*, August 7, 1974.

7. Kansu Provincial Service (Lanchow), "Lanchow Women Criticize Confucian Concepts of Women's Role," *FBIS*, August 6, 1974.

8. Chou Ke-chou, "How Our Village Got Equal Pay"; Joan Hinton, "Politics and Marriage," *New China*, June 1976. The latter is an account of the Anti-Confucian campaign in a village near Peking where Joan Hinton was living.

9. Heiliungchiang Provincial Service (Harbin), "Heilungchiang Women's Federation Holds Criticism Meeting," *FBIS*, August 7, 1974. See also, "Honan Daily Publishes Letters on New Marriage Concept," *FBIS*, January 7, 1974; "Oppose Arbitrary Marriage," *Nan-fang jih-pao* (Southern Daily), February 8, 1975, in *Union Research Service*, 79, no. 13; "Inner Mongolia Girls Criticize and Dissolve Childhood Marriage Plans," *FBIS*, March 15, 1974.

10. *New Republic*, February 27, 1965, pp. 17–23.

11. See William Parish and Martin Whyte, *Village and Family in Contemporary China* (Chicago: University of Chicago Press, 1978), p. 186.

12. See, for example, "Is a Daughter-in-law Obliged to Support Her Father and Mother-in-law?" *CKCNP*, May 12, 1962, in *SCMP*, no. 2756.

13. Deborah Davis-Friedmann, "Strategies for Aging: Interdependence Between Generations in the Transition to Socialism," *Contemporary China*, 1, no. 6 (March 1977).

14. "Preparing a Wedding the New Way," *Nan-fang jih-pao*, January 18, 1975; "Dare to Do Away with Old Customs," *Nan-fang jih-pao*, February 8, 1975, in *Union Research Service*, 79, no. 13.

15. "Dare to Do Away with Old Customs."

16. Ibid.

17. "Destroy Old Habits, Establish New Customs: An Investigation of the Promotion of Matrilocal Marriage in Ting Hsien," *JMJP*, March 14, 1975.

18. The leftist slogan "dare to swim against the tide," which was often used during the period and often accompanied calls to women and young people to "fight old customs" or "bourgeois tendencies," was cynically mispronounced as a joke in some circles. The mispronunciation rendered the meaning of the slogan, "dare to swim against whom?" (Author's interviews, 1978).

19. Author's interviews, Hong Kong, 1978. Most of the 22 "sent-down youth" interviewed were scattered in Kwangtung villages, mostly in the Pearl River delta. Parish and Whyte's interviews also indicated that the campaign was not very significant in the Kwangtung villages for which they obtained information during the period of the campaign.

20. Author's interviews with Hopeh Women's Federation cadres, Shihchiachuang, July 1978.

21. According to the Hopeh federation's statistics, 36 percent of the brigades in the province had year-round nurseries and 80 percent had kindergartens, the

majority of which had been established on a full-time basis in the wake of its campaign in 1974. In seven prefectures, 82 percent of the brigades were reported to have met the federation's criteria for implementing an equal pay policy for women. While these criteria were meaningful, they did not strictly require that men and women average the same pay. If at least 60 percent of the female work force was ranked at the highest two work-point grades (10 and 9.5 work points per labor day in most places), the brigade was considered to be implementing the policy. The percentage of men in these rankings was in most places much higher, often reaching over 90 percent of the "full labor power" male work force. (Quota work and special tasks, such as house construction, which often earn above the 10-point labor day ranking system were not included.) In 1964, the time of the last previous investigation of the federation before it was disbanded in 1966, 25 percent of the brigades in Hopeh were reported to have "basically implemented" the policy. This percentage had not improved much by 1973 according to federation investigations. Where the equal pay policy had been implemented in the mid-1970s, women's participation rates were said to have increased more than 15 percent to over 90 percent of able-bodied, working-age women.

22. Data collected by Edward Friedman, Paul Pickowicz, Mark Selden and me in Wukung brigade, Jaoyang County, in June 1978. Our household survey of the brigade's largest team, with a population of over 1,100, showed that while only 29 percent of the married women over 35 in 1978 were from within the village, over 60 percent of the married women 25 or younger were natives of the village. All of the married women 25 or younger were natives. My thanks to Mark Selden who computed the demographic data in "Profile of a Team," draft chapter for our upcoming book on Wukung.

23. The model status of the village and the desirability of remaining there are no doubt unique factors. But the village was also a model in the 1950s and 1960s when the majority of native daughters (75–80 percent) were still marrying out of their own rich villages into much poorer ones.

24. Ch'ang-an brigade in Jao-yang County, where the brigade Party secretary is a veteran woman Party member and labor model, emerged as a model. See "Pay Attention to the Development of Women's Role in 'Holding Up Half the Sky'," *JMJP*, January 8, 1974. Two other Hopeh counties, Lan-hsi and Cheng-te, were also frequently lauded as models in women's work. See, "Actively Cultivate Women Cadres," *JMJP*, March 17, 1974; "Throughly Smash the People-eating Theories of Confucius and Mencius," *JMJP*, November 24, 1974.

25. In addition to the articles cited earlier, see "Young Women of Hsiaochin-chuang Return Brigade Presents," *JMJP*, December 5, 1974.

26. Joan Hinton, "Marriage and Politics."

27. Of course, in 1978, the leaders of the Hopeh Women's Federation denied that their work had any connection to Chiang Ch'ing and her followers, who were disgraced in 1976. They in fact stressed that their work began in 1973 before the Anti-Confucian campaign on their own initiative, although they admitted their work was accelerated and greatly aided by the campaign. Indeed, throughout the province in 1978, people preferred to refer to the changes that had occurred "around 1974" rather than recall the campaign itself, due to the association of the campaign with the "Gang of Four" and their oblique attack on Chou En-lai. In 1978, it was Chou En-lai who was most frequently cited as a powerful mentor of the women's movement and in Hopeh he was credited with having encouraged the work of the federation, of which

Teng Ying-ch'ao (his wife) was a long-time leader. It is possible that these Hopeh groups were caught in the midst of a complicated political dynamic which they themselves did not fully understand. It is perhaps significant in this regard that our requests to visit Ting Hsien in Paoting prefecture were denied because, it was said, Paoting was still recovering from the political turmoil caused by the "disruptions of the Gang of Four."

28. "Raise Cotton Production to a Still Higher Level through Self-Reliance and Hard Struggle," *Peking Review*, no. 12 (March 20, 1970).

29. Parish and Whyte, Conclusion, *Village and Family. "* Also see, Martin Whyte, "Rural Marriage Customs," *Problems of Communism*, 26, no. 4 (July–August 1977).

30. See, C. K. Yang, *The Chinese Family in the Communist Revolution* (Cambridge: MIT Press, 1959).

31. See Christopher Lasch, "The Family and History," *New York Review of Books*, November 13, 1975.

32. The most notable proponent of this view is William Goode, *World Revolution and Family Patterns* (New York: Free Press, 1970). Also see Edward Shorter, "Capitalism, Culture and Sexuality: Some Competing Models," *Social Science Quarterly*, 1972, pp. 338–56. Eli Zaretsky, *Capitalism, The Family and Personal Life* (New York: Harper, 1976). These views have not, of course, gone unchallenged. For a discussion and critique of some of Goode's ideas, see above Chapter 6.

33. Author's interviews, Hong Kong, 1978.

Chapter 14

1. William Parish and Martin Whyte, *Village and Family in Contemporary China* (Chicago: University of Chicago Press, 1978), pp. 169–80; Janet Salaff, "The Emerging Conjugal Relationship in the People's Republic of China," *Journal of Marriage and the Family*, November 1973, pp. 705–17.

2. Salaff found that this was the most common type of marriage in rural areas, especially among nonelite youth. Salaff, "Emerging Conjugal Relationship." Also see, Jack Chen, *A Year in Upper Felicity: Life in a Village during the Cultural Revolution* (New York: Macmillan, 1973), pp. 72–78.

3. Parish and Whyte, *Village and Family*, pp. 169–72; Chen, *A Year in Upper Felicity*, pp. 72–78. Also see, Janet Salaff, "Institutionalized Motivation for Fertility Limitation," in Marilyn Young, ed., *Women in China: Studies in Socialism and Feminism* (Ann Arbor: Center for Chinese Studies, University of Michigan, 1973); "Will Young Women Working Together with Men Bring Disrepute to the Family?" *CKCNP*, October 27, 1964, in *SCMP*, no. 3339.

4. Senior middle schools, run at the commune level, do provide such opportunities. But only a minority of rural youth in most areas attend school beyond the junior middle school level and junior middle schools are usually run at the brigade or village level. See Suzanne Pepper, "Education and Revolution: The Chinese Model Revised," *Asian Survey*, 18, no. 9 (September 1978).

5. The revised 1980 version of the Marriage Law removed the phrase which referred to following "local customs" on the degree of exogamy required. The main purpose of the revisions was to raise the minimum marriage ages from 18 for women and 20 for men to 20 and 22 respectively, and to insert a clause stating that it is a duty of each couple to practice family planning.

6. Parish and Whyte, *Village and Family*, pp. 180–82.

7. The leader of a relatively wealthy commune said that the groom's wedding expenses were usually at least 1,000 yuan, about half of which was spent on the wedding banquet and half sent to the bride's family in cash and gifts. Expenses for the groom's family commonly went as high as 2,000 yuan, he claimed, with 1,000 yuan as bride price. Dowries were said to be very small. On the other hand, Salaff found bride prices to be less prevalent in her interviews (Salaff, "Emerging Conjugal Relationship").

8. Author's interviews, Hong Kong, 1978. Only three of my informants had spent time in Fukien villages.

9. See chapter 1, note 17, and accompanying text.

10. Ibid.

11. Sidney Gamble, *Ting Hsien: A North China Rural Community* (Stanford: Stanford University Press, 1968), pp. 379–85.

12. See chapter 1, note 17. As pointed out earlier, economic structuralist explanations of bride price and dowry systems argue that bride prices should be the norm where women's productive labor contribution is high and dowries should predominate where women contribute little to the major agricultural sector.

13. Author's interviews, Shihchiachuang and Peking, 1978.

14. See, for example, "Resolutely Oppose Marriage by Purchase," *JMJP*, July 25, 1978 (reprinted from *Che-chiang jih-pao*); "Arranged Buying and Selling Marriages in Kwangtung," *Wen-wei pao* (Hong Kong), August 8, 1978.

15. One might speculate that it would be easier for women to maintain ties to their own natal families where dowries rather than bride prices dominate, although we have no significant evidence that would allow us to test this speculation. Perhaps, however, it is not a coincidence that dowry-dominant Ting Hsien was a model area in promoting matrilocal marriage.

16. Parish and Whyte, *Village and Family*, pp. 192–99.

17. See Salaff, "The Emerging Conjugal Relationship," p. 709.

18. Official guidelines on handling divorce cases in fact encourage this process. See *How to Manage Marriage-Registration Well* (Peking: Village Reader Publishing House, 1963), reprinted in *Chinese Sociology and Anthropology*, 1, no. 2 (1968–69). Also see, Parish and Whyte, *Village and Family*, p. 194.

19. Victor H. Li, *Law without Lawyers: A Comparison of Law in China and the United States* (Stanford: Stanford Alumni Association, 1977).

20. Parish and Whyte, *Village and Family*, pp. 193–94; Felix Greene, *Awakened China* (Garden City: Doubleday, 1969), pp. 195–207; Nina Shapiro-Perl, "Divorce Trial," *New China*, 3, no. 2 (Summer 1977); M. J. Meijer, *Marriage Law and Policy in the Chinese People's Republic* (Hong Kong: Hong Kong University Press, 1971), chap. 11.

21. Parish and Whyte, *Village and Family*, p. 192.

Chapter 15

1. William Parish and Martin Whyte, *Village and Family in Contemporary China* (Chicago: University of Chicago Press, 1978), pp. 171–72.

2. Jean Adams, "The Utilization of Surplus Labor in the People's Republic of China," *Bulletin of Concerned Asian Scholars*, 11, no. 4, (1979), pp. 54–55.

3. See Deborah Davis-Friedmann, "Strategies for Aging: Interdependence between Generations in the Transition to Socialism," *Contemporary China*, 1, no. 6 (March 1977).

4. For additional ways in which the traditional family structure, and particularly the position of women in the family, aids accumulation and investment, see Batya Weinbaum, "Women in the Transition to Socialism: Perspectives on the Chinese Case," *Review of Radical Political Economics*, 8, no. 1 (Spring 1976).

5. This view is clearly expressed in Karl Marx, *The Communist Manifesto*.

6. For a discussion of this Maoist view, see Maurice Meisner, *Mao's China: A History of the People's Republic* (New York: Free Press, 1977), pp. 212–15. Of course when Mao asserted, in order to justify his Great Leap schemes, that the primary advantage was that China's peasantry was "poor and blank," like a piece of clean paper ready to have new words written on it, he was quickly proven entirely wrong. Quite the opposite has been the case, as Mao himself frequently acknowledged. The "advantages of backwardness" that have actually been utilized are those deeply etched traditional community and family orientations on which this analysis has focused.

7. Parish and Whyte, *Village and Family*, pp. 267, 290, 326.

8. As pointed out earlier this is a major theoretical point argued by Joan Scott and Louise Tilly, "Women's Work and the Family in Nineteenth-Century Europe," in Charles Rosenberg, ed., *The Family in History* (Philadelphia: University of Pennsylvania Press, 1977).

9. The case for the important role ideological forces may play in shaping change is argued by, among others, William Goode, *World Revolution and Family Patterns* (New York: Free Press, 1970) and Eli Zaretsky, *Capitalism, the Family and Personal Life* (New York: Harper and Row, 1976).

10. This view is an important part of the arguments put forward by a number of scholars, including Gayle Rubin, "The Traffic in Women: Notes on the 'Political Economy' of Sex," in Rayna Reiter, ed., *Toward an Anthropology of Women* (New York: Monthly Review Press, 1975); Heidi Hartmann, "Capitalism, Patriarchy, and Job Segregation by Sex," *Signs*, 1, no. 3, part 2 (Spring 1976).

11. For an account of a young, apolitical urban student whose modern and progressive ideals, including those concerning marriage and women's rights, led her to become an activist in land reform in 1949, see Chen Yuan-tsung, *The Dragon's Village* (New York: Pantheon, 1980).

12. It is possible that public government endorsement of the Marriage Law's principles had the same sort of significance for urban supporters which, Joseph R. Gusfield argues, federal support for desegregation had at one time for civil rights groups even though desegregation was often only token and had little tangible impact on the lives of most black people. According to Gusfield, "Desegregation is a status issue par excellence. Its symbolic characteristics lie in the deference which the norm of integration implies. The acceptance of token integration, which is what occurred in the North, is itself prestige-conferring because it establishes the public character of the norm supporting integration. It indicates what side is publicly legitimate and dominant" (*Symbolic Crusade: Status Politics and the American Temperance Movement* [Urbana: University of Illinois Press, 1963], p. 173). Also see Murray Edelman, *The Symbolic Uses of Politics* (Urbana: University of Illinois Press, 1964), pp. 24–26.

13. Mark Selden, *The Yenan Way in Revolutionary China* (Cambridge: Harvard University Press, 1971), pp. 114–15.

14. See, for example, Mao's classic defense of the peasant movement, "Report on an Investigation into the Peasant Movement in Hunan," in Mao

Tse-tung, *Selected Works of Mao Tse-tung*, vol. 1 (Peking: Foreign Languages Press, 1965). Also see chapter 3, above.

15. See chapter 3, note 22 and accompanying text above.

16. *Beijing Review*, no. 38 (September 22, 1980).

17. Leo Orleans, *China's Population Policies and Population Data: Review and Update*, prepared for the Committee on Foreign Affairs, U.S. House of Representatives (Washington, D.C.: U.S. Government Printing Office, 1981), p. 8.

18. Parish and Whyte, *Village and Family*, pp. 138–54; Janet Salaff, "Institutionalized Motivation for Fertility Limitation," in Marilyn Young, ed., *Women in China* (Ann Arbor: Center for Chinese Studies, University of Michigan, 1973), pp. 129–34.

19. Ibid. Also see, William Parish, "Socialism and the Chinese Peasant Family," *Journal of Asian Studies*, no. 34 (1975).

20. Orleans, *China's Population Policies*, p. 10.

21. Davis-Friedmann, "Strategies for Aging."

22. See Parish and Whyte, *Village and Family*, p. 147. Author's interviews with family planning cadres in rural areas in 1978 produced similar findings.

23. For details of the current policies on rewards and punishments, see Orleans, *China's Population Policies*.

24. On the emotional pressures and abuse women may suffer in these pressurized circumstances for failing to produce a son on the first or second try, see, for example, "Wife Beater Sent to Chinese Prison," *Korea Herald*, September 18, 1980; Tung Tung "One Baby for You, One Baby for Me," *American Spectator*, January 1981.

25. For recent indications of female infanticide, see Lucien Bianco, "Birth Control in China: Local Data and Their Reliability," *China Quarterly*, no. 84 (March 1981), p. 131; Orleans, *China's Population Policies*, p. 31; Jay Mathews, "Odyssey of Love," *Washington Post*, August 17, 1980.

26. Orleans, *China's Population Policies*, pp. 31–32.

27. R. Cassen, "Population and Development: A Survey," *Journal of World Development*, no. 4 (1976), pp. 785–835.

28. See chapter 1, note 3 and accompanying text above.

29. Vera Schwarcz, discussing her work-in-progress on the legacy of May Fourth, presented a view of the May Fourth cultural revolution and its fate similar to the one argued here. "May Fourth: The Enduring Challenge of Enlightenment" (Lecture presented to the New England China Seminar, Harvard University, May 6, 1981).

Index